This Is REAL Feng Shui

Once you have experienced the positive effects of improving your environment with feng shui, you will need no convincing about its effectiveness. What you are likely to want, though, is someone who can take you beyond the basics and into the artistic domains of feng shui.

Happily, Henry B. Lin, a native of China, has stepped up to this challenge. The successful result of his advanced understanding is *The Art and Science of Feng Shui*. Here you will find the universal principles that are the foundation of this method of human improvement, and see that the real masters of feng shui are those who go beyond the forms and rules, and use their imagination, intuition, and creative understanding.

Lin reveals how feng shui bridges the illusory divide between the metaphysical and the practical, and delivers a wealth of knowledge that can be of immediate use, whether you are buying property, building office space, or just rearranging a room.

About the Author

Henry B. Lin has been a health/life/feng shui consultant for many years. Profoundly studied in traditional Chinese culture, he provides quality services to people from all over the world: natural health care and self-healing consultation, instruction of Chinese fitness exercises and martial arts, feng shui design, and astrological readings for life and business planning. For almost thirty years, he has been a close student of Dr. Wan Laisheng, the great modern Chinese martial artist and medico-athlete, who is also a famous medical doctor and philosopher in China. Mr. Lin has published articles in local periodicals such as *The New Times* and *Seattle Journal* and is the author of *What Your Face Reveals* and *Chinese Health Care Secrets*.

To Write to the Author

If you wish to contact the author or would like more information about this book, please write to the author in care of Llewellyn Worldwide, and we will forward your request. Both the author and publisher appreciate hearing from you. Llewellyn Worldwide cannot guarantee that every letter written to the author can be answered, but all will be forwarded. Please write to:

Henry B. Lin
℅ Llewellyn Worldwide
P.O. Box 64383, K436-7
St. Paul, MN 55164-0383, U.S.A.

Please enclose a self-addressed, stamped envelope for reply, or $1.00 to cover costs.
If outside the U.S.A., enclose international postal reply coupon.

Many of Llewellyn's authors have websites with additional information and resources. For more information, please visit our website at
http://www.llewellyn.com

The Art & Science of Feng Shui

THE ANCIENT CHINESE TRADITION OF SHAPING FATE

Henry B. Lin

2000
Llewellyn Publications
St. Paul, Minnesota
55164-0383

FIRST EDITION
First printing, 2000

Cover design: Anne Marie Garrison
Cover illustration: Robert Schmitt
Illustrations: Carrie Westfall
Talismans, Chinese characters, and floor plan layouts: Henry B. Lin
Editing and book design: Christine Snow

Library of Congress Cataloging-in-Publication Data

Lin, Henry B.
 The art & science of feng shui: the ancient Chinese tradition of shaping fate / Henry B. Lin.
  p. cm.
 Includes bibliographical references and index.
 ISBN 1-56718-436-7
 1. Feng-shui. I. Title: Art and science of feng shui. II. Title.

BF1779.F4 L555 2000
133.3'337–dc21   00-030970

Llewellyn Publications
A Division of Llewellyn Worldwide, Ltd.
P. O. Box 64383, Dept. K436-7
St. Paul, MN 55164-0383
www.llewellyn.com

Printed in the United States of America

Other Books by Henry B. Lin

What Your Face Reveals (1999)
Chinese Health Care Secrets (2000)

Dedicated to my dear parents.

Contents

Illustrations and Tables

Introduction

The breeze of feng shui is swaying the continent of North America with irresistible appeal. Its growing influence on American thinking can be seen in an article published in a 1997 issue of *Economics* magazine shortly after the 1996 United States presidential campaign. The following is an excerpt titled "The Right Vibes":

> *The Republicans apparently did not think of feng shui for their convention in San Diego. If they had shown more respect for this ancient Californian custom, they might be doing better now. Feng shui—literally, wind and water—is the ancient Chinese art of placing things in harmony with their surroundings. To its practitioners in Asia, such as the builders of the towering Hong Kong and Shanghai Bank in Hong Kong, it is serious stuff.*

Put a shop at 219. 375 degrees off from north, and you face "destruction and decay"; but put it at 331. 875 and you get "brilliance and peace." In New York City, the Guggenheim Museum and the Lincoln Center both have splendid feng shui. This sort of thing has, of course, been taken up hugely in California.

Here, the author blamed the failure of the Republicans to recapture the White House on the bad feng shui of their headquarters located in San Diego, including the arrangement of sofas and tables in it. Is it true that the arrangement of furniture in a house can affect the fate of individuals and even that of a major political party? To answer this question, we need to know more about feng shui—the ancient Chinese art of shaping fate.

Feng shui is also known as geomancy, which is a means of divination composed of finding auspicious sites for construction of a house or a business or for burial, then configuring and orienting the building, and finally locating and designing individual rooms, arranging furniture, and other internal details of a building. Feng shui consists of two branches: one for the living and the other for the deceased. The branch concerning the residential and commercial buildings is known as the "yang-house feng shui," while the branch concerning burial

grounds and tombs is known as the "yin-house feng shui."

Literally, feng shui means in Chinese "wind" and "water," which are two of the major concerns in the design of feng shui. But this is just the beginning. Feng shui is a much more involved subject of study than its literal meanings can suggest. Alternatively known as *Kun-yu*, or literally "heaven" and "earth," feng shui seeks to find or create a harmony among heaven, man, and earth, with the overriding objective to benefit humans by taking advantage of the natural resources available. That is to say, it aims at finding or creating harmonious and auspicious environments for humans. Thus, feng shui takes as its subjects the study of heaven, of earth, and of humans as well. Of course, there are macro- and microenvironments, as well as interior and exterior environments. As such, wind and water can only suggest half of the meaning, i.e., the macro or external environment of a building. We still have the tasks of orienting, configuring, and furnishing the building, and so on.

Feng shui is a highly practical and metaphysical study that seeks to harmonize humans and the natural environment in which they live, with the purpose of benefiting humans and enhancing their happiness. It is regarded as both a divination method and a magical tool to mold or modify fate, so that good luck will come to people in various aspects of life, from finance to career, from romance to relationships, from marriage to family life, from health to intelligence, from interpersonal skills to social position, etc. In extreme cases, it can even mean the difference between life and death.

Practiced in China for almost 3,000 years, the art of feng shui has exerted a profound influence on the appearance of China's landscape and on the Chinese mind. Most Chinese believe that fate is predetermined to a large extent, first, by one's own moral actions in a prior life, and second, by the Qi energy of the living environment. In other words, fate is not totally determined by heaven (meaning supernatural force), and that we ourselves also have the power to shape and even change our fate. Feng shui is the primary tool that can provide us with such marvelous power. By carefully choosing a location to build a house, designing the house in the light of orthodox feng shui principles, and if possible, burying our ancestors in auspicious locations, we can add a lot of good luck to our fate in this lifetime. In fact, many wise people have already done that and have handsomely reaped the rewards of feng shui.

For instance, in 1985, a Hong Kong newspaper carried an article in which the author cited the example of how Taiwanese billionaire Wang Yungching became the country's plastic czar. Wang came from a poor family and was a 100 percent self-made man. One day a friend told him that feng shui could change his fate and make him rich. Wang was introduced to one of the best feng shui masters in Hong Kong, who advised Wang to reallocate his father's remains to another auspicious burial ground in Taipei. Wang reluctantly agreed and thus, the remains of his father were reburied. Not long afterward, Wang's business experienced a dramatic takeoff. He kept on expanding it until he owned more than 10 percent of Formosa Taffeta Corporation, 30 percent of Formosa Chemical and Fibre Corporation, 10 percent of Formosa Plastic Corporation, and 16 percent of Nan Ya Plastic Corporation, placing himself on the eye-catching list of billionaires in the world. His financial good luck seems to be growing with age. As the twenty-first century unfolds, Wang's business empire is aggressively expanding, from Taiwan to the mainland China, from plastics to electrical power and telecommunications.

It is hard to imagine that the reburial of an ancestor's remains to a new site could make such a dramatic change in the fortune of the descendants. According to the law of conservation, matter does not become extinct; it just changes in place and form. Thus, when a man dies, his body returns to the earth. The departed spirit will maintain a tacit tie with its dear, living ones, thus affecting the fortune of their posterity. Therefore, if a relative is buried in an auspicious location with strong Qi energy in the environment, his or her descendants will benefit from the same Qi energy in and around the burial site. However, if a relative is buried in inauspicious land with little live Qi energy, disaster and ill luck will fall upon the descendants. Feng shui theory holds that the skeleton will absorb the Qi energy of the earth and pass this on to the descendants.

This belief of the magical power of feng shui has developed into a way of life for the Chinese. When they want to build or buy a house, set up a business or office, or bury their dear ones, they seek expert opinions from feng shui masters regarding the location, environment, orientation, interior layout, and even the color of the house as an integral part of the project. This kind of intellectual investment is considered as important and valuable as the real property itself. In fact, many have openly admitted that they owe the art of feng shui a huge debt of gratitude for their success and prosperity.

Not surprisingly, this belief and practice of feng shui on the part of the Chinese naturally extends to the administration of the nation. In China, fathers of a new dynasty would spend a lot of time and money consulting feng shui masters on where to locate the capital, how to line up the palace with the surrounding mountains and rivers, if they were present, and how to lay out the interior and exterior environments of the palace including which direction the throne should be facing, what kinds of flowers and trees to plant, what kind of pictures and mirrors to hang on the walls, and so on. Especially when locating a national capital, ancient Chinese would make absolutely sure that it was a site looking like a coiling dragon and crouching tiger, where the royal Qi energy permeated and condensed.

Much effort has been put into selecting burial grounds and designing tombs for emperors in order to prolong their dynasties. The Ming Tombs—the graves of thirteen emperors of the Ming dynasty located in the outskirts of Peking—the Sun Yat-sen Mausoleum in the outskirts of Nanjing, the Yuan Shi-kai Mausoleum in Peking, and the Chiang Kai-shek Mausoleum in Taipei are all masterpieces of burial feng shui. A careful study of them can provide us with profound insights into the art of geomancy.

Recently, feng shui is rapidly finding its way into Western societies. From Europe to America, school after school of feng shui has been set up, and feng shui titles are moving steadily in bookstores. Here, the underlying belief seems to be that we are all humans, and therefore what works for the Chinese should be able to work for other ethnic groups as well. Just like feng shui has changed the physical and mental landscape of China, it may very well do the same for Westerners. Developments in science may be able to provide modern ground for ancient geomantic theories. To be sure, feng shui will play a bigger and bigger role in the personal, social, and political life of people in the West, and its power to shape and change human fate will become more and more confirmed throughout the world.

The subject of feng shui is preoccupied with the relationships between humans and nature, and between a residence and its environment. It aims at reaching harmony with nature and the environment. For the Chinese believe that harmonious human-nature equilibrium is highly desirable for, and ultimately indispensable to, the enhancement and promotion of the quality and fortune of life. It takes little imagination to realize that the environment in which we live and work has a direct impact on the quality of our life. Numerous facts bear evidence to the truth that feng shui has significant influence on the outcomes of human affairs. Little wonder Chinese fathers paid so much attention to the environment in which they lived.

It is no exaggeration to say that in feng shui, knowledge is power and wealth. Admittedly, feng shui has brought wealth and prosperity to many Asians. Armed with the essential knowledge of what makes a good site and what makes a bad one, we are able to find auspicious localities for ourselves and improve the quality of life, materially and spiritually.

Editor's note: Unless otherwise noted, all translations of foreign book titles and quotations are the author's.

Chapter 1

A History of Feng Shui

The practice of feng shui in China can be dated back 4,000 years, almost to the origin of the Chinese civilization. It is recorded in the epochal *Historical Annals* by Si MaQian:

> *When the Yellow Emperor first started to divide the country into cities and provinces, he consulted Qin Niao Tse on the project because the latter was adept at geomantically surveying the landform.*

The Yellow Emperor was one of the first emperors of China who reigned a loosely combined empire in the now northern part of China, along the Yellow River valley, around 2600 B.C. This valley was the cradle of Chinese civilization. Even today, all Chinese, both at home and abroad, proudly consider themselves the "children of the Yellow Emperor," obviously identifying the Yellow

Emperor as the father of Chinese civilization. Thus, Qin Niao Tse is regarded as the originator of the art of feng shui. For this reason, feng shui is sometimes referred to as the "art of Qin Niao Tse."

Although Qin Niao Tse is regarded as the father of feng shui, none of the books he had written had been passed down through history. The first book available about feng shui, however, is *Book of Burial* by Guo Pu, a famous author and interpretative critic of ancient texts of the Jin dynasty (A.D. 265–420). This classic by Guo Pu is widely regarded as the groundbreaking work of feng shui, which is still very influential in the field. Consequently, Guo Pu is considered by many as the father of feng shui, if only because it was Guo who first coined the term "feng shui."

The ancient Chinese made the arduous efforts to study feng shui because they were preoccupied with molding and improving their fate as reflected in the welfare and well-being of human beings. After all, man is accountable for his own behavior. It is the Chinese belief that auspicious burial grounds or residential sites belong only to those who have done a lot of good deeds in their lives. A popular saying goes: "To obtain an auspicious land site, one must first till the land of the heart." Here, "till the land of the heart" means "cultivate morality" or perform a lot of good deeds.

Chinese fathers believe that heaven, man, and earth form a universal trinity, and that man's well-being is determined not only by his own decisions and efforts, but also by heaven above him and the earth beneath him. This vague or superstitious feeling became an unshakable belief later on and triggered a wide range of research in traditional China, all aimed at discovering how, why, and when heaven and earth exert their influence on human affairs. Feng shui is one of the most outstanding products of this research.

Feng shui is a means of divination aimed at promoting human fate by first finding auspicious grounds for building a tomb, house, or a city, and then building and arranging the structure in ways that find harmony with the environment. In the beginning, there was little theoretical guidance to train geomancers in their practice. People acted largely on their instinct and experience with the aid of I-Ching, the oldest book on divination. For instance, Chinese fathers knew that a house with a southern exposure was the most desirable because the house was positioned to absorb the maximum amount of sunlight during the winter and to avoid as much of the heat of summer as possible. Similarly, they knew that living close to water had a number of advantages, many of which are, indeed, vital to life itself. In the same way, they were aware that a house situated in a beautiful landscape or environment could lead to better health and good luck.

Since the second century B.C., the Chinese have regarded the earth as a living organism, similar to the human body. Just as the human body incorporates channels along which life energy and blood flow, so it is believed that the earth contains similar channels, called "the veins of the dragon" in feng shui litcrature. The wide variations in the topography of the earth determine favorable and unfavorable sites, or auspicious and inauspicious sites. Auspicious sites are thosc that lie at points where "channels" converge, bringing with them an abundance of natural energy from the earth known as Qi, or lie at points where the mountains merge with water, creating a contained pool of Qi energy. Inauspicious sites are those that lie on flat plains with no mountains or water in sight, subjecting themselves to the merciless blow of ill winds; or those that are faced with roads or water running straight into them.

Formative Period

The development of feng shui over the past 3,000 years can be grouped into five distinctive periods. The first is the Formative period. This period roughly started with the reign of the Yellow Emperor about 4,600 years ago, and ended sometime during the Jin dynasty. In this period, especially in the Jin dynasty, primitive theories of burial and residential feng shui grew up as two separate but related branches from the same trunk of Chinese culture. In particular, they were closely linked to the Taoist theories of yin-yang and the five elements, but the practice was scattered and application was limited to the privileged few such as royalty, dignitaries, and wealthy people.

The first name mentioned in history about geomancy is Qin Niao Tse. As mentioned before, he was an officer in the court of the Yellow Emperor about 2600 B.C. Qin Niao Tse was said to have written three books on geomancy: *Classics of Burial Geomancy, On Reading Graves,* and *How to Examine the Earthy Bones.* Allegedly, these are the earliest books on geomancy. Unfortunately, all of them were lost.

The earliest books available on the subject were written by Guo Pu (A.D. 276–324). These include *Book of Burial* and *Ancient Burial Classics.* For this reason, Guo is alternatively regarded as the father of feng shui, even though his focus was on burial instead of residential feng shui.

A highly literate man born in northwestern China, Guo's knowledge was amazingly wide and profound; he was adept at politics, geomancy, astrology, fortunetelling, history, literature, and even military strategy. His reputation as a master of feng shui was so influential that even the emperor came in person to observe his practice. In his *Book of Burial*, Guo described the inconceivable power of feng shui: "Hence (by means of feng shui), a gentleman can prevail over God's work, change his own fate, and instantly create fortune or misfortune." Obviously, Guo believed that feng shui could have supernatural power in the shaping of human fate. Judging Guo from these words, we can justifiably say that Guo Pu possessed strong scientific spirit.

What is more, Guo repeatedly verified his belief with amazing facts. One story tells that shortly after Guo had master-minded the burial of his client's father, the emperor arrived in disguise at the burial ground. He asked the son of the deceased: "Why bury your father at this specific location? I am told that such a site is called the Horn of Dragon, which will cause the destruction of the entire family." The son replied: "Guo Pu told me that by burying my father in this specific ground, the emperor will come in person to ask me questions in three years." The emperor was deeply surprised by Guo's foresight and geomantic skills.

The last part of Guo's life saw him serving as the military advisor to a duke named Wang Dun. Wang had been har-boring the ambition to replace the emperor of the Jin dynasty. Before he rebelled, Wang asked Guo to predict the outcome of his forthcoming uprising. Guo's divination boded ill for Wang. Wang became so furious that he killed Guo to prove his own invincibility. Of course, the rebellion was crushed. It is said that Guo's body disappeared hours after his execution.

In terms of geomancy, Guo stressed that in siting a grave, one should first select a location full of lively Qi energy, and then measure and determine the ideal exposure of the grave based on both natural and human factors such as mountains, waters, forests, roads, bridges, the birthday of the deceased, and so on. The idea is to not only take advantage of the strong Qi reserves in the land, but also to strike a harmony between the grave, the deceased, and the burial environment.

Heyday Period

The second phase in the history of feng shui can be called the Heyday period. This period lasted about 600 years, from the Tang dynasty (A.D. 618–907) to the end of the Song dynasty (A.D. 960–1179). Characteristic of this golden period in the development of feng shui was the forma-tion and maturity of geomantic thinking. Significantly, this period witnessed the division of geomantic thought into two major schools—the Situation school and the Direction school—in addition to widespread acceptance of feng shui doctrine by people from all walks of life. It is no mere coincidence that the Heyday period of feng shui should occur in the Tang and Song dynasties, for these were the two dynasties in China's history that boasted the strongest, freest academic atmosphere and the greatest achievements in art and literature. Many of the greatest Chinese poets and literary people were born during this period. Among the better known names are Li Bai and Du Fu, the two greatest Chinese poets of all time, as well as great authors such as Han Yu, Liu Zhongyuan, Su Shi, and Ou Yang Xiu. This would not have been possible without the presence of more liberal and enlightened emperors, who sponsored academic research and granted greater freedom of thinking to the people. The frequent natural disasters and social turmoil in China also prompted people to seek haven in feng shui for the protection and promotion of their own welfare.

Feng shui is an art form, a metaphysical art, if you want. Like any art, there are always different opinions and schools. In feng shui, the split of theory and practice into two major schools—the Situation school and the Direction school—happened in this period. Neither school,

however, ever escapes the theoretical framework of Taoism. Their differences lie mainly in the emphasis each puts on different sets of Taoist thinking. Thus, the focus of the Situation school is on the topography and environmental elements around a site, stressing the supreme importance of the shapes and height of mountains, and the speed and curves of the watercourses. The Direction school, in contrast, focuses on the accurate alignment of the site and the building with the appropriate stars. This alignment is strictly based on the theory of the five elements and the eight characters of birth, as well as the eight trigrams of the I-Ching.

Practitioners of the Situation school must be guided by strong observation, intuition, and imaginary power when it comes to surveying the topography of the land. Students of the Direction school have to rely heavily on a complicated tool known as a geomantic compass or a Luopan. It is specifically designed for the purpose of helping students decide on the appropriate alignments.

It is said in Meng Hao's *Verses of the Heart of Snow*, a feng shui classic of the Situation school, that "all depends on individual's intuition to ponder over the appropriate height of mountains, and his reasoning power to determine which exposure to take." For students of the Situation school, there would be no space without topography, nor would there be time without topography. To them, land form or topography is the substance, in the absence of which no feng shui exists. Advocates of the Situation school declared that "one does not need a geomantic compass as he climbs a mountain" and that "so long as the situation is right, direction will take care of itself."

The fathers of the Situation school are Yang Yun-song and his disciples Zen Wenshan and Lai Wenjun. The fathers of the Direction school are Wan Ji and Cai Yuanding. Since Yang, Zen, and Lai were natives of Jiangxi province, the Situation school came to be known as the Jiangxi school. Similarly, the Direction school of feng shui became known as the Fujian school because Wan and Cai were from Fujian province.

Just like the two geographically adjacent provinces, these two major feng shui schools often borrow from and overlap each other. This is the case in actual practice at least. The difference, as I see it, lies mainly in emphasis. Therefore, a complete picture of feng shui must include both situation and direction. Moreover, since geomancy is first and foremost a study of the earth, it follows that landforms and the environment of the earth should occupy a more prominent place than the direction or orientation of a

building or tomb. Indeed, to seek direction at the expense of situation is to take the branch for the root, so to speak.

Yang Yun-song served briefly as a high-ranking official in the later Tang dynasty, responsible for astrological and geomantic affairs for the empire. When the peasant revolt occurred, he escaped into the Kunlun Mountains for the rest of his life. From then on, he was completely separated from politics and devoted all of his energy to the study and teaching of feng shui.

He traveled thousands of miles from province to province, studying the topography of the country and, in particular, helping poor people by using his geomantic skills so that they could become more prosperous. Actually, most of those who were lucky enough to get his help turned out to be much better than before. For this reason, Yang won the name of "Mr. Savior for the poor."

Yang Yun-song is widely regarded as one of the earliest and most influential fathers of feng shui. Indeed, he was one of the most prolific writers on feng shui. His works include *Han Long Jing* ("Shaking the Dragon"), *Yi Long Jing* ("Verify the Dragon"), *Methods of Dao Zhan* ("Methods of Mr. Yang"), *Jing Han Jing* ("The Golden Classics"), *Tian Yu Jing* ("Books of Heavenly Jade"), *Qing Nan Ao Yu*

("Secret Words of Mr. Qing Nan"), and *Du Tian Bao Zhao Jing* ("Precious Classics that Light Up the Heaven"), all original works that have exerted profound influence on the development of feng shui up to this day. Yang's creative works not only included the scattered theories from previous generations, but more significantly, paved the way for later development and research on the subject.

Yang's name is further honored by the enormous success of his disciples, such as Zhen Wenshan, Wu Kechen, Wu Jinluan, Liao Yu, and Zhang Ziwei. In a cultural tradition where teachers are held in high esteem, it is not difficult to understand why Yang became the father of feng shui.

Lai Wenjun was an official in Fujian province in the Song dynasty. He became so preoccupied with and, indeed, addicted to the art of feng shui that he resigned from his position and devoted the latter half of his life to the study and practice of feng shui. Since he downgraded himself from an official to a common man, he was also known as "Lai, the Common Man."

As the dominant school in feng shui, the Situation school is concerned with the quality of the following major geographic and topographic objects: waterways and bodies of water, mountain veins and individual hills, and land sites for construction called "dragon lairs." Clearly, this school is preoccupied with the quality and quantity of Qi energy itself, in its natural form, for water, mountains, hills, and land sites are natural carriers, containers, and reservoirs of Qi—and Qi is what feng shui is about.

By contrast, the focus of the Direction school is how to strike a harmony between a location, its residents, and the environment by aligning a building or a tomb in accordance with the owner's year of birth as well as the directional structure based on the I-Ching. Thus, the Situation school represents the macromanagement of geomancy while the Direction school tends to micromanage the issue.

On the surface, they are contradictory to each other, but are actually complementary. Both are needed, although the Situation school should normally take precedence. This is because location or situation is the basis or source of Qi energy, which is the primary concern of feng shui. There has to be Qi in the first place for us to work with. No amount of directional fine-tuning can create the earthly Qi that travels with mountains and water. Direction exists only when there is a physical situation or landform. In the absence of this, direction becomes totally meaningless. Here, geographic situation can be likened to the skin on our bodies, while direction and orientation can be likened to the hair that grows on the skin. Without skin, what can hair grow on?

A genuine feng shui master typically would examine both the topographical situation of a site as well as the alignment of its direction with reference to the heavenly stars. This means that a feng shui master must possess knowledge and skill of both worlds—the physical topography and the metaphysical astrology. In feng shui, more than in any other field, a little knowledge is dangerous. A geomancer has to make some compromise between situation and direction. This is also the time when art is most called for in the practice of feng shui.

While the Situation school relies on the artistic perspective of the geomancer, the Direction school borrows generously from the research in the classic I-Ching for theoretical guidance. In the Song dynasty, the study of the I-Ching and numerology was the fashion of the day. During this period, the eight trigrams of I-Ching were significantly elaborated on by Zhu Xi and Shao Yong, two great neo-Confucian scholars. The results of their creative study on I-Ching was readily borrowed by feng shui scholars who, with some modification, developed the theory of the "eight karmas" and the corresponding "eight houses" in feng shui.

Interestingly, feng shui was originally a product of Taoism, but it ignited strong enthusiasm in the domain of Confucianism, which used to reject feng shui as groundless and heathen. The greatest compromisers in this regard are neo-Confucian sage Zhu Xi and his outstanding student, Cai Yuandin, of the Song dynasty. Both were deeply drawn into and immensely fond of feng shui, and both emerged from their study with profound insights into the subject. Indeed, few could resist the geomantic fashion of the day, something that related so intimately with personal welfare and happiness. Cai Yuandin was a brilliant student of Zhu, but Zhu openly acknowledged that Cai was his peer in scholarship. In fact, Cai even exceeded his teacher in astrology and divination. Part of the reason why Zhu and Cai were profoundly absorbed in the study of feng shui was because they resided in a geographically and geomantically extraordinary area amidst the famous Wuyi Mountains in northern Fujian province. Personally, I spent many years in the same area, which boasts of magnificent mountains and clear, beautiful waters, offering a convenient and wonderful opportunity for on-the-spot study of feng shui theory. Coincidentally, it is during this period that feng shui and other aspects of traditional Chinese culture was exported to Japan, Korea, and Southeast Asian countries, which were on their way to becoming more and more under the political and cultural influence of China.

Follow-Up Period

The third period in the history of feng shui can be called the Follow-up period. This period lasted about 600 years, from the Yuan dynasty (1270–1368) to the late Qing dynasty (1644–1911). Marking this period was the general lack of original development of feng shui theory, although there were extensive summaries and illustrations of feng shui theories put forth by the previous masters. For example, *What Every Son Should Know about Geomancy*, coauthored by Xu Shan-ji and his brother Xu Shan-shu, is an optimization of the major works on feng shui found in the past. Significantly, the names of the two brothers, Shan-ji and Shan-shu, literally mean "good at inheriting and expounding the past tradition." Another book by Ding Ruipu in the early Ming dynasty titled *Solving Puzzling Issues in Feng Shui* made a tremendous contribution to the documentation of feng shui.

There are several more authors famous for their achievements in feng shui research during this period: Xu Si-ke, the author of *A Collection of Heavenly Secrets*; Jiang Dahong who wrote *Classics of Watery Dragons*, *Essential Quotations on Geomancy*, *Debates on Geomancy*, and *Ancient Poems on Feng Shui*; Liao Ping (1852–1932) who authored *Questions and Answers in Geomancy*; Zhang Jiuyi, the author of *The Axe for Carving Jade*, *Genuine Inheritance of Thorough Truths* and *Bullets of Geomancy*; Ye Jiushen, the author of *Secrets of Directions*, *A Complete Book of Geomancy* and *Annotations for Six Classics on Geomancy*; Yao Ting-luan, the author of *A Collection of Burial Feng Shui* and *A Complete Book of Burial and Residential Feng Shui*; Wei Qingjiang, the author of *Random Talks on Residential Feng Shui*, *Formulae for Residential Feng Shui*, and *Choose the Right Timing and Create Your Own Fate*. These authors, though mainly focused on expounding and clarifying the feng shui principles laid down by their predecessors, also developed their own brilliant ideas.

One of the outstanding examples was Mu Jiangzen of the Ming dynasty who, based on the unique discovery of the I-Ching secrets by a neo-Confucian scholar named Shao Yong, developed a timing theory of feng shui. According to Mu Jiangzen, the luck of individual lands and grounds (just like the fate of individual people) shift and change with time. What was considered auspicious land 100 years ago may become inauspicious at this point in time. This idea has given rise to a popular saying in China that feng shui keeps on rotating; for the first thirty years it favors the land to the east of the river, but for the next thirty years it favors the land to the west of the river. This timing theory of Mu's gave feng shui, for the first time, an additional dimension—the dimension of timing.

It is only natural that feng shui caught the attention and affection of Chinese rulers ever since its birth. In China, fathers of any newly founded dynasty would seek advice from feng shui masters on where to locate the capital, how to line up the palace with the surrounding mountains and rivers, if they were present, and how to lay out the interior and exterior environments of the palace, including which direction the throne should be facing, what kinds of flowers and trees to plant, and what kind of pictures and mirrors to hang on the walls. The structure and layout of the Forbidden City and indeed the entire city of Peking are a brilliant illustration of these principles of feng shui.

It is told that when Zhu Yuanzhang became the first emperor of the Ming dynasty (1368–1644), he decided to establish his capital in the city of Nanjing, then called Jinling. He consulted his chief military advisor, Liu Ji, who happened to be a great master of feng shui, on where to build the inner walls for the city so that the empire would last for a long time. As loyal to his boss in geomantic issues as in

military affairs, Liu gave Zhu valuable advice. Zhu thereupon ordered the drawing of the city boundaries in accordance with Liu's teaching.

Upon returning home, the emperor told the empress what had happened. The empress said: "Now that you have conquered the world by yourself, why leave to other people the decision of the boundary of your capital?" Regrettably, the emperor ordered the old boundaries to be wiped out the next day and replaced by new boundaries that he and his wife had drawn. After that, Zhu invited Liu to inspect the new city boundaries. Knowing that any attempt to change the emperor's mind would only arouse suspicion and court disaster, Liu smiled and commented casually: "Sure, this is very good, except that your capital will be moved to some other location in the future." Almost immediately after the death of Zhu Yuanzhang, the Ming dynasty capital was moved to Peking at the order of his second son.

Equal amounts of effort had been put into the selection of burial sites for Chinese emperors in order to prolong the life of their dynasties. For instance, the following are all masterpieces of feng shui: the Ming Tombs—the graves of thirteen Ming emperors in the outskirts of Peking; the Sun Yat-sen Mausoleum in the outskirts of Nanjing; the Yuan Shi-kai

Mausoleum in Peking; and the Chiang Kai-shek Mausoleum in Taipei. A careful study of these graves can provide insight into the art of geomancy.

The Chinese believe that these considerations will affect the well-being and life expectancy of the dynasty as well as the common people. Several short-lived dynasties have been blamed on the misplacement of their capitals.

Declining Period

The fourth period is the Declining period. It lasted about 150 years, from the late Qing dynasty all the way to the 1970s. This was the most socially turbulent and destructive period in China's history, during which the Chinese people witnessed great upheaval: the destructive Taiping Rebellion, which spread over more than half of the country and lasted more than ten years in the mid-nineteenth century; the Boxer's Movement; the Eight-Power Allied Forces invading China; the Revolution of 1911, which toppled the Qing dynasty; the Japanese occupation of China; World War II; the civil war between the Nationalists and the Communists; and the Cultural Revolution.

During this period, feng shui fared badly. Faced with disasters and persecution, few had the time and courage to delve into the theory of feng shui. After the establishment of the People's Republic of China in 1949, feng shui was banned as a superstitious practice aimed solely at cheating people. There was little to boast of in terms of original works in geomancy.

The general lack of theoretical creation during this period, however, was partly made up for by widespread practice. Chinese dignitaries, in particular, took feng shui seriously as a means to ensure good luck. One story relates to the prosperity of Yuan Shi-kai (1859–1916). Yuan was a powerful warlord and the first president of the Republic of China. Coming from a common family background, Yuan started his career as a soldier while in his twenties. In less than twenty years, he became the head of state. It is said that his great-grandfather, Yuan Fangxian, was a gentleman with high morals and a deep believer in feng shui. In particular, he liked to buy captive fish, birds, and animals and set them free, as long as he was financially able. For decades, he spent quite a lot of money doing this. Nothing pleased him more than seeing the animals, birds, and fish regain their freedom.

In his sixties, Yuan made a trip with his servant deep into the mountains in his native province of Honan. They walked for many miles along the banks of a beautiful brook flanked on both sides by a grove of trees. They came to a point where huge rocks on both sides of the brook merged to form a "big door." Entering this rocky door, he was amazed by the sight of a magnificent mountain facing him. The mountain looked like a great general sitting in his office, directing the war. Knowing that this was an auspicious feng shui feature, he couldn't help but start to climb the mountain despite his age.

Halfway up the hill, he was so exhausted that he had to sit down on a stone for rest. Turning his head, Yuan saw a huge rock with a hole in it with the appearance of a pavilion not far away from him. Intrigued by this strange view, he seemed to forget all his fatigue, and climbed to the hole. Sitting in the hole, he saw a clear spring coming out incessantly from the ground below, and peak after mountainous peak appeared in his sight. These peaks assumed various images; some looked like dragons, lions, tigers, horses, warehouses, banners, drums, pens, and swords. All these peaks seemed to stand in respect for the hole, as if guarding it. Green trees and pretty flowers gave more life to these mountain peaks.

Strongly attracted by this wonderful scene, he wanted to stay there overnight to fully enjoy the sight. He asked his servant to go home and bring enough food, clothing, and some of his favorite books. As the servant headed home, Yuan laid down on the stone and fell asleep. A strange dream intruded into his sleep, in which he saw a dozen pretty virgins entering his bedroom and telling him in a coquettish tone: "This is the ground for emperors. If you can get it, yours will be the first family in the country." Upon saying these words, the group of virgins disappeared in a cloud of smoke. Awakened by the dream, Yuan walked out of the hole in search of the virgins, but it was in vain.

At this time, his boy servant had just come back with what he requested. Yuan had a vague feeling that he had received a heavenly omen from the dream. He quickly came to the decision that the opportunity could not be lost, or he would rue it. He asked his servant to run one more errand, this time with a very unique mission—to bring the ashes of his parents, which were kept at his home.

Once the boy brought the ashes, they dug a hole in the ground inside the rocky hole. As they dug three feet into the ground, a glittering stone appeared. The stone was so flat and smooth that it could accommodate two people. There was also a small hole in the center of the stone, out of which a stream of warm vapor kept rising. Yuan put his parents' ashes into the small hole of the stone, and covered everything with soil.

As soon as the burial was completed, the spring in the rocky hole stopped flowing. From then on, the financial situation in his family improved, and more and more grandchildren were born into the family, until eventually his great-grand-child, Yuan Shi-kai, emerged as president of the Republic of China in 1912. Four years later, he claimed himself an emperor, realizing the prophesy of the virgins in the dream. This experience made Yuan a profound believer of feng shui. The design of his mausoleum also bears witness to his belief.

Chiang Kai-shek, leader of China from 1926–1979, was found to be another devoted believer in feng shui. A 1997 issue of *Min Kuo Chun Chiu* magazine ("Chronicles of Republic of China") carried an interesting story about Chiang's fascination with geomancy. Perhaps the most amazing fact about him was that Chiang started seriously considering his own grave site in the apex of his political career in his thirties. When his mother died in 1921, Chiang employed several feng shui masters in a joint venture to find a highly auspicious burial site for his mother. Once the grave site was pinpointed, he told his sister, Chiang Rui-lian, that he himself would like to be buried next to his mother, so that he could be "eternally accompanying and attending to mother's spirit." But this is just an excuse. The real reason is because he thought such an auspicious grave site would enable his descendants to continue

his brilliant political career for generations to come.

Chiang's real intention became more and more clear as time went by. After he was promoted to commander-in-chief of the Nationalist Army and successfully led the Northern Expedition, a grand military campaign that resulted in the unification of the country, he returned triumphantly to his birthplace. What mostly preoccupied his mind during this short vacation was the selection of a highly auspicious burial ground for himself. Chiang was forty years old at that time, still a rising star in the political arena, both at home and abroad. Although he had said that he would like to be buried next to his mother, it did not take him long to fall in love with another piece of land.

This new piece of land that fascinated Chiang tremendously was situated in a high mountain, surrounded by nine smaller hills, embraced by two rivers, and accompanied by a natural lake at the center of the nine hills. Such a lake located high in the mountains is known as a heavenly pond, a very auspicious sign in geomancy. Chiang personally named the mountain lake Benevolent Lake. The entire landform surrounding the grave site possessed the image of "nine tortoises visiting water"—another extremely auspicious symbol. He also ordered a mountain road to be constructed around the auspicious landform as a reminder to potential competitors for the land that it already had an owner, and a formidable one at that.

After the defeat of the Japanese in 1945, he returned as a national hero to the prewar capital city of Nanking, located on China's eastern coast. Almost at the same time, he started another round of romance with feng shui, and the object of his love this time was a piece of spacious land beside the Lake of Sunset Clouds amid the Golden Purple Mountains in the suburb of the capital. As decidedly as before, he ordered a pavilion to be built on the bank of the lake and personally named it the Pavilion of Healthy Spirit. His intention was exactly the same as when he named Benevolent Lake: for his descendants to continue in politics.

Afterward, Chiang told his subordinates that this special piece of land had an altitude lower than that of the Sun Yat-sen Mausoleum but higher than that of the mausoleum of the founding emperor of the Ming dynasty, both of which were located in the region. The remark had political overtones. Chiang was the portage of Dr. Sun Yat-sen, the father of the Republic of China, who led a revolution that overthrew the rule of the Manchus. Throughout his political life, Chiang had never stopped claiming him-

self as a disciple of Sun Yat-sen. As such, it made perfect sense for his potential grave site to be lower than that of Sun's.

Chiang, especially after the surrender of the Japanese, also thought of himself as greater than the founding emperor of the Ming dynasty, Zhu Yuanzhang, who had boasted of a similar feat in driving the descendants of Genghis Khan out of mainland China. Feeling superior to Zhu, Chiang's grave site should then be higher than the emperor's.

Another reason Chiang stood above the Ming emperor was that Zhu ordered the arrest and, afterward, poisoned to death his own mentor and advisor Liu Ji (1311–1375), even though Liu deserved a lot of credit for the establishment of the Ming empire. It was merely out of jealousy that Zhu had found a burial ground with excellent feng shui for himself. From this perspective, Chiang deserves a grave site with a higher altitude than the Ming emperor.

Chiang's romance with feng shui lasted throughout his life. Not only did he seek geomantic favor for himself, but he also sought such favor for his royal subordinates. It is told that Chiang had been rather tight-fisted when it came to money, even when it involved his most beloved followers. But a rarely known fact about Chiang was that he liked to express his sorrow and bestow special favor on his most trusted subordinates upon their death in a very unique way—to find a burial site for them with excellent feng shui features. Sometimes he did this in person, sometimes he hired the best-known feng shui masters in the country to do the job in his stead.

For instance, when Dai Li, his head of secret police, died in a plane crash in 1945, Chiang, in person, twice inspected the site of burial for his loyal student and general, insisting that Dai's corpse be placed in a north-south direction. When Chen Chen, vice president of Taiwan and another of his most reliable students and generals, died in Taipei in 1966, he hired a master of feng shui to find an auspicious burial site for Chen.

Another great leader of modern China, Mao Tse-tung, also believed in the power of feng shui. It is told by some of his subordinates that Mao insisted that his bed always be aligned in an east-west direction, so his head would always point to the east when he slept. (This was because the "useful spirit" of his karma was wood, which corresponded with the direction of east.) His father had deliberately picked the name "tung," which literally means "east." His name and his insistence on his head pointing to the east may have contributed to his revolutionary success. Interestingly enough, despite his own belief in feng shui and divination, Mao strictly banned his people from reading feng shui books, to say nothing of practicing feng shui, because of feudal superstition.

Resurgent Period

The last period in the history of feng shui is the Resurgent period, which we are currently in. It started in the 1980s after China opened its doors to the outside world (i.e., trade), and academics in the country began enjoying greater freedom of speech. After a long period of hibernation, talk of feng shui once more could be heard in the air. However, the greatest boost to the revival of feng shui in its home country was not greater academic freedom, but the so-called "China enthusiasm" in the West. This enthusiasm was for almost everything traditionally Chinese—from foods to herbs, from acupuncture to taiji (a form of exercise), from martial arts to military strategy, from astrology to feng shui.

In an effort to be more appealing to the world, and attract more foreign investments and hard currency, the government tacitly encouraged the study and export of traditional Chinese culture, including feng shui. Thus, feng shui enjoyed a robust comeback, igniting enthusiasm about the ancient art throughout the world.

It is possible that as feng shui extends its influence deeper into modern life, more scientific tools will be employed to study the theories behind it. In particular, physics shares some essential common ground with feng shui in its interpretation of nature. One of the similarities is their mutual understanding of electromagnetic fields. In physics, these fields are defined as a collection of electromagnetic waves. As such, the more concentrated these waves are in a field, the stronger the field will be.

Similarly, feng shui defines a site or locality as a reservoir of earthly Qi energy. Thus, the more Qi contained in a site, the more auspicious the site, or better feng shui. If you compare Qi to electromagnetic waves, both of which are sources of energy and subject to change in quantity, quality, location, and direction, you will see that feng shui can begin to be tested scientifically.

In modern Taiwan, almost all dignitaries and business tycoons have consulted feng shui experts in their purchase of residential and burial sites, as well as in the layout of their houses and offices. For instance, James Fu Qian of Taiwan, the foreign minister of Republic of China (ROC), is a devoted believer in feng shui.

This Harvard-educated Ph.D. minister has an unshakable faith in the ancient art. It is said that wherever he goes to work, either in his ministerial office in Taipei or in the embassy building in Washington, D.C., he always hires geomancers to design his offices. Apparently, one door in his ministerial office has never been used since he's been there, apparently out of geomantic consideration.

It must be pointed out that feng shui is a double-edged sword in that it can be used artificially to bring not only good luck but also disaster. It has been a horrible weapon in the hands of some who seek to destroy their enemies. There are almost as many negative stories related to feng shui as positive ones.

For instance, it is documented in *History of Wu* by Chen Shau that the Beginning Emperor of the Chin dynasty (221–207 B.C.) once made an inspection tour of the city of Nanking after he had united the country. With him on the trip was a geomantic advisor, who was so amazed by the magnificent landforms surrounding the city that he described it as a city of "coiling dragons and crouching tigers"—a formidable strategic point with great potential for producing at least one emperor or becoming a national capital. This analysis and prediction painfully worried the Beginning Emperor, a cruel dictator who had burnt most of the books available at the time and buried alive hundreds of innocent intellectuals for fear that true knowledge in the hands of the people would lead to the overthrow of his totalitarian regime. This worry was not lost on the smart geomancer, who suggested a feasible method to sabotage the city's feng shui. The emperor gladly followed the advice and immediately ordered that a vital portion of the Zhong Mountains surrounding the city be hewed. This severely damaged the dragon Qi of the city. As a consequence, no emperor has ever come from Nanking throughout China's history.

Although the city had been the national capital during several dynasties, these dynasties were all short-lived, including the Nationalist government headed by Chiang Kai-shek, which was founded in 1911 but was toppled by the Communists in 1949. The reason why Nanking still served as a national capital for these dynasties was mainly because the Yangtze River curves and twists through the metropolis and the magnificent mountain landforms in the area.

Feng shui is rapidly gaining recognition and popularity in the Western world because it is offered as a pragmatic way to improve one's fate and combat the bad influences in the environment. In the United States, for instance, from small towns to large cities, Americans are embracing feng shui as a way to enhance their happiness and offset misfortune. The sale of octagonal mirrors (*ba-gua mirrors*) and amulets (talismans) has been booming in the United States, and feng shui books move steadily out of bookstores. More than a dozen specialized feng shui schools in America are now offering certification programs. The Feng Shui Institute of America in Wabasso, Florida, alone has graduated more than 1,000 students since opening in 1995. Established organizations like the American Institute of Architects and the American Society of Interior Design also sponsor workshops on feng shui. These workshops are often crowded with enthusiastic and curious audiences. Perhaps it is not an exaggeration to say that feng shui is a merging point where East meets West.

In its long history, feng shui has seen its share of ups and downs, but it has shown its strong survivability and great practical values. It can be expected that the subject will continue to expand and enjoy wider popularity well into the future.

Chapter 2

Guiding Principles of Feng Shui

As a product of Taoism, feng shui draws heavily upon many Taoist theories. For instance, Taoism advocates the theories of the five elements, of the yin-yang dichotomy, and the heaven-man-earth trinity. Even though the theory and practice of feng shui later split into two major schools—the Situation school and the Direction school—neither one ever escapes the theoretical framework of Taoism.

The Situation school uses the theory of the five elements to classify mountains, while the Direction school employs the same theory to determine the proper alignment and orientation of a house or tomb. Indeed, it is Taoism that has given feng shui the theoretical muscle to grasp the visible variations in topography and invisible connections between man and heaven, man and earth, heaven and earth, the living and the deceased.

It is a traditional Chinese belief that man's fate is determined to a large extent by how well he accommodates himself to the natural surroundings and the eternal rhythms that are in sync with the movements of heaven, man, and earth. Based on such a set of principles and their intuitive application, feng shui masters are able to define the auspicious and inauspicious properties of a land site. These principles are powerful tools in the hands of practitioners of feng shui. Anyone serious about studying feng shui will have to start with understanding these principles.

The following paragraphs discuss the guiding principles governing the practice of feng shui. They should be thoroughly understood and firmly kept in mind, because they pave the way for successfully practicing feng shui.

Principle of Yin and Yang

The ancient Chinese concept of the yin-yang dichotomy is a prevalent principle in traditional Chinese culture. In other words, the principle of yin and yang is the principle of principles. This concept classifies everything in the universe—materialistic, spiritual, spatial, and temporal—into two basic poles: yin and yang. To the ancient Chinese, the origin of the universe is *taiji*, or the Great Ultimate, which is the primitive nebulous Qi energy in the universe. It does not quite lend itself to the classification of yin and yang, since yin and yang existed in a mixed, unidentified state in taiji. Thanks to the constant evolution of taiji itself, the classification between yin and yang became possible and clear as time went by. In traditional Chinese thinking, this is the first classification of the universe. For this reason, yin and yang are called the Two Standard Powers.

In traditional Chinese culture, yin is conceived to be the collective representation of all forces in the universe that spring from the earth, while yang is the collective representation of all forces that emanate from heaven. By nature, yin is still and cumulative, while yang is mobile and circulating. Everything in the universe is the product of reaction and integration of these two kinds of Qi energy, which are at once opposite and complementary to one another. For example, yin stands for things feminine, dark, cold, weak, gentle, interior, and conservative, while yang stands for things masculine, bright, hot, strong, violent, exterior, and aggressive. Night is of yin nature, while day is of yang nature; winter is of yin nature, while summer is of yang nature.

According to the I-Ching, "Yin cannot give birth to things by itself, just like yang alone cannot grow. Tao is nothing but yin and yang combined in a harmonious way." By way of illustration, females alone cannot conceive (with the exception of St. Mary), not to mention males. But as yin meets yang, changes take place. It is the ongoing reaction and interaction between yin and yang that have created this immense universe full of a tremendous variety of things.

The images of the trigrams in the I-Ching convey to us this sense of interaction between the two standard powers. (See Figure 9-1, page 97, for an illustration of the trigrams. Yang is shown by a solid line, while yin is a broken line.) Of the eight trigrams, only two are pure forms: Qian, which is pure yang, and Kun, which is pure yin. (Notice that the trigram Qian is represented by three solid lines, the trigram Kun by three broken lines.) Statistically, this means that in six out of eight cases, yin and yang are mixed in the same thing or object. The probability for pure yin or pure yang is only 25 percent (two out of every eight). In other words, yin and yang combined is the norm, while pure yin and pure yang are exceptions.

It is only natural that feng shui should build part of its theoretical base on this principle. One way in which feng shui describes mountains and waterways is in terms of yin and yang: mountains are conceived to be yin in nature while water is conceived to be yang. Mountains are considered static—stability is the character of yin; water moves—mobility is the character of yang. Thus, from a feng shui perspective, mountains should be moving, so to speak, whereas water should be stable. Of course, this is a broad generalization. In fact, like almost everything in the universe, mountains and water have yin and yang elements. Therefore, some mountains are considered yang mountains as compared to others, exactly like some rivers are regarded as yang rivers as compared to other rivers.

For instance, while mountains are conceived to be yin in nature due to their stability, mountain ranges full of peaks and valleys (ups and downs) are considered yang-mountains, since their up and down shape imitates motion, which is characteristic of yang. For the same mountain, the front is considered yang while the back is considered yin. This is because the front receives the morning sunshine while the back is exposed to the afternoon sun. Since the morning is regarded as yang and the afternoon as yin, the front and back of a mountain correspond, respectively.

Similarly, while water is conceived to be yang in nature, because water is mobile and flowing, water that curves and stops in certain areas is considered yin-water, as compared to straight, fast-flowing water. Thus, ponds and peaceful lakes are largely regarded as yin-waters due to their relative stability.

This classification of the same objects into yin and yang is significant to the practice of feng shui. This alone tells us that Chinese geomancy is a profound art rather than a strict science. So much depends on the intuition, imagination, creative understanding, and flexible application of the same set of broad principles on the part of individual geomancers. In feng shui, changes and variations are the norm, the successful handling of which calls for artistic taste in addition to the solid understanding of basic principles.

If the existence of the universe depends on the harmonious combination of yin and yang, as is held by Chinese fathers, it stands to reason that good feng shui must reside in places where yin meets yang, or yin contains yang, and vice versa. Auspicious land sites are found wherever yin changes to yang or yang changes to yin. Thus, a flat mountain range is a dead dragon with little geomantic value, because such a mountain range symbolizes yin in its pure form which, according to I-Ching, cannot yield. However, if there are ups and downs in the mountain range, it turns into an active dragon full of life. By the same logic, a rapidly flowing river symbolizes yang in its pure form

and therefore cannot accumulate or gather. In a geomantic sense, it is not auspicious feng shui. However, when the river is checked by layers of mountains and is forced to slow down or even stop, it becomes a yin river which, when combined with its general nature of yang, will be very productive. Therefore, grounds and sites situated in the neighborhood of yang-mountains and yin-waters are auspicious sites.

In actual application, fathers of feng shui advocate that sites should be 60 percent yang and 40 percent yin. Yang should slightly outweigh yin in topography, not the other way around. If a location has more yin factor than yang factor, it is not considered to be very auspicious because it can bring about setbacks and frustrations to its residents. Of course, the disparity should not be too broad either, otherwise the situation of pure yin and pure yang occurs, neither of which is auspicious. Here again, we can see the artistic requirement of geomantic practice.

Principle of the Five Elements

The ancient Chinese believed that there are five basic elements from which everything in the universe is made, including human fate. These elements are water, fire, wood, metal, and earth. Two kinds of relationships exist among these elements—

mutually productive and mutually destructive. (See Figure 2-1.)

On the productive side, water nourishes wood, wood feeds fire, fire generates earth, earth creates metal, and metal yields water, completing a cycle of mutual production. On the destructive side, water vanquishes fire, fire melts metal, metal cuts wood, wood penetrates earth, and earth stops water, thus completing a cycle of mutual destruction. It is the productive cycle that is desired, and the destructive one that is to be avoided. This is the principle of the five elements in feng shui.

These five basic elements exist in various forms and manifest themselves in numerous ways such as shape, color, and direction. Professional feng shui practitioners should go a long way in identifying the elements contained in different objects in and around the location concerned. How meticulously they examine each mountain and river, even each stone and rock within sight, from the viewpoint

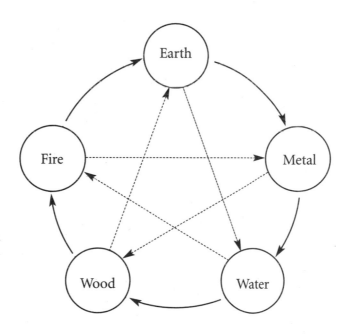

FIGURE 2-1
Productive and destructive relationships between the five elements
(solid lines = productive; dotted lines = destructive)

Element	Color	Shape	Season	Business
Water	Black	Round	Winter	Fishery, laundromat, seafood store, video store, travel agency
Fire	Red	Pointed	Summer	Restaurant, grocery store, department store, barber shop, beauty salon, clothes store
Wood	Green	Straight	Spring	Pharmacy, stationery store, bookstore, flower shop, fruit store, hospital, clinic, publishing house, furniture store
Metal	White	Square	Autumn	Auto shop, jewelry store, electronics, car rental, bank
Earth	Yellow	Flat	Two weeks between the four seasons	Rice store, accounting firm, attorney, construction, real estate, antique shop, funeral home

TABLE 2-1
Correspondences of the five elements

of the five elements is important. For example, in Table 2-1, page 24, the shape of fire is pointed. Therefore a stony ground with pointed rocks is predominantly a "fire" location which, if used to build a house, will have a good chance of causing fire in the building.

To better appreciate how this theory of the five elements can be applied to feng shui, we have to understand what these elements stand for. Table 2-1 illustrates what these five basic elements correspond to in terms of color, shape, season, and type of business.

According to Chinese fathers, man's fate, or karma, is realized at the time of birth which, in turn, is encoded in terms of the five elements, called the eight characters of birth. Since no karma is perfect, there is always some element in excess or deficiency. It is within the power of feng shui to create balance. For instance, if someone has too much water element in his or her karma, one way in which the person can overcome this disadvantage is to live in a place that is predominantly "earth" in nature, since earth can stop and absorb water. If one's karma favors metal, it would be inauspicious for him or her to live in a building painted red, because red represents fire, which can melt metal.

However, this is not to say that two mutually destructive elements, such as fire and water, must be bad when combined. Destruction in the context of Chinese divination, including feng shui, does not necessarily mean something bad. Actually, such a combination can be highly desirable under special circumstances. For example, summer is the season of fire and is a season when water is most needed. The same logic is applied to winter, which is the season of water. It is in this season of water that fire becomes indispensable to survival. Thus, we see the perfect combination of two mutually destructive elements: fire and water.

It is not so much the individual elements themselves as the specific circumstances in which different elements come into play that count. Hence, each situation—year of birth or land site—must be studied on a case-by-case basis.

Principle of the Heaven-Man-Earth Trinity

As mentioned before, Chinese fathers thought of heaven, man, and earth as a trinity. The technical term for feng shui is *Kun-yu*, which literally means "the heaven and the earth." The location, the environment, the structure, the interior decorations, and the direction that a house faces all fall under the dimension of earth. Most feng shui books only discuss these areas, at least in the case of most English literature on feng shui. It should not be forgotten that there are two other dimensions to the art of feng shui—man and heaven.

Man is the most active element in this trinity. It is he who builds the house, lives in it, arranges the furniture, and possesses the power and tools to change its appearance and configuration. Feng shui is one of the most effective tools where man can hope to change his fortune. In the final analysis, this influence exerted by man over a house through arrangement and location comes back to himself, and is reflected in his own well-being and good or bad luck. With a powerful knowledge of feng shui and an investment of time and energy, man can hope to prevail over heavenly forces, which very much determine our karma.

To prevail over heaven, or more exactly, to mold and improve our own fate, we must study each individual and each location carefully; that is how feng shui becomes an art. For one thing, the same color can mean different things to different people and can exert different influences on their lives. Another example of individuality is the orientation of a house, the appropriateness of which depends on the owner's year of birth. Bear in mind this principle and you will find it easier to come to terms with the fact that the same house can bring for-

tune or misfortune to the different owners living in it.

Heaven in feng shui means both astrology and timing. Chinese ancients believe that the stars in the heavens can affect the Qi energy of a location, depending on the relationship a location has with specific stars. The idea is to strike a balance among heaven, man, and the earth, so that the Qi energy in the environment can be further enhanced and utilized to man's advantage.

However, not all feng shui practitioners agree with this idea. Some, in fact, are against it on the grounds that stars alter their position from time to time, while the location of a house remains unchanged. If stars must be taken into account in the analysis of a house, then a good house may have to be dismantled sometime down the road in order to fit into the star position.

Still others maintain that the incorporation of stars into feng shui analysis unnecessarily complicates the whole matter, with little to be gained in the end. While the jury is still out on the issue of stars, the relevancy of timing to feng shui design is beyond any doubt. We will talk about timing later in this chapter.

Principle of Balance and Harmony

Balance and harmony are dominating concerns in traditional Chinese thinking. It could even be said that the Chinese are preoccupied with them. The principle of balance and harmony regarding a house has several dimensions. For example, a large house with only a few residents, a small house with big windows, or a large house with small doors are all considered out of balance.

This principle is another reason that motivates a geomancer to find a landscape where yin and yang are combined, so that a balance can be struck between yin and yang. For example, stability is a feature of yin (mountains), while mobility is a characteristic of yang (water). To strike a balance between mobility and stability, yin and yang, and mountains and water in a location, masters of feng shui employ several methods depending on individual situations.

One of the methods is to find a location with a combination of mountains and water in the surroundings. Thus, stability (mountains) and mobility (water) come together in harmony. While it is ideal to have both water and mountains in the same location, not all locations are gifted with both. In cases where there are only mountains but no water, or only water and few mountains, fathers of feng shui proposed the idea of seeking stability in mobility or vice versa. This means that in the cases where there is only water and no mountains, one should try to find a location where the water curves and turns as frequently as possible. This is because whenever the waterway curves, it automatically slows down, which is an image of stability, thus balancing with the mobility of the water. Similarly, if there are a lot of peaks and valleys in a mountainous location but no water, the mountains themselves seem to dance and move, which gives an image of mobility. This balances the stability of the mountains.

For instance, when there is flat ground among undulating mountains, or a bump in a vast expanse of flat terrain, or a pause in a course of rapids, a geomantic balance is found.

Land sites with good feng shui are always limited in number. Anywhere in the world, a good land site usually costs a lot of money. Worse still, money alone often is not enough to obtain such land. To make up for the natural shortage of good land supply, feng shui resorts to alternate means of design in the form of artificial mountains, fountains, gardens, and the like. The purpose is to make the land a more balanced, harmonious site. This is one of the major reasons why the Chinese are so sophisticated in the art of gardening, which has a distinctive mark of feng shui consideration in it. This is not yet the case in North American countries where the practice of feng shui is largely limited to the interior design and arrangement of a house.

Principle of Timing

Timing remains a crucial factor in feng shui. Indeed, timing is an essential factor in everything we do, because timing is an integral dimension of the universe. This idea, first proposed by Chinese ancients, is scientifically confirmed by Einstein in his broad theory of relativity.

The relationship between the time of construction of a building and its Qi energy was first proposed by a famous scholar during the Ming dynasty named Mu Jiangzen. Mu combined the nine palaces with the eight trigrams and developed the theory of *yuan-yun*.

In this theory, time is grouped in feng shui by periods of 180 years. Each period is further divided into three subperiods known as yuan. The first subperiod is called the "upper yuan," the second the "middle yuan," and the third the "lower yuan." Combined, a full era consists of nine yuans. Thus, we are in the upper yuan (1984–2043) of the lower epoch in our era. Thus, a school of feng shui that has timing as its primary focus is known as "three yuans feng shui."

A popular feng shui proverb also attests to the significance of timing in feng shui. This proverb says: "Feng shui keeps on rotating. It favors the land to the eastern bank of a river for the first thirty years, but shifts its favor to the land to the western side of the river for another thirty years." While we cannot take this proverb on its face from a numerological perspective, we must keep in mind that the Qi energy of a location does change with time. In a broad sense, nothing is constant in the universe; everything changes. This is the central theme of I-Ching, the Book of Change.

The above proverb originates from the ancient unit of timing, yuan, proposed by the great neo-Confucian scholar, Shao Yong, of the Song dynasty. Shao put forward the concept of yuan together with *hui*, *shi*, and *yun* as different measurements of time. According to him, our universe consists of three yuans. Each yuan consists of twelve huis. Each hui consists of thirty yuns. Each yun consists of twelve shis. Each shi lasts for thirty years. Thus, the life span of the universe is 388,800 years. This may sound ridiculous to most, but it has been so influential a concept in history that some geomancers could not help but believe it.

The law of timing is a universal one. For instance, we have different seasons for the sowing of crops, which have to be followed strictly. Violation of this law of timing will result in poor harvests and possibly even famine.

In feng shui, however, the concept of timing is more involved with five different meanings. First, timing refers to the homeowner's birthday or the birthday of the deceased (regarding the grave site). It was assumed by the ancient Chinese that a person's birthday determines his or her horoscope and, therefore, his or her fate. This horoscope, in turn, determines the person's lucky direction and location on earth. However, there is no such thing as a forever auspicious direction and location for everybody, if only because the birthday horoscope varies from one year to another and from one person to another.

Second, timing refers to the date of construction or the age of a building. Third, it refers to the time when a new owner moves into a building. Fourth, it relates to the length of time it takes for a site to show its geomantic effects, good or bad, auspicious or inauspicious. Fifth, there is the issue of how long a land site can keep its good luck, say, for only one generation, or two or more generations. These multiple meanings of time in feng shui have contributed to its highly dynamic nature.

How long it takes a site to manifest its geomantic effects, good or bad, once it is occupied for burial or residential pur-pose, largely depends on the geomantic features of the site and its surroundings. My teacher calls it the "strength of the earth," which is just another way of describing the Qi energy of the land site. The stronger the Qi reserves in a land site, as manifested by its surroundings, the sooner good luck will come to its inhabitants or their descendants. Likewise, the more malignant the geomantic environment of a land site is, the sooner misfortune will visit.

For instance, the longer and more undulating a mountain vein near a specific site is located, and the taller the surrounding mountains with favorable shapes (such as a tiger, dragon, lion, general, pen, drum, or warehouse), the more powerful the Qi energy reserve of the site will be. Therefore, the sooner good luck will come to those who live there. In contrast, the faster and louder the water flows away from a site without being checked, the sooner misfortune and disaster will visit. Even the distance between a site and specific mountains is another factor that helps determine the timing of geomantic effects. Thus, the same auspicious mountains, if located close to a site, will cause the site to manifest its auspicious effects quicker than if they are located far away from the site.

As to how many generations a site will bring good luck to its residents is a more complicated issue. Basically, two factors account for the length of time a site will continue to bring good luck to its residents. One factor is the strength of the earth in the site itself, and the other is the type of good luck, i.e., a million dollars or becoming president.

As a general rule, the greater the strength of the earth, or the stronger the Qi energy of the land site, the longer a site will be able to bring good luck. Also, the smaller amount of good luck that is enjoyed by one generation, the more Qi energy will remain in the reserves and therefore last for more generations. For example, if the maximum amount of good luck that a site can yield is $1 billion, and you take a lump sum, you should not be surprised to find that the land is less and less favorable each passing day. On the other hand, if you only take $1 million for a generation, the same land would be able to support your family's financial luck for 1,000 generations. That is why villages in China that had given birth to founding emperors were often found afflicted with famine and flood, since the Qi reserve of the land had been largely consumed during the course of creating founding emperors.

Principle of Topography Flow

This principle deals with the general flow of the topography in terms of water and mountains: "being with or at odds with the flow." It is one of the single most important principles in the selection of sites. Li Mozai of the Ming dynasty, for instance, underscores the importance of this principle in *Pi Jin Jing*, his insightful book on feng shui:

> *To be with or at odds with the general flow is the most vital consideration in the practice of feng shui. All other considerations will become illusory if one does not understand the meaning of going with or against the flow. Ordinary feng shui practitioners may have five years of experience and yet still ignorant of what are meant by "with" and "at odds." They are like blind people leading others to proceed. What nonsense!*

The term "flow" in this principle should be understood in a broader sense. It refers not only to the direction of the water flow, but also to the direction a mountain range runs, or a coastline, as well as the general topography. "Being with the flow" means to go in the same direction as the mountain range or watercourse runs. "Being at odds with" means to go in the opposite direction that the mountain range or watercourse runs.

For instance, mountains are considered to be with the trend if they are largely flat, straightforward, with little undulation, and curving. Likewise, water that runs directly away from a land site without being checked is considered being with the trend. By contrast, mountains full of rises and falls, peaks and valleys, curves and turns are considered being at odds with the trend. So also is water that is checked by mountains, stones, or islands, so that the water is forced to slow down, stop, or turn around.

As a general geomantic principle, we must look for land sites that are "at odds with the flow" in an area that largely "goes with the flow," or vice versa, look for land sites that "go with the flow" in an area that largely is "at odds with the flow."

This is a secret of feng shui that has been kept for centuries. Only the wise feng shui masters can understand and appreciate it. If a geomancer is ignorant of this secret of "being with versus being at odds with" regarding the topographic flow of a site, beautiful mountains in the surroundings would be to no avail. But if a geomancer follows this secret, ordinary mountains can be of great value. In other words, such a location will bring good luck for three generations.

Water is mobile. Checked (blocked), it will stay with you; unchecked, it will run away from you. Since water stands for wealth in feng shui, we certainly want it to stay with us. If water flows away unchecked, it is like allowing money to leak from a pocket unguarded.

The ideal situation then is a terrain that goes with the watercourse while having some mountains downstream that somewhat check the water flow, forcing it to turn and slow down (at odds with).

There are various ways to block the flowing away of water. For instance, if there are hills downstream, they can provide effective checks or blocks. If hills or mountains are located far away downstream, then they must be big and tall in order to provide efficient blockage to the water flow. In the absence of hills and mountains, checks can still be found in the form of graded pads (similar to pads for growing rice that look like stairs) downstream that slightly change the course of flow to make it less abrupt. If the checking objects are close enough that you think you can touch them, you will have both wealth and power.

If the water flows from the right to the left of a site, then you need to see whether there are high mountains on the left (downstream). If not, see whether there are large, tall trees in that direction. These objects are good protectors called "promoting spirits," and the taller they are, the better the feng shui will be. On the other hand, if mountains or trees are found on the right (upstream), they are considered "demoting spirits," which have a bad impact on the residents. With such a terrain, nothing will remain in the end even if you now own ten thousand acres.

Note: To know which direction is right or left, stand in front of the site and look outward, away from the site.

However, water that turns and flows back to a site must be evaluated on a case-by-case basis. This is because not all "returning waters" are good, if you do not know how to correctly choose a site where there is returning water. Again, this idea is clearly elaborated by Li Mozai as follows:

> *The kind of lands that can quickly bring tremendous good luck to their residents are those that have waters coming back to them after flowing away in the front. However, returning waters can also cause fast failure and disasters to the residents. This is because a land site facing a returning water is usually located at the end of a mountain. As such, it often lacks sufficient protection on the sides. Particularly, the bright hall is often so large that Qi energy gets dispersed. Of course, if the returning water is accompanied by several branches of curving mountains, or there are mountains on both flanks of the site, or there is a huge mountain guarding the Earthly Door of the water down the stream, or there are three to five small mountains standing in the Bright Hall, this becomes a best site. Needless to say, such a land site is very hard to find. Short of an ideal landform, a site can still be auspicious if there are a couple of mountain branches turning inward like pincers to intercept the water in-between, plus one or two hills guarding the water gate down the stream. To say the least of it, there must be one mountain guarding the water gate down the stream. Otherwise, residents on the site are vulnerable to alternations between success and failure.*

Thus, we see the importance of taking into account the topography of a land site. This will help identify whether a site is with or at odds with a waterway in the vicinity. The original purpose of feng shui is to find a site of construction that can store and contain, rather than disperse and waste, the lively Qi energy in the environment. If the terrain of a location runs parallel to the course of water, the lively Qi energy will be beneficial to the inhabitants. On the contrary, if a location bears the brunt of oncoming water, evil spirits will hit the location and its inhabitants head-on as well.

Another creative application of this principle is to select a piece of land in a relatively flat area among a series of mountains that descend in height until they flatten out. This downward slope represents the run of the mountains and therefore "goes with the flow." In this case, if there is no water present in the area, it is all right to build on the site with the front of the building facing the descending mountains. Since the descending trend of the mountains is the direction in which mountains go, to build a house with its front facing this direction is to go at odds with the flow. This technique of pinpointing a site is known as "riding a dragon backward" in feng shui.

Principle of Normality and Abnormality

This principle is an extension of the previous principle of going with or at odds with the flow. It is actually a shortcut to the laborious task of finding auspicious sites for construction. Auspicious feng shui sites are most easily found by looking for abnormalities amid the normality of a landform. Abnormalities are considered auspicious since normal stands for commonplace while abnormal stands for extraordinary.

An abnormality refers to the uncharacteristic features of a landform. For example, the dominating feature of a flat site lies in the flatness of the landform, and therefore flatness is the norm. In contrast, in mountainous areas, the normality is the undulation of the landform. If flatness is the norm, then protrusions are abnormal. Likewise, if undulation is the norm, then flatness becomes abnormal. Using the same logic, a piece of dry land in a country abounding in rivers and lakes is considered abnormal, whereas a lake becomes the abnormality in a dry land such as a desert.

This principle of normality and abnormality includes the contrasts between long and short, high and low, etc. For instance, there are long and short mountains. In an area where long mountains abound, it is a feng shui principle to look for auspicious sites located in short mountains, and vice versa. By similar token, if an area is characterized by high mountains, this principle advises us to look for auspicious sites located in relatively flat lands.

Chapter 3

Burial Feng Shui

Traditional Chinese culture stresses filial piety to one's parents and ancestors. However, it is not this consideration that led the Chinese fathers to study burial feng shui. Actually, it was a very selfish concern that motivated them to learn the art of burial feng shui: to bring good luck to themselves.

It is the Chinese belief that even if one is dead, one will still be connected to his descendants for at least three generations. The means of this connection is the mysterious Qi energy. This kind of connection can directly influence the fate of the descendants. Therefore, if the remains of ancestors are buried in auspicious grounds, the descendants will be happy and successful in life. On the other hand, if ancestors are buried in inauspicious grounds, such as one that is wet or the gathering place of ants, the descendants will be star-crossed and miserable in life.

It is this understanding that led to a profound study on the art of burial feng shui, with the focus on finding how different topographic and environmental features of burial grounds could affect the life and fortune of the living. A Taoist named Qin Niao Tse (475–221 B.C.) wrote a book on burial geomancy titled *Examining the Burial Ground*, but the book was lost.

However, the art of burial remained an oral tradition in China for many generations until another Taoist, Guo Pu of the Jin dynasty, summed up this oral tradition and added his own research and experience. The result was his monumental *Book of Burial*. It is in this epochal book that the term "feng shui" was first used. Guo said: "In terms of priority, the first thing in geomancy is to secure shui (water), and the second thing is to shield away from feng (wind)." That is to say, the secrets of feng shui lie in getting water in the first place, and protecting against the blow of wind in the second place. From then on, feng shui came to stand for the art of Kun-yu, and gradually replaced it as a household name for geomancy in China.

The Chinese culture holds that a person should never forget where he or she comes from. The Chinese like to say: "When you drink water, think of its sources." This means, first of all, taking care of one's ancestors even if they are no more. By way of feng shui, this means burying the remains of one's ancestors at auspicious feng shui sites.

Of course, filial piety is not the sole reason why the Chinese want to bury their ancestors at auspicious burial grounds. More important than filial consideration is the consideration for self-benefit. They believe that our bodies are an extension of our ancestors. Therefore, our fate is determined to a large extent by the Qi energy in and surrounding the graves in which our ancestors rest.

Modern science tells us that if our parents are strong and healthy, we will be born strong and healthy. If they are intelligent and well educated, most likely we will be born with a higher IQ. Hence the Chinese saying that "dragons beget dragons and phoenixes beget phoenixes." In fact, this biological connection between parents and children doesn't just exist at physical and intellectual levels. It also exists with regard to fate. Chinese fathers hold that we are influenced by our ancestors for at least three generations. Therefore, the well-being of our ancestors will indirectly affect our own fate through feng shui.

It is believed that the soul of the dead is divided into several parts, each of which has to be dealt with appropriately before the deceased can rest beneath the earth. The remains of the ancestors form a big reservoir of yin forces (hence the branch of feng shui governing the rules of burial is known as the feng shui of the yin-house) which, when buried underground, can absorb the Qi energy in the burial grounds and the environment in the surroundings, and exert significant influence on the welfare of the living relatives and descendants. If ancestors can rest comfortably under the ground, they can help bring good luck and happiness to their children. Otherwise, their children will suffer from misfortune, simply because they are still linked to their ancestors for many generations. Understandably, many wealthy Chinese have been making an incredible amount of effort to auspiciously site the graves of their ancestors. This is especially the case in the southern part of China, where the bones of important ancestors are often dug out of the original graves and moved to more auspicious burial grounds meticulously selected when such sites become available, usually as a result of financial success on the part of the descendants.

As a keynote, Guo Pu said at the beginning of *Book of Burial:* "Since our bodies are derived from our ancestors, it becomes inevitable that if their remains gain the strong Qi energy from the environments, we descendants will benefit accordingly." Guo lost no time in pointing out that the first criterion of a burial site was the quality and quantity of the earthly Qi energy contained in the ground. Guo continues to say:

> The objective of burial feng shui is to take advantage of the Qi energy of the deceased. . . . For life is nothing but the reaction of Qi energy, which is condensed into the skeleton as one ceases to be. Flesh decays and disappears but the skeleton remains. At that time, Qi energy returns to the bones and remains in the grave for a long time to come. That is why the deceased can protect and benefit their descendants.

We owe our physical existence to our parents. That is to say, we are the physical extensions of our parents' bodies. Thus, if the skeletons of our parents receive strong and good Qi energy in the environment, our own bodies benefit as a result. This is an example how Qi reacts and interacts—that the deceased can benefit the living. Mountains and rivers have spirits but no owners. Skeletons have owners but no spirit. The combination of the two results in various fortunes depending on what kind of Qi is absorbed by the skeletons, which affects the living in various ways.

In other words, the ancient Chinese believed that parents and children are related to each other like the trunk and branches of a tree. A strong trunk yields good branches, whereas a weak trunk gives birth to weak branches. This relationship exists long after the parents have passed away, realized through the feng shui or Qi energy of the burial grounds of ancestors. The Qi energy of the burial ground serves as a conduit between the deceased and the living members of the family. If the deceased are buried in good sites full of live Qi energy, they can transmit this auspicious Qi energy to their offspring and enhance their fate. However, if they are buried in inauspicious locations vulnerable to ill winds or are barren of grass and trees, their offspring will suffer as a consequence. Some geomancers think this interaction between the living and the dead is caused by electromagnetic effects in the earth.

All this is the result of Qi, and Qi is critical to the living and the deceased alike. It is the Qi that connects the living and the deceased in a mysterious way. This is a two-way street in that the living choose the burial site for the deceased and the deceased pass on the Qi they receive from the burial ground to the living members of the family. Depending on the quality and amount of Qi received by the deceased, this process of Qi transmittal can be beneficial or harmful to the living. If the burial site is full of lively Qi, which is well protected by mountains and water, the living members of the family will be healthy, happy, and successful, because the auspicious Qi energy in the surroundings of the burial ground can be transmitted to the descendants.

Many great personalities in history have benefited from the strong Qi energy surrounding the burial grounds of their ancestors, such as Yuan Shi-kai, Chiang Kai-shek, and Mao Tse-tung.

In modern terms, this phenomenon can be interpreted in terms of radio waves and receptors. Radios are tuned to different frequencies to receive different messages. Members of the same family use the same biological frequency in their communication. Even if some of the family members are deceased, their remains keep emitting radio waves that can only be received by their dear survivors and even remote descendants. If their remains are buried in an auspicious land full of Qi energy, the radio waves they emit are received by their survivors and descendants, thus benefiting their lives.

Thus, the feng shui of our ancestors' burial grounds is believed to be one of the most important factors in determining our own well-being. Nowadays, people are so selfish that they only care about their own comforts as they can see it, to the total ignorance and neglect of the comfort and security of their ancestors in their resting places. They fail to realize that this is not only a selfish, but also foolish behavior on their part, because the well-being of their deceased ancestors bears on their own well-being.

This connection between the deceased and the living can also be reflected in our faces. That is to say, our faces reflect the geomantic quality of the burial grounds of our ancestors. Chinese ancients believed that our faces are a recorder of our fate, which in turn is a reflection of the burial feng shui of our ancestors. Thus, by simply looking at a person's face, an experienced Chinese geomancer would be able to tell the geographic and topographic features of the burial ground of that person's ancestors. For example, if a man possesses an outstanding nose with a high, straight nose bridge, a pair of thick eyebrows, and high cheekbones, his ancestors must be buried at a site that has mountains resembling a banner, drum, or tank in its surroundings. The man with such facial features is or will be a great general, for a burial ground with the geomantic features described above is bound to generate great soldiers. Similarly, if a person possesses a broad, high forehead, a pair of thick, long ears, and a fleshy nose or a thick chin, that person's ancestors must be buried at a site surrounded by staying, curving waters, or flanked and faced with mountains with the shape of a warehouse. Both the face and the geomantic features of the ground suggest that he is or will be a very rich man. By the same analogy, if a person has irregular facial features, say a crooked nose or mouth, or a pair of ears of obviously unequal size and length, that person's ancestors must be buried at a site that is biased, and surrounded by pointed, slanting mountains. This correspondence between a person's face and the burial ground of his or her ancestors' is inevitable.

In a sense, the burial feng shui is more critical to the shaping of fate than residential feng shui. A burial ground is more stable and lasts longer than a residence, which can change from time to time. Especially in the modern world where mobility is a keynote of life, we may change houses many times in our life. Because the effect of Qi is cumulative, the more stable a location, the greater and more lasting its geomantic impact on our fortune. That is the major reason why the Chinese pay so much attention to burial feng shui.

Chapter 4

Key Factors in Feng Shui

The following are seven key elements of consideration in feng shui: Qi, mountains, water, wind, soil, direction and orientation, and timing.

Qi

Qi is a vital concept in feng shui, as it is in many other traditional Chinese fields. For instance, traditional Chinese medicine holds that Qi is the essence of life, and that the quality and quantity of Qi a person possesses largely determines his or her health status and life span. The Chinese speak of young and healthy people as "full of Qi," of the weak as "short of Qi," and of the dead as "out of Qi."

In feng shui, Qi is a geographic substance. It is contained in the earth and moves around along the mountain ranges, beneath the ground. This kind of Qi is different from the Qi energy in our body.

Qi in the universe was originally an entity called taiji. Taiji is divided into two polars—yin and yang—which are further broken down into the five elements. It is this Qi that gives birth to everything in the universe. Although Qi moves in the air, it is actually accumulated on earth. Wherever it gathers and accumulates, the essences of yin and yang are combined and condensed. This traditional understanding is basic and essential to feng shui. In the absence of it, all practice of feng shui becomes groundless and nonsensical.

Qi is at once a universal concept as well as a multidimensional one. It is said in the *Book of Burial*:

> *The Qi energy made of yin and yang can assume various forms. It can blow as wind, ascend to become clouds, fall in rain, travel under the ground as lively Qi, which gives birth to everything on earth. . . . Earthly Qi travels under the ground. The manner in which it travels varies with the topographic situations of the ground. As the situation stops, Qi accumulates there. Therefore, the secret of burial lies in taking advantage of the stops in topographic situations (i.e., flat land). To detect and recognize such stops, one has to study the origins of mountains, which cause topography to change. Thus, in plain areas, one has to follow the "pulse" of the earth. In mountainous areas, one has to study the "spines" or "backbones" of the mountains, which sometimes head towards the south, sometimes turn to the east, sometimes run towards the west, and sometimes extend to the north. Mountains over 1,000 feet in height and areas over one square mile in size are considered situations, while smaller mountains and lands are considered forms. As Qi energy travels with situations and comes to a stop with forms, forms become reservoirs of Qi. Burial grounds should be chosen at such reservoirs.*

Thus, the fathers of feng shui believe that topographic changes—changes in mountain forms in particular—are what cause the earthly Qi to become stronger. (An example of a topographic change is if a mountain range approaches the ocean and eventually stops in front of it.) Qi reservoirs are formed when Qi stops or slows down. Auspicious sites must be places where earthly Qi energy stops and accumulates. Only where Qi gathers can life prosper and good luck come.

Another vital thing about earthly Qi is that it should be continuous. In fact, the longer Qi energy travels uninterrupted before it comes to stop, and the more undulating the topography along the way, the greater will be the Qi reserve, and therefore, the more auspicious it will be. However, when a mountain range is suddenly obstructed by a natural feature such as a valley, river, or ocean, or a man-made construction project such as a tunnel, highway, or canal, the earthly Qi underground is interrupted and jeopardized.

Note: When I say that Qi should stop or slow down, I mean Qi should stop or slow down after the dragon (mountain range) has traveled for a long distance. However, it is bad for Qi to be interrupted before it has traveled a long way.

Fathers of feng shui say that whenever the topography suddenly changes from a group of undulating mountains into a vast plain, the movement of Qi will slow down if not completely stop there. This often happens when a mountain range is interrupted by water.

Feng shui distinguishes between earthly Qi and heavenly Qi. Earthly Qi is the Qi energy hidden under the ground of a land site, while heavenly Qi is the Qi energy permeating the air of the environment surrounding the land site. Fathers of feng shui tell us that a land site with strong earthly Qi energy must be located close to curving or still water, on high ground, or surrounded by green, lush mountains on all sides. This is because water and mountains can stop the loss of Qi energy, while a high land position suggests the land is, so to speak, pushed up by Qi energy, which must be strong and powerful at the location.

As for heavenly Qi, it is manifested in a landscape surrounded by magnificent and lush mountains, and/or encircled by curving waterways. Even common sense suggests that such an environment must be full of Qi in the air, for mountains covered in lush, green forestation are symbolic of strong life energy, while water is one of the most essential elements of all lifeforms.

Since earthly Qi energy is so vitally important to feng shui, a geomancer should know what kinds of landforms contain strong Qi energy.

- Mountains that look like a thousand horses galloping in the air must be full of earthly Qi energy.

- If an area is dominated by a group of mountains that look like dragons flying and phoenixes dancing, the area must possess plenty of Qi energy.

- If there are a series of peaks, each one rising higher than the other, as if like waves, the area must have an abundance of Qi energy.

- If the mountains look like a dragon descending from the sky, or look like layers of houses lining up one after another, or are surrounded by curving waterways and vegetation, this must be an area that abounds in Qi energy.

- If the mountains in the surroundings look like plants and trees, people related to the land will be prosperous.

- If the topography is suggestive of a person putting on his or her clothes, landlords or successful realtors will be born there.

The following are landforms that deplete Qi energy.

- If the area looks like a snake getting ready to bite, or if the mountains are uneven (leaning) and pointed, such a locality will lead to bankruptcy and even discontinuation in the family line.

- If the mountain peaks are suggestive of swords and spears, sharp and jagged, such a place will cause the residents to die a violent death.

- If mountains or rivers resemble rapid, straight-flowing water, the residents or descendants of the buried will suffer from starvation.

- If the mountains look like a boat turned upside down, they will bring various diseases.

- If the mountain looks like a sandbag, houses built nearby will burn down some day.

Mountains

In feng shui, mountains are held to be the main carriers of Qi energy in the earth. Since the image of a mountain vein suggests the shape of a dragon—long and bumpy (peaks and valleys)—mountains are called "dragons." Two reasons account for this widespread use of the dragon image. First, the dragon is thought to be the most powerful and auspicious animal in traditional China. Second, the general terrain and shape of a mountain range is best described in terms of a dragon among all other animals—prolonged, vibrating, fluctuating, full of ups and downs as well as twists and turns. Indeed, no other animal comes as close as the dragon does to the image of a mountain range.

Mountains provide two vital functions. First, mountains carry Qi energy underground to various land sites in their journey, enabling these land sites to bring good luck to people. Second, mountains protect land sites from the attack of evil winds, which can include storms and hurricanes, so that the precious lively Qi energy in the site can remain and nourish the land and its residents.

How well mountains can perform the first function depends largely on the length of the dragon and the shape of *shas* (small hills). Dragons refer to mountain veins, while shas refer to individual mountains and hills. Whether mountains can do a good job in protecting a land site from the attack of evil winds depends on how close they are to a land site and how flat and open the area is.

Of course, the dragon is not the only image that is widely used in feng shui. Quite a lot of other images are also employed to help understand the geomantic significance of individual mountains. For instance, there are images of ox, tiger, lion, dog, wolf, bear, deer, eagle, horse, tortoise, phoenix, ape, monkey, crane, rat, cock, and so on. The total number of such images used in feng shui exceeds 200.

Besides animal images, the images of plants and people of different walks of life are also employed. For instance, we find the following images also appearing in feng shui theory and practice: lotus flower, rose, drum, boat, pencil, flag, general, soldier, dancer, women, and so on. Some geomancers liken a group of mountains and hills to interrelated muskmelon vines. Thus, the main peaks of the mountain ranges are perceived to be the roots of the melon vines, and the surrounding hills are thought of as branches of the vine, grown out of the trunk. The open land and plateau among these hills are thought of as the leaves in the spreading branches. Animate or inanimate, all these images have the basic function of revealing the hidden geomantic meaning of topographic situations.

Water

It is no mere coincidence that water stands for wealth in feng shui, which holds that an ideal site must have some water in its surroundings. The importance of water can be readily appreciated from the term "feng shui" itself. Literally, it means "wind and water" in Chinese, which geomantically means "to get water" and "to be protected from wind." Chinese fathers put these two concepts together because wind is considered a counterforce to Qi energy and should therefore be avoided, whereas water is a favorable force for Qi energy and should be sought out.

Of the two major considerations in feng shui analysis—water and mountains, some geomancers hold that water is of greater importance than mountains. Others hold that the emphasis shifts from one topography to another. Thus, in mountainous areas, dragon pulses—the peaks and valleys in mountains—are more important than water, because the shapes of the mountains very much determine the feng shui of a location. In flat areas, however, water becomes more significant than mountains. (These factors will be discussed later on.)

Water serves two major functions in feng shui. First, it can create wealth, and secondly, it can protect Qi energy from being blown away by the wind.

As a general rule, the bigger the construction site, the larger the body of water that is desired. Therefore, we often find major cities built along seacoasts or on the banks of major rivers. In China, for instance, there is Shanghai, Nanjing, Hong Kong, and many other major cities situated by water. The significance of water is not lost to urban designers in other countries. There are many metropolises built along bodies of water: St. Petersburg, Russia; Lisbon, Portugal; Tokyo, Japan; London, England; Dublin, Ireland; Rome, Italy; Calcutta, India; Sydney, Australia; as well as many in the United States such as New York, Miami, Boston, Seattle, San Francisco, and Los Angeles. The continuous prosperity of these cities bears witness to the validity of this feng shui principle.

The importance of water lies in that water can readily absorb Qi energy in the universe. A body of water effectively checks or slows down the flowing away of Qi. An interesting analogy can help bring to light this "magical" function of water. Police dogs are very helpful in tracking people, because these dogs have a very keen sense of smell. However, if the object being tracked crosses a river, dogs quickly lose track of the scent. It is because of the water. This experience demonstrates that water can effectively stop the flow of Qi. In other words, it can form an effective check for the flowing away of Qi energy. In the presence of water, Qi will linger and accumulate in an area. In the absence of water or mountains, however, Qi energy will disperse easily when the wind blows. Therefore, an ideal site should have both mountains and water.

Wind

It is a feng shui understanding that the wind can blow away Qi energy. The stronger the wind, the greater harm it will do to a site and its residents. Not all winds are bad, though. A mild breeze from the south in the summer is a very desirable thing to have. Actually, it is the most benevolent kind of wind, welcomed by all. By contrast, the most malignant wind is the bitter northern wind in the wintertime. This is one of the reasons why the Chinese want to build houses with a frontal exposure toward the south, so they can benefit from the benevolent southern winds. From a feng shui point of view, there are many more malignant winds than benevolent ones. Therefore, to risk overgeneralization, wind is to be avoided. The most effective way to avoid strong winds is to have a land site located in the midst of mountains and/or surrounded by water.

Land

An auspicious land site is known as a "dragon lair" in feng shui, meaning "a locality where a dragon rests." A dragon lair is full of auspicious Qi energy. I tend to compare a land site to an acupoint on the human body. An acupoint is a focal point where bodily Qi energy gathers. Touching this point can affect the Qi energy balance in the body, bringing about healing or disease in a person, depending on how that balance is affected. Similarly in feng shui, a dragon lair or auspicious land site is a location where earthly Qi energy gathers, which can affect the fortune of the residents. Dragon lairs are the reservoirs of earthly Qi energy.

Fathers of feng shui have classified auspicious land sites into four basic types: protruding, nest, pincers, and breast. The first type of dragon site is called a protruding site, which is literally a small protrusion in a flat area.

The second type is known as a nest site, which is characterized by flat land in the front, with some kind of protrusion in the rear, and mountains on both sides for protection.

The third type of dragon site is called a pincer site, which is similar to a nest site but has longer "embracing" or curving mountains on both sides, which look like the pincers of a lobster.

The fourth kind is called a breast site, because it is hidden between two tall mountain peaks, similar to the shape of a woman's breasts.

Soil

The soil of a land site also has meaning in feng shui. From a scientific viewpoint, the quality of the soil at a construction site directly affects the stability of the building, or the preservation of the coffin and body buried in it. If water and stones can be likened to the blood and bones in the body, then soil is the flesh. Blood circulates in the flesh, not in the bones. Therefore, a land site full of stones does not have good feng shui, because such soil hinders the circulation of earthly Qi. Similarly, soil containing a lot of tree roots is not auspicious, nor is soil that is too dry or too wet. High-quality soil should be solid but moist, yellow or red in color, clean, and unpolluted.

Direction and Orientation

Almost all projects on earth have a dimension of direction. Which way is it facing? What stands in its view? What objects are to the right, left, back, or front? These are questions a homeowner should know the answers to.

The direction of the topography should also be considered. For example, rivers have their direction of flow, as do mountain veins. In analyzing a mountain vein, note which direction it flows into a specific land site. Similarly, in surveying a body of water, know which direction the water flows. While a mountain or a river may be auspicious in itself, its auspiciousness will be reduced if a house is built with the homeowner's desirable direction running counter to the direction of the mountains or water.

Of particular importance is the frontal exposure of a building. As mentioned before regarding the wind, the frontal exposure of a building should face the south. The wind coming from the south is the mildest and gentlest, and therefore is considered a favorable and welcome wind. Such a favorable wind can bring lively Qi energy to the house, rather than taking away the lively Qi energy from the house; bring about good luck for the residents rather than causing trouble for them. This is especially true for residential buildings, for in the winter the sun shines at the house from the south whereas in the summer, the sun casts its light on the house from the west. A house thus built can accept the maximum warmth from the sunshine during the winter, while avoid most of the heat during the summer. Yet another important reason for a southern exposure is the south-north alignment. This corresponds to the two poles of the earth, where the strongest electromagnetic waves of the earth are to be found. As has been mentioned before, Qi energy is a kind of electromagnetic wave. As such, the building will be able to absorb the maximum Qi energy hidden beneath the earth in addition to the Qi brought about by the southern wind.

Although it is generally desirable that the front of a residence faces south, the issue is more complicated. Three factors determine the appropriate orientation of a residence. These factors are the terrain of the land, the location and shape of the mountains and water in the environment, and the birthday of the owner. We have briefly touched on the terrain and topographic shapes, leaving the topic of the owner's birthday to be discussed.

Timing

The dominant feature of timing is change, which is also characteristic of feng shui, since the whole universe, including earth and human beings, are in a constant state of change. Since feng shui is an art that seeks to benefit humans, it is inevitable that man plays a central role in feng shui design. This is reflected in the ancient Chinese philosophy of heaven-man-earth trinity. The human factor of feng shui is first and foremost reflected in the birthday of the owner of the residence or business for whom feng shui is designed.

This factor of timing determines, to a large extent, the appropriate orientation of the house, the correct layout of the bedrooms, kitchen, living room, bathrooms, and so on inside the house, the desirable colors to paint a house with, as well as the timing of when a house should be built and moved into.

Due to the role individual owners play, the same residence can have a very different impact on the welfare of its residents. Thus, the same residence may fit one family very well, but cause a lot of trouble for another family. This is similar to the foods people eat. The same kind of food may agree with some people while causing indigestion in others.

The birthday of the homeowner is more important than the other residents in a house is because the homeowner is typically considered the head of the household, who is responsible for the livelihood and well-being of the family. The role he or she plays in the residence is similar to that of a chief executive officer or chairperson of a company. Both are mainly responsible for the success or failure of the group of people under them.

The direction or location a person's year of birth falls in is known as his or her "karma palace," or "original palace." This is in light of the nine palaces in correspondence with the eight trigrams of I-Ching.

For instance, if a woman was born in the year 1950, her karma palace is Kan or north. However, if a man was born in the same year, his karma palace is Kun or southwest. We will come back to this issue of birth year in chapter 9 (the *ba-gua* system). For the time being, know that everyone is born with an individual karma, which should be an integral factor in the overall feng shui design.

Chapter 5

Exploring Qi

Qi is on top of the list of key feng shui elements. The ancient Chinese regard Qi as the most original, fundamental raw material, the basis of which everything in the universe is created. Thus, Qi bears on a person's fate, health, and life. Not surprisingly, Qi is also the central concern in the art of feng shui. In fact, all efforts in feng shui design can be boiled down to the goal of promoting and conserving the Qi energy in a site.

Since humans live on earth, inevitably, they are all influenced by the earthly Qi energy in the environment. It takes little imagination to see that if the Qi reserve in the ground and in the surroundings is strong and abundant, residents will be born strong and abundant, and will have good luck in life. On the other hand, if the Qi reserve is low and polluted, residents will have ill luck and a frustrated life.

Besides earthly Qi, we are also influenced by heavenly Qi, which flows in the air. In recent years, radio astronomers have discovered that Qi is a kind of microwave radiation, including celestial electromagnetic radiation, in the background of the universe as it was first created. One article agreeing with this theory is titled "Cutting Through the Chatter About Feng Shui, Physics, and the Forces of the Universe" by Jawaharlal Nehru. Thanks to developments in science, we have been able to get a modern interpretation of this most mysterious element in feng shui.

Generally, this kind of microwave radiation cannot be physically seen or felt by people. However, there have been people who can physically see or feel the movement of Qi energy in the environment. Queen Lu, the first wife of Liu Bang, first emperor of the Han dynasty (206 B.C.–A.D. 220), possessed this special ability to sense the flow of Qi. It is said that before Liu Bang became emperor, he had extramarital affairs, but his wife, Lu, was able to tell exactly where he was at specific times, even though he was hiding deep in the forests or high in the mountains. Repeatedly, Liu was surprised by his wife's ability to keep track of him tens of miles away from home. Once found by his wife

deep in the forest after being away for two days, Liu asked his wife: "How did you know I was here?" Queen Lu replied: "Wherever you go, there is always some special Qi energy following you in the air. This special Qi is made of five different colors. I just follow the Qi and have been able to locate you."

History books seem to suggest that her ability was inherited from her father, because it is told that he also possessed such an ability. Queen Lu's father was the owner of a small liquor store, which Liu Bang liked to visit often before he became emperor. He often drank too much and, as a result, he slept in the store for a few hours. Several times while Liu was asleep, his future father-in-law could see a special aura of colorful Qi lingering around his head. Sometimes, a white tiger showed up amid the aura. This convinced him that Liu possessed the Mandate of Heaven, and was going to establish a dynasty of his own. This prompted him to propose marriage between Liu and his only daughter, even with the full knowledge that Liu Bang was not only an alcoholic, but also a pauper and a womanizer as well. The deal went through, to the pleasure of all three parties involved—Liu Bang, Queen Lu, and her father.

Coincidentally, one of Liu's key political enemies also possessed the supernatural ability to see the movement of Qi. He was Fang Zhen, the premier and chief military advisor to the king of Chu. Based on his understanding of the special Qi that followed Liu all the time, Fang Zhen insisted that the king of Chu kill Liu Bang without delay, otherwise Liu would usurp his power sooner or later. A physically brave but kind man, the king of Chu hesitated over Fang's suggestion and failed to act on several occasions. Infuriated at the king's hesitation and aware that Liu Bang was going to be the winner in the bid for supreme power of the nation, Fang submitted his resignation to the king and tried to hide himself as a recluse in the deep mountains for fear of persecution by Liu, but he did not succeed. The combined effect of prolonged anger, fear, and frustration had caused a cancer to develop in his body, and he died on his way home. True to his forecast, the king of Chu was driven by Liu to commit suicide by the River of Wu two years later.

Another famous detector of Qi energy in China's history was Yuan Tiangan, one of the greatest feng shui masters. The story goes that one day Yuan Tiangan went to see Emperor Yang of the Sui dynasty (A.D. 581–618) and told him that he had detected Qi with five different colors in the sky in the northwestern part of the country. The cloud sometimes took the shape of a dragon and sometimes the shape of a phoenix. According to Yuan,

such Qi was indicative of the Mandate of Heaven, and therefore a change in the dynasty. But the emperor was not convinced: "Qi is something intangible. How can it determine the rise and fall of a dynasty?"

As Yuan went into detail describing various Qi with various significances, hinting that the emperor's dynasty would end in the hand of someone born in the northwestern part of China, the emperor became infuriated. He asked Yuan to identify the person who was going to take over his empire, so that he could kill the person. Although Yuan knew how to find this person, he could not do so, because this was a serious violation of the Mandate of Heaven. Therefore, he just told the emperor that the person might not have been born yet. Upon hearing this, the emperor burst into laughter: "You are really worried too much. What is the point worrying about things yet to happen in 500 years?!"

Seeing that it was no use to further argue with the emperor, Yuan left the palace and said to himself: "It won't be long before the collapse of the Sui dynasty. This special Qi of five colors should be in the district of Taiyuan, the capital of Shanxi province. Who can the son of heaven be other than Li Shimin? It looks like the genuine dragon will arise to power soon. The Mandate of Heaven just cannot be disobeyed." Making up his mind, Yuan Tiangan left Yangzhou, the capital of the Sui dynasty and headed northwest towards Taiyuan. There, General Li Shimin, who immensely admired Yuan's talents, enthusiastically received him. Shortly afterward, Yuan became a key advisor to Li Shimin who is none other than the founding emperor of the Tang dynasty, which replaced the Sui dynasty.

Earthly Qi and Heavenly Qi

Feng shui distinguishes Qi energy into two broad categories: earthly Qi and heavenly Qi. As the names imply, earthly Qi travels in the ground and is manifested by changes in topography, especially the rise and fall of mountains, while heavenly Qi flows in the air.

Different projects give different weight to these two kinds of Qi. In burial feng shui, the major concern is earthly Qi. Because the deceased are buried under the ground, they are thus little exposed to and affected by heavenly Qi. By contrast, residential and commercial feng shui has to take into account both kinds of Qi. This is because houses are built above the earth and are directly affected by heavenly Qi in the air, as well as the earthly Qi under the ground.

Earthly or heavenly, Qi is of such a nature that it disperses when blown by the wind and lingers when heading into the mountains or waterways. In particular, earthly Qi travels with and is carried forward by the mountains until it is interrupted or checked by some big objects.

Objects that can interrupt or check the flow of earthly Qi include mountains, bodies of water (rivers, streams, lakes, ponds), highways, tunnels, and so on. As a general rule, any location where Qi flow is checked is considered an auspicious site for construction.

Of course, not all localities carry the same amount and quality of Qi. Here are some basic rules to follow:

- The longer a mountain vein, the taller the mountains in it, therefore the more powerful the earthly Qi.

- If a mountain peak is shrouded in mist or haze most of the time, this mountain must contain plenty of Qi energy, earthly and heavenly.

- If a mountain is covered by green trees and grass, has some spring water or brooks flowing on it, the soil is fertile and full of moisture, and the stones and rocks in it are magnificent and well-shaped, this mountain must contain an abundance of Qi.

- If a mountain is dry and bare, devoid of trees and grass, with only rocks on it, this mountain must be an inauspicious mountain low in Qi.

Chinese ancients must have come to the above conclusions by means of analogy. Since Qi is an intangible substance that is invisible to most people, there are some objects of reference available to judge the quality of mountains. Clouds, haze, mist, water, trees, and grass are good objects of reference and all signify auspicious Qi. Trees and grass are also products of Qi energy as is everything else in the universe. The more Qi there is under the ground and in the environment where these trees and plants are located, the more luxuriant and strong they will be. Therefore, a mountain with a rash of trees and grass must be full of Qi, just like a barren, rocky mountain is considered devoid of Qi. If a mountain cannot even produce trees and grass, how can it be expected to contribute to the good fortune of humans?

It must be noted that all Qi does not have a continuous flow throughout the course of a mountain vein, or from the head to the tail of a dragon. In fact, its flow is often interrupted and obstructed. This happens, for instance, when the mountain is "stopped" by a big lake, an ocean, or severed into two branches by a river, an artificial tunnel, or highway. Interruption of Qi flow normally is a bad omen, as in the case of health. However, such an interruption in the flow of earthly Qi is not necessarily a bad thing. As a matter of fact, it can be a very good thing, so long as the interruption is caused by a naturally formed object, such as an ocean or a valley. With the exception of artificial causes, a geographic location where Qi flow is blocked is an auspicious site for living or burial, because the precious Qi will come to stay and accumulate there. It is the accumulation of Qi that makes an auspicious site.

However, if the interruption of Qi flow is caused by artificial objects such as tunnels and highways, Qi is not only interrupted but also injured as a consequence. Qi is injured because it is taken away by the traffic which travels fast and straight along the highway. For this reason, there can hardly be any good feng shui sites immediately along the highway.

Even if a major mountain vein is intercepted by a river, there should be small hills and mountains lying along the riverbank downstream. The more hills and mountains there are along the waterway, the better for feng shui because Qi energy flowing down along the river can be effectively checked and contained. For the same reason, there should be hills in the front of a house (facing mountains, i. e., table and worshipping hills) to check the flowing away of the water that carries the Qi energy of locations in the upper stream. When such mountains are present, the water flow will most likely have to curve ahead or even turn around in its journey forward. If this is the case, there are bound to be excellent dragon lairs situated along the banks of the water. No matter how far these mountains are from a specific site, they are good mountains that serve to check and prevent the dispersing of precious Qi.

Mountains on the exterior side of facing mountains are collectively known as the Encircling City. These mountains serve as the second guardian of the precious Qi energy to make sure that it will not be lost or carried away by water or wind. This is the second line of defense for Qi energy. Thus, Qi energy in and around a location is preserved and protected by means of appropriate landform in the environment. Qi resides in certain landforms, and a landform determines the quantity and quality of Qi energy.

Since mountains bear heavily on Qi energy, let us spend some time exploring them.

Chapter 6

Exploring Mountains

As has been discussed before, mountains receive close attention in feng shui because they are the major carriers of earthly Qi energy. Mountains are referred to as dragons and auspicious sites full of Qi energy are called dragon lairs. To the ancient Chinese, the very image of a dragon invokes the connotation of good luck, power, authority, and wealth, as well as security. The reason why mountains are so called is explained by Xu Jishan and his brother in their book, *What Every Son Should Know About Geomancy*:

> *Why do feng shui masters call mountains "dragons?" This is because mountains have various shapes and forms: some smaller, some bigger; some high, some flat; some rising, some falling; some conspicuous, some hardly visible. . . . Dragon is the only*

animal that comes so close to these characteristics of mountain veins. Hence the name.

Actually, there is another meaning to this analogy between dragons and mountain veins. Both are considered the catalyst and carrier of Qi energy, and Qi is what feng shui is concerned about.

Since there are so many different mountains, there are also various kinds of dragons, the quality of which can vary vastly from one to the other. In fact, some mountains can even carry evil Qi, which can do a lot of harm to people living in their shadow. Feng shui cares a lot about the shape and quality of the mountains because much of a person's fortune is determined by the kind of Qi energy and the strength of that energy embodied by mountains.

To live up to the image of a dragon, mountain veins should be undulating, full of peaks and valleys, and covered by trees and grass. Preferably, the dragon must have easy access to water resources, because in Chinese culture, the supernatural power of a dragon is, to a large extent, dependent on whether or not it can access water. Flat, dry, and bare mountains are not considered lively dragons of high quality.

Because of this, we cannot get a complete picture of mountains without also talking about water. In feng shui, water is considered latitude and mountain veins longitude. In fact, major mountain veins in China are classified by the major waterways between them (listed from north to south): Yalu River, on the border between China and North Korea; the Yellow River in northern China; the Yangtze River in central China; and the Pearl River in southern China. Corresponding to these waterways are three major mountain dragons: the northern dragon, which runs between the Yalu River and the Yellow River; the central dragon, which stretches between the Yellow River and the Yangtze River; and the southern dragon, which extends between the Yangtze River and the Pearl River.

All three major mountain dragons in China have their common origin in the Kunlun Mountains. As Chinese fathers view it, the Kunlun Mountains are the pillars of the universe from which all major mountains in the world develop and extend. Hence, the Kunlun Mountains are regarded as the mother mountains. These three major dragons all reach the ocean on the eastern coast of China. Thus, the northern dragon extends into the Bohai Sea, the central dragon runs into the East China Sea, and the southern dragon into the South China Sea.

All mountains in China are broadly classified into three types, depending on their distance from the mother mountains of Kunlun. The first type is known as remote ancestors mountains. These are mountains that lie close to the Kunlun Mountains. The second type is called close ancestor mountains, which are mountains located close to the ocean. The third type is called old ancestors mountains, which are those that lie between remote and close ancestors mountains, in terms of their distance from the Kunlun Mountains.

Geomantically, this classification has great significance for guiding the practice of feng shui. It is spatial as well as temporal. According to feng shui theory, the closer a mountain is to its origin, i.e., the Kunlun Mountains, the older the mountain is, and the less Qi energy it carries with it, just like an elderly man will not have as much Qi energy as when he was young. That is why we hardly ever hear of a business tycoon or great political leader (equivalents of wealth and social position) in China coming from the deserted areas close to the Kunlun Mountains in the northwest part of the country. There is simply not enough Qi energy in that area to support the birth of such dignitaries. Mountains close to the Kunluns are considered older because the Kunlun Mountains are considered the origin of all mountains (also known as the Mother Mountains).

The Kunluns extend in various directions in various distances. As a result, a sundry of mountains have come into being, in a chronological order measured by their distance from their common origin. Thus, the farther a mountain is from the Kunluns, the newer it is (measured by the time it came into being), and therefore, the younger it is. Also, the further away a mountain is from the Kunlun Mountains, the closer it is to the ocean, or the end of its journey, and therefore, more Qi energy has been carried forward into it. For example, most dignitaries and wealthy people in China have come from coastal areas or areas not far from the ocean. The amount of Qi a mountain carries is determined simultaneously by the age of that mountain and by the distance between that mountain and the Kunlun Mountains.

Mountains and Hills

Dragons

There are four kinds of dragons (i.e., mountains) defined by their relative height and forestry: progressive, lucky, retreating, and sick.

A progressive dragon is a group of mountains that gradually get bigger and taller as the dragon progresses and advances into the background. Viewed from a specific location, the hills get higher and higher, one after the other, as they recede into the background, as if they are stairs leading to the sky. This is the most desirable of the four kinds of dragons, because it contains the strongest type of Qi energy and therefore brings good luck, prosperity, and improved financial and social positions to many generations.

The second kind of dragon is a lucky dragons. A lucky dragon is a group of mountains surrounding a land site. These mountains vary in height and offer an undulating landscape. According to feng shui fathers, lucky dragons will bring good luck to the people living in the area, although to a lesser degree than progressive dragons.

Next is the retreating dragon. It is a group of hills with the exact opposite characteristics of a progressive dragon. The mountains decrease in height as they gradually retreat into the background. Retreating means retiring. A man at the age of retirement is generally short of Qi energy and near the sunset of life; not much can be accomplished anymore. Such a dragon can cause the residents to gradually lose their financial and social positions.

The most undesirable kind is the sick dragon. A sick dragon is a group of mountains with grotesque shapes (skinny, leaning, or in the shape of inauspicious animals such as a snake, rat, or wolf) that are barren, dry, and sandy. They scatter around loosely like sick men standing around, short of spirit and strength. As the name implies, a sick dragon will bring diseases, disasters, financial trouble, and even discontinuation in the family line for those residing in the area.

A simpler and convenient way to classify mountains is to divide them into two broad categories: living dragons and dead dragons. We have already mentioned that some mountains can be harmful to people since they carry evil Qi. Those mountains that can hurt rather than benefit people are known as "dead dragons." These are mountains that are flat, dull, inflexible (meaning the mountains are all about the same height), barren, devoid of trees and grass, and just plain ugly in appearance. By contrast, living dragons are mountains that are flexible and undulating in topography, full of rises and falls, abundant in forestry, have access to water sources, and are magnificent and pleasant to look at. Living in the vicinity of such dragons can enhance one's fortune, whereas living in the environment of dead dragons can lead to health problems and bad luck.

FIGURE 6-1
A seal hill has a broad base and a pointed peak, often seen in the middle of a lake or river

Five Elements Mountains

Another system of classification for mountains is based on the theory of the five elements. Under this system, mountains are associated with one of the five basic elements: water, fire, wood, metal, and earth. Since each of the elements has a characteristic shape and appearance, many mountains fit well into this ancient philosophical system.

Water mountains: These are somewhat wavy in appearance with a flat top (jade belt mountain).

Fire mountains: These have a broad base and a pointed peak (seal hill).

Wood mountains: These look straight, high, and slim (pen hill).

Earth mountains: These have a round body and a flat peak (drum mountain).

Metal mountains: These are round on the top and square (bell mountain).

The real significance of this system of classification lies in that it correlates individual mountains with individuals living in the environment, specifically the homeowner. The birthday of the home or business owner is traditionally recorded in the same system of the five elements.

FIGURE 6-2
Pen hills are straight, tall, and slim with rounded peaks

This creates a convenient common denominator between man and his environment. This common denominator has enabled geomancers to correlate people with topography, and find out the relation between the two, facilitating the task of feng shui design.

For instance, if a business is of the fire nature such as a restaurant, then a wood mountain in the neighborhood will have some positive impact on the business, since wood produces fire. However, if the same business is located in the vicinity of a water mountain, the business will be negatively affected because water quenches fire.

Using the five elements system and the owner's year of birth, we can also determine what the "desired spirit," or "useful spirit," is in the karma of the homeowner. This also tells how compatible a specific mountain is with a specific house. Thus, if the useful or desired spirit of a homeowner is the element of fire, and the residence happens to be located close to or facing a fire mountain or a wood mountain, the family's fortune will be improved because fire is exactly what the homeowner wants, since wood feeds fire. However, if the same residence is located by or facing a water mountain, the family's fortune will be negatively affected because water conquers fire, an incompatible situation for the residence.

Note: For a better understanding of the five elements, refer to chapter 2 on the principles of feng shui and also to chapter 9 on determining the owner's karma. As to what business corresponds to which element, refer to Table 2-1, page 24.

Mountain Veins

Besides the basic issues of shape and height, the length of mountain veins is also an important parameter of the quality of mountains. As a rule, the longer a mountain vein runs, the longer will be the good luck that the mountain vein can bring to the residents. This theory holds that the longer a mountain vein is, the more time is consumed in creating it, and therefore the more Qi energy is contained in it. Also, the longer a mountain vein is without interruption, the more powerful the Qi energy it carries. On the other hand, if a mountain vein has gone through many interruptions during its course of travel before it comes to a stop, the Qi energy in it is damaged and reduced. Indeed, the more interruptions there are, the less Qi energy a mountain contains.

This is a top secret of feng shui which, unfortunately, has been used for political sabotage in history. A story goes that towards the end of the Ming dynasty, a massive peasant rebellion broke out in northern China under the leadership of Li Zicheng, a native of Shanxi province in northwestern China. This rebellion forced the last emperor of the Ming dynasty to commit suicide right behind the Forbidden City in Beijing, ending in the collapse of the Ming dynasty and the invasion of Manchurians. While Li Zicheng was busy conducting his peasant army against the Ming army, the emperor secretly ordered local officials in Shanxi to dig into the mountains in which Li's ancestors were buried, so as to destroy the feng shui of Li's family tree and consequently the good luck that Li had been enjoying in the battlefield. (What happened afterward is that shortly after the suicide of the Ming emperor, Li's own subordinates killed him. All his rebellious efforts only served to pave the way for the establishment of the Qing dynasty by Manchurians.)

While I was a child, I often heard elders talk about the feng shui of my hometown, the coastal city of Fuzhou. They said that the municipal feng shui had been deliberately and seriously sabotaged by Ye Xiang-gao, a famous premier in the Ming dynasty who was from FuQing, a neighboring city to Fuzhou. Ye did it out of his jealous fear that the auspicious feng shui of Fuzhou would enable the city to produce competitors to go against him and his descendants. So he ordered the digging of the West Lake at the expense of the continuity of the mountain chain. As a consequence, the dragon pulse (the flow of earthly Qi) in the city was injured and nobody from the city has ascended to the position of a premier ever since.

During World War II, Japanese troops were trying to storm a tightly fortified mountain village in Laos. After suffering huge casualties, the Japanese decided to take it by strategy rather than by force. They sent a spy into the village, who spread the rumor that there were a lot of treasures hidden under the main mountain. Eager to strike it rich, many villagers went on a gold rush and heavily dug into the mountain. As a result, the dragon Qi in the mountain was miserably damaged. Shortly afterwards, the fortified mountain village was taken over by the Japanese without much fighting. Believe it or not, these stories highlight the importance of the continuity of earthly Qi energy traveling with mountain ranges. As you can tell, Qi is a powerful material and feng shui a powerful tool in the hands of geomancers in shaping human fate.

Mountain Vegetation

There are many ways a mountain possesses strong Qi energy or not. Chinese fathers tell us that if the top of a mountain is permeated with mist, or if a mountain has a lush growth of trees and grass, as well as some clear water flowing in it to moisture the soil and nurture life-forms in it, this mountain must have an abundance of Qi energy. It is therefore a lucky thing to have such a mountain in our living and working environments. It takes little shrewdness to imagine that a mountain full of trees and grasses must possess strong Qi energy. Such a mountain is capable of not only conserving its own earthly Qi but also attracting heavenly Qi in the environment.

To verify, just compare the temperature on a barren mountain with that on a lush mountain in the same geographic area. We know that in the summer, the temperature on a barren mountain is much higher than that on a mountain covered by forestry. In winter, it is just the opposite.

In contrast, a mountain devoid of forestry must be short of Qi energy. Indeed, many of them are considered to possess evil energy. If a mountain cannot even support the growth of its own grass and trees, how can we expect it to contribute to the happiness of our life? Thus, feng shui contains a lot of common sense.

These principles are described in *Qin Lan Hai Jiao Jin* ("Blue Bags and Seabirds") as follows:

> *Good mountains are flexible like dragons flying, with its soil warm and air evaporating, a rash of trees and*

*grasses in it growing, which are so
exuberant as to be overlapping.
You can see spring water flowing by,
And magnificent rocks gallantly lie.
Around its top in the morning and
evening, a sea of clouds and haze is
permeating.*

As a footnote to the above poem, the author added:

*Especially in the mid-summer and
mid-winter, after the morning and
evening rain, there will be a canopy
of Qi ascending in the mountains.
Such a mountain must be full of Qi
and therefore very beneficial to people living in it and nearby. Qi canopy
can take various forms and assume
different meanings. If it looks like a
bird, high-ranking officials will be
born in the neighborhood. If it looks
like a tiger, great generals will come
out from the place.*

Shas

Smaller hills are called *shas*. Shas serve similar purposes as mountains:

- Protecting the precious Qi energy of a construction site from being blown away by winds.

- Cumulating of wealth.

- Promoting the social position of the inhabitants.

- Enhancing the intelligence of people living in it.

Four Animals

Fathers of feng shui also paid close attention to the mountains on the four sides of a locality. To them, these mountains have the greatest impact on the welfare of the residents in the locality. In feng shui, these four hills or mountains are figuratively referred to as the "four animals." It is Guo Pu who first pointed out the special significance of these hills and personally coined the terms.

Black tortoise: This is the major mountain found in the background of a site. Located at the immediate rear of a building or grave, it is supposed to be the tail of a "coming dragon."

Red phoenix: Red phoenixes refer to the hills or mountains in front of a land site. These hills should assume the shape of a hovering bird with its wings fully extended.

Green dragon: This refers to the hill or mountain that lies to the left of a site. Such a hill serves to protect the site from the attack of the wind coming from the left.

White tiger: This is a mountain situated on the right side of a land site. As a counterbalance to the green dragon, the white tiger provides a shield for the house, protecting it from evil winds coming from the right.

Note: To determine which direction is left or right, stand in front of the house facing it. The side to your left is considered left, and the side to your right is considered right.

Let's look at these four animals in more detail. While highly desirable for land sites of all purposes, black tortoises vary in quality, just like mountains differ in quality. Indeed, some are excellent, some are just so-so, and others may even be bad. For a black tortoise to be auspicious, it should gradually slope toward the back of a land site as if bowing to it. Feng shui describes such a submissive topographic situation as "a tortoise kowtowing to the people in its front." This signifies the acceptance by and support of the black tortoise.

However, if the tortoise holds up its head, so to speak, in a steep and arrogant manner without a gradual slope toward the site, this indicates that the tortoise is unbending, unfriendly, and unwelcome to the residents. As such, little help or protection can be expected from this mountain.

This distinction is significant. Since the black tortoise stands for the tail of a major dragon (a major mountain vein), it is filled with the precious lively Qi energy carried all the way by the dragon during its course of travel. Whether or not the dragon is willing to transmit the Qi energy to a location very much depends on the shape of the black tortoise. If the tortoise assumes a "bending" manner towards a location, reflected in its gradually descending slope leading to the location, this shows that the dragon is willing to pass on its precious Qi to the local people and benefit their lives and businesses. However, if the black tortoise is found in the form of a lonely, steep peak, this shows that the dragon is not willing to transmit its precious Qi to the location and the residents there.

It is also preferable that the black tortoise be located closer to the residence than the other three "animals," i.e., the green dragon, the white tiger, and the red phoenix. It gives the building a strong sense of protection, especially since the rear or back is the most vulnerable part of the site, just like the body. In fact, many a glorious military victory in history was won by surprise attack at the rear of enemy lines. A tall, close mountain in the rear of a house offers the residents a strong line of defense against the blow of ill winds from behind.

The red phoenix refers to the hills or mountains in the front of a land site. While generally auspicious, if the hill is flat and tedious, it is considered a sick bird and will not do much good to the residents. For this reason, when examining a site, feng shui masters always make sure there are large hills in the front of the site. It does not matter how far away these hills are from a site; so long as they exist, the area will benefit.

Feng shui further distinguishes two kinds of red phoenixes:

Table hills: A hill or mountain that lies close in front of a site.

Worshipping hills: A bigger hill or mountain that lies farther back in front of a site, but still within sight.

The names come from the ancient Chinese who thought of the hill close to the front as a table—so close that it can be easily "touched" and conveniently used. They thought of the big mountain farther away from a site as a guest who is coming from afar to worship a dignitary at the site.

Table hills are generally desirable because they provide a buffer in the front. This is especially true if a site features a northern exposure. In such a case, the presence of a table hill becomes indispensable. The northern wind is the most violent and destructive of all winds and is

regarded as the most evil and malignant wind of all. It must be checked by all means, especially when it blows at the front of the house. Therefore, the first condition for a good site with a northern exposure is the presence of a table hill. The only exception is when a site is located at the center of a Qi reservoir of some major dragon (mountain vein). In this case, the Qi energy in the locality is strong enough to offset the negative effects of the northern wind.

In most cases, a table hill is highly recommended. Hence, geomantic proverbs say: "If you can touch the table hill from where you live, you will have tons of money"; "I would prefer a small hill in the near front of my residence to layers of magnificent mountains far away from my residence"; "Better to have a homely hill close by than to have beautiful mountains far away." In addition to its being close to the site, a table hill should be relatively small. A big hill in the near front of a residence will interrupt the visibility of the residents, and interrupted visibility means lack of foresight and limited future, not encouraging signs in geomancy.

The following objects are used to convey the image of an auspicious table hill: a table, a piano, a horse, a lion, or a suitcase. In addition to being close and small, a good table hill should also be shaped well and even. If it is crooked and slanting, or pointing away from the site, it becomes a bad hill, which will do more harm than good to the residents.

If there is a waterway flowing away from the front of a site, a red phoenix becomes a "locking mountain" or a "door mountain" to the waterway. These mountains serve as doors or checks to block the water, which is symbolic of money. Remember that water stands for wealth in feng shui. Therefore, we do not want to see water flow away from us unchecked (even if it is a natural inevitability), exactly as we do not want to see our wallet or purse left open or the safe unlocked. The presence of a good table hill downstream is an effective check on the loss of wealth. Preferably, there should be a pair of table hills on both banks of the waterway to be double sure that wealth is not lost. Better still if there is a mountain standing in the middle of the waterway down the stream. Such a hill or rock is known as a "seal hill" in feng shui, and is a very auspicious sign for sites located upstream.

Compared to table hills, worshipping hills are usually larger and taller, and located farther away from a specific site. However, no matter how big these hills are, they are always considered guests while the mountain closest to the site is considered the host. Therefore, their presence is likened to officials coming to worship an emperor, or guests coming to pay respect to a host. In a practical sense, worshiping mountains provide additional protection for a locality. In case there is water flowing away from a site in the front, such mountains farther downstream can serve as a second layer of checks against the leakage of wealth. It is said that "affectionate worshipping mountains ensure the generation of premiers and generals." Like table hills, worshipping mountains should also be straight and well-balanced to be auspicious.

Green dragons are hills or mountains that lie to the left of a land site. However, not all mountains to the left of a land site are considered auspicious, at least not of the same degree of auspiciousness. For a green dragon to be auspicious, it should be bigger and taller than the white tiger, located close enough to the site to be able to shield and protect the site. More importantly, it should extend a friendly welcome gesture towards the land site. This means the green dragon should curve and gradually slope towards the land site located to its right side.

However, if the green dragon stands up abruptly, or is the same width from top to bottom, such a dragon is called a "legless dragon"—not an auspicious sign. If the green dragon is turning away from rather than in toward the site, it is considered to be a jealous green dragon, which will bring nothing good.

According to traditional Chinese culture, Qi energy is the combined product of yin and yang, the two broad polarities in the universe. The left side stands for yang while the right side stands for yin. This translates to mountains, with those on the left side of a site symbolizing yang while those to the right of a site symbolizing yin. Mountains on both sides of a locality turning toward each other are symbolic of such a yin-yang combination.

In feng shui, the green dragon (located on the left side) and the white tiger (located on the right side) turning toward each other represent the merging of yin and yang, a very auspicious sign signifying the creation and preservation of a lot of Qi energy in between. Therefore, it is very important that the green dragon and the white tiger turn their heads down and in toward each other, as if to shake hands with each other and collectively embrace the site between them. They should not turn outward away from the site, which is a sign of being "not affectionate and unfriendly" towards each other and especially towards the site. Nor should they hold up their heads in an arrogant, unbending manner, lest they usurp the host's role played by the mountain on which the site is located.

If there is more than one single layer of mountains to the left of a locality, those mountains in the innermost layer are called "inner green dragons," which is the most relevant mountain to the well-being of the residents due to its closeness to the house. Mountains in the outer layers are known as "outer green dragons," which are of secondary importance due to their distance from the house.

A white tiger is the mountain situated at the right side of a land site. It provides a shield for the house, protecting it from evil winds coming from the right. Not all mountains found on the right of a land site can be considered auspicious. For a white tiger to be auspicious, it must meet the following conditions. First, it must be lower than the green dragon. Second, it must be relatively flat and static as compared to the green dragon. In other words, it should not be too undulating with rises and falls, which is a good quality for a green dragon but not for a white tiger. This is based on the Chinese understanding that an active tiger will hurt or eat people while an active dragon will bring good luck. Third, it must be "tamed" and "submissive" in that it bows, so to speak, to the land site by gradually (gently) sloping. If, however, the white tiger holds its head high, it is a menacing tiger and will hurt rather than help the people living in its vicinity.

The black tortoise, red phoenix, green dragon, and white tiger are the four key mountains in the environment that serve to protect a site from ill winds. Of the four basic mountains in the surroundings, the black tortoise is the most important. This is because the tortoise lies in the rear of a land site, which is normally the least guarded and defended, and therefore, most in need of protection.

Lower Passes

There is yet another type of mountain that is extremely essential if there is a watercourse flowing by and away from the site. This kind of mountain is known as a "lower pass," because they are located downstream from the land site (also known as an earthly door). As a matter of principle, whenever there is a waterway flowing away from a site, there should be some hills or mountains downstream to symbolically block its flow, so that wealth will not flow away unchecked. Remember that water is money in feng shui. Yang Yun-song said: "Only lower passes can save you and your descendants from poverty." Indeed, the more lower passes there are, the tighter the family's wealth will be safeguarded, and the less likely they will suffer from poverty. Occasionally, there are some huge rocks standing midstream. Such rocks are known as "northern stars," and their presence is an extremely auspicious sign for the residents living upstream.

Better still if these hills and rocks (lower passes) can assume the images of a lion, a tiger, an elephant, a phoenix, a banner, an umbrella, or a pen. Such a landscape will give birth to great personalities. This is because the shape and landscape of mountains in the surroundings count a lot, too. It is a feng shui belief that a mountain signifies what it looks like. Thus, mountains with the appearance of a tiger or a lion signify military authority, indicating a generation of great soldiers in the neighborhood. Similarly, mountains with the shape of a pen or pencil signify literary talents, indicating the birth of great authors or top ranking civil officials. Mountains that look like a warehouse signify financial strength, indicating the birth of millionaires if not billionaires in the area. This may sound too simplistic. Like it or not, its truth is repeatedly verified in actual life. Indeed, one cannot be too imaginative when coming to feng shui. It is interesting to know that some geomancers liken mountains to human bodies. Thus, they refer to stones in a mountain as bones, soil of the mountain as flesh, water in it as blood, and the forestry on it as skin and hair. This shows once more that feng shui in the true sense of the word is an art of high caliber.

Mountains and Water

Water assumes the additional role of mountains on top of its original roles. Even in the presence of mountains, water remains a vital factor in the assessment of the quality of mountains. Big mountains need big waters to border and balance them, just like small mountains need small waters such as brooks and ponds for the same purpose. The bigger and longer the watercourse, the more powerful and abundant the Qi resources, and therefore the bigger uses to which these locations can be put. What you need to do is to follow the waterways until they slow down in a curve or turn around to form a waterbody, such as a pond or a lake. These are the places where genuine dragons rest and earthly Qi energy abounds, and are therefore excellent locations for sites.

What can be done if the land is a vast plain with few mountains in sight? Are there still dragons in the land? The answer is yes, but they are more implicit and therefore harder to find than in other areas. The clue to finding dragons in flat country lies in water (which is the object of exploration in the next chapter). Water takes the place of mountains in flat areas. So long as there is water, there is a dragon.

Generally speaking, the existence of the following objects are indicative of an auspicious locality or genuine dragon lair:

- The general topography of the land is flat or gently sloping forward.

- A table and a worshipping mountain are in the front of the site.

- The green dragon and the white tiger mountains are on both sides, curving toward each other.

- The bright hall is bright and spacious. (See chapter 10.)

- Waterways flow by or are in the vicinity.

- Mountains in the environment have the shape of a banner, drum, pen, horse, dragon, tiger, lion, seal, or warehouse.

Although in many situations water and mountains merge in the topography, the subject of water is another key factor in feng shui that deserves attention. In the next chapter, we will explore this subject in detail and take a close look at its various forms and significances.

Chapter 7

Exploring Water

Water is vital to all life forms, human beings in particular. Physiologically, deficiency in water can result in various kinds of health problems, including death. Water is also essential to the living environment in that it helps modulate the temperature and cleanse the environment. Not surprisingly, water is also one of the greatest concerns in feng shui.

In feng shui, there is a division of duty between mountains and water. Mountains are in charge of the population of the family living nearby while water is in charge of wealth. The relationship between the two is a close one. Mountains are likened to the body and the bones of the body, while water represents the blood vessels and the blood flow inside the body. While the blood supply is fresh and sufficient, one is able to enjoy good health. A loss of blood can be a threat to the life of the body. This physiological rule applies equally well to geomancy. The more water there is in an area, the more auspicious it is. Such an area is usually highly developed in its economy with picturesque scenery.

As the geomantic symbol of wealth, water can bring materialistic affluence and financial success to residents in its neighborhood. Many of the world's major cities are located close to the water: New York, Los Angeles, San Francisco, Miami, Seattle, Tokyo, Osaka, Shanghai, Hong Kong, Taiwan, Bangkok, Vancouver, and Sydney.

Of the two most basic elements of feng shui—water and mountains—water is regarded by many as even more important to feng shui. It is held that water should come prior to mountains in terms of feng shui consideration. No land site can be considered perfect without water, but a land can still be excellent in the absence of mountains as long as there is water nearby. There is a classic feng shui saying to the effect that one should look for water gates while entering mountains; in the absence of water one should not seek residence at all.

Why is water so essential to feng shui? Fan Yibin of the Qing dynasty says the following words in his *Annotations on the Burial Book*:

In the absence of water, Qi disperses when the wind blows. In the presence of water, Qi cumulates and wind stops. Therefore, "feng" (wind) and "shui" (water) are the two most significant words in geomancy, with lands encircled by waters as the best choice and those protected from wind by mountains come next.

Therefore, an ideal location for residence or burial site should possess both water and mountains. Water collects and preserves Qi, while mountains protect the site from wind.

However, such an ideal location is not easily available. In fact, it can be quite difficult and expensive to get. Most likely, either water or mountain is absent in a landscape. If we must choose between the two, many feng shui masters vote for water, if only because most people prefer wealth (brought about by water) to a big family (brought about by mountains).

Another strong argument for water over mountains lies in the fact that water possesses some of the vital functions of mountains, such as carrying the earthly Qi to a place and protecting Qi energy from dispersing. For this, feng shui fathers sometimes refer to water as the "watery dragon." This concept of the watery dragon is crucial to feng shui practice in flat lands where few mountains are present. Under such circumstances, there seems to be no dragon at all in the environment, but in actuality, the dragon is none other than water. Find the water and you will find the dragon.

Water is mobile by nature, and its greatest geomantic beauty lies in its stability, which is what feng shui seeks in water. This is in accordance with the principle of yin-yang harmony. In fact, the deeper and larger a water body is, the more auspicious and prosperous will be the land in its vicinity. Similarly, the longer a water course has traveled before it comes to a land site, the more Qi energy will there be under the land, and the longer this land will bring good luck to its residents. For this reason, it is geomantically advisable to reside in lower reaches (downstream) rather than upper reaches (upstream) of a river. Lower reaches of a river are often close to the sea into which the river runs. This provides great advantage to trade and cultural exchange. Different degrees of cultural and economic development between eastern China (lower reaches of the Yellow River and the Yangtze River) and western China (the upper reaches of the Yellow River and the Yangtze River) offer us an interesting case in point.

Feng shui defines various kinds of waterways and waterbodies. Chinese fathers observed that seas and oceans often mark the end of mountain veins. Therefore, waterfront areas are considered locations where Qi energy concentrates, because a dragon has traveled so long before it comes to the waterfront. It is the feng shui belief that the longer a mountain vein travels, the more Qi it carries. No wonder there are many more wealthy people in coastal areas than inland.

Compared to oceans, rivers are usually more rapid in flow. Since fast-flowing water is not an auspicious thing to have in feng shui, we should look for a river with portions that have more twists and turns, which can slow down the water and even cause it to stop its course of flow. Land sites near such parts of a river are therefore auspicious locations for construction, capable of bringing prosperity to the residents for generations.

With regard to small streams and brooks, the geomantic principles state that they should also be curving and twisting, slow and silent in their flow. If a stream or brook is rapid and noisy, it is considered evil and disastrous.

Lakes are considered the reservoirs of water. Compared to rivers, they are much more stable and static. This is exactly where their greatest beauty lies. As water stays, so also will wealth and prosperity.

Water, no matter what kind, so long as it stays and lingers in the front of a land site, is of great geomantic value. However, we have to watch out for water that makes a lot of noise. Such water is known as a "crying red phoenix," which is an inauspicious sign signifying sorrowful events such as funerals.

Water staying and lingering in front of a land site can mean either a sudden turn in the watercourse, which causes the water flow to significantly slow down, or a body of water that is largely static in front of a site, such as a lake or a pond. Because most places do not have such a geographic feature, a lot of room remains for artificial creation and improvement. For instance, one commonly used method of improving feng shui in China is to dig a pond in front of a residence or building. Of course, this may not always be feasible, legally or financially. Other minor measures of improvement include the installation of a water fountain or the placement of a golden fishbowl in the front of a building. If you tour China, you will be surprised to find that pond after pond, fountain after fountain, and numerous fishbowls are strategically placed to make up the deficiencies of water in the environment. A classic example is the sizable pond in front of Mao Tse-tung's old residence. Another obvious example is the brook called the "Golden Water," artificially created to encircle the Forbidden City in Peking, in addition to the famous Lake of the North Sea bordering on the Forbidden City, as well as a number of smaller ponds inside the palace.

Water is flexible and has no fixed shape in itself. Its shape is largely determined by the landform through which it flows. Thus, a mountain vein with big undulations will lead to water with big falls. On the other hand, a flat landscape will create water that runs relatively smoothly. Of course, all waters are not good; some are considered evil with respect to specific localities. Everything depends on the shape, direction, and speed of the water.

The quality of water is a big issue in feng shui, and differences in water quality mean variations in fortune. As a matter of general principle, feng shui recommends lingering rather than fast-running water, and curving rather than straight-flowing water. Ideally, a locality should have mountains in the front that serve to check the flow of water downstream. It is better still if the mountains themselves curve toward the ground, causing the water to flow back a little before resuming downstream. At any rate, there should be at least one mountain in front of a site for it to be called auspicious, so long as there is a fast-flowing waterway going by.

Feng shui has different names for different kinds of water:

Facing water: Water that flows to the front of a site.

Heavenly pond: A pond or lake high in the mountains.

Lying bow water: Water that curves and "embraces" a site in the front.

Pulling cow water: Water that runs straight away from the front of a site.

Surface gathering water: Water that stays gently in the front of a site.

Surging breast water: Water that passes by the front of a site in a surging manner.

Dry flowing water: Water path that is dry except when it rains.

Waters that break the heart of heaven: Water that runs rapidly against the site.

Cutting-the-feet water: Water that runs slowly against the site.

Water that shoots the ribs: Water that runs at frontal sides of a site.

Water that pounds on city walls: Water that runs perpendicular to the flanks of buildings.

Back protecting water: Water that curves at the back of a site.

Entering mouth water: Water that runs away from a site but is checked.

Royal street water: Water that curves often in the front of a site.

Hidden water: Water that cannot be seen directly from the front of a site because it lies to the other side of worshipping mountains.

Injecting water: The spring water on either side of a site.

Pushing face water: Water that runs rapidly against a relatively small site.

Attacking coastal region water: Water that flows against a site from either flank.

Shampoo water: A waterfall in the rear of a site.

Water that jumps over the trough: A waterfall in front of a site.

Bottoming up water: Two rivers that merge in the front of a site.

Sending dragon waters: two waters that run parallel to each other on both sides of a site.

Ringing water: Water that falls into a rocky hole and makes a deep, rich sound.

These metaphorical names are very suggestive of their geomantic meanings. Water that "breaks the heart of heaven" must be bad. It will cause the family line to be interrupted in three generations (i.e., after three generations no boy will be born into the family). Water that "pounds on city walls" will cause the residents to go bankrupt. Indeed, water can bring wealth and honor as well as poverty and disaster to people.

Perhaps the most extraordinary kind of water is the heavenly pond, which is a sure sign of the existence of a genuine dragon and is often credited for the generation of heads of state in neighboring areas. For instance, it is said that the ancestors of the emperors of the Qing dynasty were buried high in the Tianshan Mountains between two heavenly ponds. High up in the famous Lu Mountains in Jiangxi province of China, I saw three natural lakes of considerable size hidden in the mountains. This is, of course, by no means a unique phenomenon to China. In Washington State, there is a similar geographic feature. Spirit Lake is located on Mount St. Helens, close to Washington's southern border. The lake is one-and-one-half miles in diameter, which is quite a spectacular size for a heavenly pond. Who knows if there will be a head of state coming from this area.

Water does not have to be visible. Water can be near or far, visible or invisible. The fact that you cannot see water from a residence does not mean that there isn't any water in the environment. Second-rate geomancers know only visible waters. To them, only visible waters can bring good luck to people. This understanding, however, is superficial. In fact, some geomancers even suggest that houses and graves be built on grounds where water is not immediately visible. That way, water can bring good luck to the residents while all its potential evils are absorbed by the shielding mountains between them and a residence. (The logic behind this is that since water can be good or bad, and it is not always an easy thing to tell good water from bad, it may be safer to just hide behind mountains.)

Great caution must be exercised when there is water running headstrong, so to speak, against a land site, as is the case of houses built on the waterfront of an ocean. These houses will bear the brunt of the lashing waves, as well as the violence of typhoons and hurricanes. While the view of a waterfront is beautiful, the potential risks can also be high. Hence, it is not geographically and geomantically advisable to build small, individual houses on the waterfront. The remedy is found in mountains that lie close and serve as shields against the impact of the striking water. Thus, if you must build a house on the waterfront, it is best to build on top of some coastal mountains. Otherwise, the "heart and shoulders" of the house will be "broken" by the water, leading to various misfortunes.

FIGURE 7-1
A river with many curves or turns is considered very auspicious and very desirable for a land site

There is another kind of water known as "dry flowing water." It is a term for lower terrain next to or near higher terrain. Higher terrain is like a hill while lower terrain is like water. Water flows to the low places, and the low terrain is dry except when it rains, hence the name "dry flowing water." The watercourse should still be curving so the flow is not rapid or straight. Dry or wet, the function of water is the same—to carry the Qi energy of the site located on the higher terrain.

Earthly Doors and Heavenly Doors

The direction in which a waterway comes and goes is another factor of consideration. Feng shui calls the direction water comes from—upstream—the "heavenly door," while the direction water flows—downstream—is the "earthly door." This is because water flows from high land to low land, so the high land is thought of as heaven, and the low land as earth. According to feng shui theory, the heavenly door should be wide open, so that wealth and good luck can flow unimpeded to people living downstream. However, the earthly door should be kept narrow and closed, so that wealth will not flow away easily. For this reason, it is considered highly auspicious when the downstream flow of water from a site is hardly detectable. There must be layers of mountains downstream to check or stop the quick flow of water away from a site.

Apparently, we can do little to change the quality of a heavenly door or an earthly door. The best that we can do is to find a location that already features a wide open heavenly door and a closely guarded earthly door. This is no small task in feng shui design, and it takes a lot of time and effort to find such a site.

To show their special interest in the earthly door, fathers of feng shui have given different names to mountains located downstream, as well as those standing in the midst of a waterway. For example, mountains found downstream on the right bank of a waterway are called "tortoises," and those on the left bank of a waterway are called "snakes." Together, tortoises and snakes form a natural lock, checking the flow of the water. Big rocks or small hills standing in the middle of the water downstream are "respectable stars" or "seals floating in the water." Such rocks or hills further strengthen the earthly door, checking the flow again.

If the heavenly door is narrow while the earthly door is wide open, local residents can hardly hope to accumulate wealth. Their money will flow away like the water. Even if they are wealthy when they first move into the area, their financial situation will deteriorate soon. Very likely, the third generation descendants in the family may be so poor that they need to beg. In this regard, Li Mozai has the following message:

To check means to stop. This is a geomantic knack that has been kept secret for centuries. . . . Flowing is the nature of water. If there are objects to check the flow of water, it will stay. Otherwise, it will rush down a thousand miles unimpeded. As water stays, so also will wealth. If water is allowed to flow away unchecked, how can one accumulate wealth? This is exactly what is meant by the ancient sayings that "as water flows away and mountains fly, money disappears and family divide. . . ."

Of course, the word "check" has multiple meanings. The best land site is one in the near front of which, a water is forced to slow down and turn back in its flow. The next best situation will be the existence of prolonged mountains on both sides of a land, which extend themselves down the stream to form a semi-scissors to intercept, so to speak, the water flow. The third best scenario is to have terraced fields lying down the stream which force the water to curve somewhat. If you integrate the classical remarks on the bright hall, table mountains, and mountains down the stream, the significance of checking becomes self-evident.

It is said in *Adventures of Geomancy* by Ye Jiusheng:

Finding a good construction site is not so difficult if you know how to examine the mountains down the stream of a water. . . . Before you examine the coming dragons, you should first see whether there are mountains down the stream in your front. Before you put any project on a land, you should ask yourself if the mountains down the stream are standing close by. If mountains down the stream can check and stop the flow of water, your children will be able to buy all the farming lands in the country. . . . The only thing that can spare your children from being poor is a mountain down the stream. . . . Therefore, there must be mountains in the bright hall to check the flowing away of water. As you combine and study these remarks, you will be able to tell how essential it is to check the free flow of water.

Not only is the presence of mountains on the banks of a waterway essential to feng shui, the manner in which the water runs also matters. Thus, if water runs in a straight course for a long distance, it is considered evil water, even though it is considered good and convenient for transportation from an economic point of view. Feng shui tells us that no good site exists in the vicinity of such a watercourse.

Good feng shui sites along or near a waterway only exist where the water flows quietly and slowly, through twists and turns, and seems to linger in the front of a location. A slow flowing, curving water brings about wealth and good luck just like a rapidly, straight flowing water takes away wealth and brings in poverty and misfortune. Genuine dragons can only rest in places where water makes turns and stays there for a while. This is the situation of a lake, a pond, or a harbor. Sometimes, waters are not directly visible from a site, because they are hidden behind facing mountains. Such a site is an auspicious site notwithstanding.

Qualities of Water

There are several dimensions of the quality of water. These are (in order of importance) the direction of flow, the speed of flow, the shape of the watercourse, the depth of the water, and the sound the water makes.

In terms of the direction of flow, a waterway should not run directly against a site where a house is built (such as a river islet), nor should it run parallel to the mountain vein in the surroundings. Otherwise, the water cannot bring in the Qi energy from the other side of the waterway in the mountain. A waterway should instead flow from an auspicious direction to an inauspicious direction.

What, then, is an auspicious direction and an inauspicious one? There is no hard and set rule in this regard. Auspicious and inauspicious directions vary from person to person, depending on each person's birthday and gender. For instance, a man born in the year 1962 has as his auspicious directions west, northeast, northwest, and southwest. All other directions are considered inauspicious. For a woman born in the same year, however, the opposite is true. Her auspicious directions are south, north, east, and southeast. For detailed information on finding auspicious directions, refer to chapter 9.

The speed of water should be low. In fact, the slower a river or stream flows, the better it is for the local residents, for such a waterway can generate more wealth and good luck for the local residents. Feng shui describes the ideal speed of water flow as a young lady on her way to marry a husband far away from her hometown. Out of her lingering affection

for her parents and her home, she keeps turning around for another final look at the familiar faces and buildings, as if fearing that she may not be able to see them again in her life. The affectionate attitude of this young lady, according to feng shui fathers, should be the manner in which a water flows away from a locality.

Third, the water flow should be in an embracing shape rather than a straight line. An embracing or curved flow is more likely to exist on the inner side of a waterway than on the outer side. In fact, sophisticated feng shui masters always look for dragon lairs at the inner side of the curves of a waterway. There is a lot of scientific reason for this practice. Modern hydromechanics tell us that as a result of the inertial momentum of water, the inner side of a water curve will become bigger and bigger as time goes by. For exactly the opposite reason, the outer side of the water curve will gradually lose its ground. Thus, if a house is built on the outer side of a waterway, it runs the risk of being rushed away by the water. On the contrary, an expanding land base means greater stability and development, which every reasonable person wants.

Fourth, water should run deep rather than shallow. The deeper the water runs, the slower and quieter it will be. Generally, most areas where waters run deep are thriving, whereas most areas where waters run shallow and fast are economically underdeveloped.

Concerning sound, feng shui holds that the softer and gentler the sound that water makes, the more auspicious it is for the land in its vicinity. In this regard, feng shui identifies four kinds of inauspicious water and their sounds: beach water, waterfalls, rocks and stones, and rocky holes. Of course, this does not mean that the entire watercourse is bad. In other words, only the portions of the watercourse that make loud noises are considered inauspicious.

Shorelines have constantly moving water which makes loud noises due to the tides, all the more so if there are rocks on the beach. A waterfront generally is not recommended for residential buildings, because the ocean keeps on lashing it day and night. The noise pollution is harmful in itself.

Waterfalls are not good to have in the neighborhood. The waterfalls that are worst of all are those that fall right in front of a house or grave. The louder it is, the worse it is. Thus, if a waterfall sounds like thunder, it is bound to bring disaster to the residents in the area.

The third kind is water that runs past the rocks and stones that are in it. The geomantic meaning of it is the same as a shoreline, albeit the lesser of the two evils.

The fourth kind of water falls into large holes in rocks. A detailed analysis is needed in interpreting such waters based on the specific sounds they make. Some of them may sound like people laughing, others like people weeping. The rule of thumb is this: a laughing sound is preferable to a lamenting sound, a lamenting sound is preferable to a weeping sound, and no sound is preferable to all. This is exactly what Meng Hao says in his *Verses of the Heart of Snow*: "A noisy water turns a beautiful landform into a poor site for residence."

If there are more than two watercourses, they should preferably cross and intertwine with each other, rather than run parallel to one another.

To sum up, water is the first element in the Chinese system of five elements. It is also the first desirable thing to have in feng shui design. Water not only provides the necessity of life, but also the infrastructure for economic development. From a feng shui point of view, water is the blood of mountains and the wealth of the earth.

Chapter 8

Exploring Wind

Unlike water, which is generally considered an auspicious element to have, wind is largely regarded as something to be avoided in feng shui. Wind can blow away the Qi energy of a location, and finding and accumulating Qi energy is what feng shui is all about.

However, not all winds are considered bad. The nature and quality of the wind depends on the direction from which it blows. To better understand the individual effects of wind from different directions, fathers of feng shui have distinguished eight kinds of wind corresponding to the eight directions defined in the I-Ching, i.e., the eight trigrams: Li, Kun, Dui, Qian, Kan, Gen, Zhen, and Xun. (See Figure 8-1, page 87.)

The stronger the wind, the more destructive it is to the Qi energy of an area, and therefore the more harmful to the residents in that area. If wind can blow into a location from all directions, it is called an open location without protection. Such an area is considered inauspicious except when it is a vast plain. The reason why a vast plain is an exception lies in the understanding that a plain vast enough contains strong energy in itself, and is therefore capable of standing up to various winds. It is also desirable that there are watercourses running through it, because watercourses can preserve the Qi energy in the face of wind.

In mountainous areas, however, it is absolutely necessary that a residence have some protection from the wind. Such protection comes in the form of neighboring hills or forests. In the absence of these protective objects, wind can easily blow through a location, carrying away its precious Qi energy and rendering it an inauspicious place for living and working.

Figure 8-1, page 87, correlates eight types of wind with a specific direction. The nine palaces are also correlated in this figure. Since wind cannot come from within a house itself (wind generated by an electronic fan is an exception unknown to feng shui fathers), the Attraction Palace at the very center of the illustration can be ignored. Only the remaining eight palaces are of significance.

At the top of the illustration, Kan, or north, correlates to the Hibernation Palace, which stands for a very strong wind coming from the north. The Heavenly Palace in the south, Li, stands for a very weak wind. The Warehouse Palace in the east, Zhen, stands for a baby wind, a weak wind. The Fruit Palace in the west, Dui, generates a strong wind. New Luo Palace in the northwest, Qian, generates a very strong wind that can break things (hence the name "broken wind"). The Reserve Palace in the northeast, Gen, generates a fierce wind. Yin Luo Palace in the southeast, Xun, also generates a weak wind, while scheme wind, or evil wind, comes from the Mysterious Palace in the southwest, Kun.

It is a feng shui observation that the weaker and warmer the wind is, the better will be its impact on a location. Chinese fathers hold that weak, warm winds are good winds that will not destroy the Qi energy of a location. It is the strong and cold winds that are malicious and therefore should be avoided. With this in mind, we can tell from Figure 8-1 that there are three benign winds in nature: the baby wind coming from the east, the weak wind coming from the southeast, and the very weak wind coming from the south.

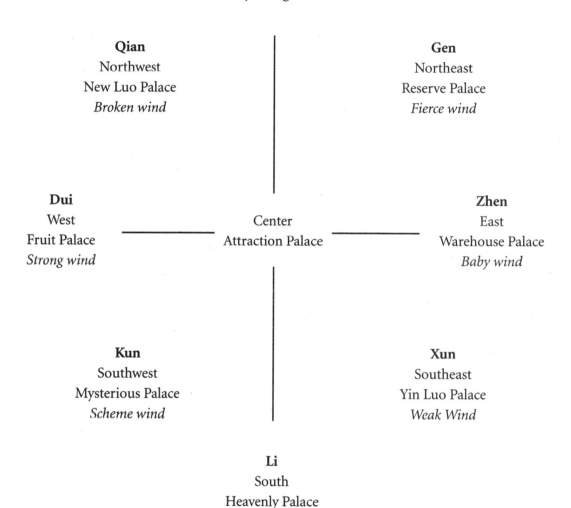

FIGURE 8-1
Wind correspondences

The rest are considered bad or inauspicious winds.

For this reason, a good location for a house should have something (hills or tall buildings) standing to its southwest, west, north, northwest, and northeast as protection, while leaving its southern, southeastern, and eastern sides relatively open. Such a design forms an image of a semicircle, with its front facing the open directions.

This understanding about the quality of wind is very much in line with human experience. Most people know that the southern and southeastern winds are gentle winds that blow during the summer and blow away the heat. Western and northern winds usually blow during the winter season, adding frost to the snow. This information has been incorporated into the design of residential feng shui in China for centuries. Almost all wealthy and noble Chinese people build their residences with a southern or southeastern exposure, while covering up the other sides with natural or artificial objects. As long as it is financially and geographically possible, the Chinese choose a southern exposure for their houses.

Winds blowing from different directions carry different geomantic meanings for a location. If you can feel the wind blowing hard against you from the back, it indicates that there is not enough protection in the rear. Such being the case, you will suffer from financial trouble and your life will not be long if you continue to live there. If the wind blows hard on the left side, it indicates your spouse will die before you and you will have to live a lonely life. If there is a strong wind attacking you from your right, it indicates that there is no white tiger in that direction, i.e., the lack of protective hill to your right. As a result, you will either be left without a child or your children will fail in life. If the front of your residence bears the attack of severe wind, the consequence is that you will gradually lose all your money and go bankrupt, or that your family line will be cut short in your generation, leaving you without a child, which is considered a great misfortune in traditional Chinese society because there will be no one there to take care of your tomb and offer sacrifices to you after you have ceased to be.

Besides the eight trigrams, some feng shui masters also classify winds in terms of yin and yang. In other words, winds can be categorized as yin-wind and yang-wind, just as everything in nature can be so classified. Here, yin-wind is defined as the wind that can destroy the Qi energy of a land, and is therefore inauspicious. Yang-wind is described as a favorable wind that will benefit the people.

Ye Jiushen of the Qing dynasty was the first feng shui master to point out the vital differences between these two fundamentally different kinds of wind. According to Ye, winds that blow along a river or ocean are of the yang nature, which can benefit residents there. Also, as a long mountain range passes through a watercourse, it brings in the yang-wind, which is needed to dispel evil spirits. Not all winds are bad. In the absence of wind, air will become stagnant, just like a house without windows. Therefore, it is highly important to be able to tell yin-wind from yang-wind. Yin-wind is bad but yang-wind is good. As to the degree of damage that yin-wind can inflict on a site, it depends primarily on the strength of Qi in the location, just like the immune system of a person. The stronger the Qi reserve in the area, the less damage yin-wind can bring to it. Just like the stronger the immune system a person has, the less likely he or she will become ill. Thus, when yin-wind blows at large, long-running mountains, little damage results from it. But if it blows at a small hill, the effects can be very disastrous Therefore, one needs to distinguish different kinds of wind.

Thus, we cannot indiscriminately regard all winds as vicious. An insightful, distinguishing eye is needed on the part of a feng shui practitioner to tell what is really bad, what is neutral, or even good.

Chapter 9

Exploring Direction

Direction is a significant issue in geomancy as well as geography. We know that the direction in which major waterways and mountain veins run has a significant impact on the atmosphere, agriculture, and cultural life of people living around them. For instance, even people of the same nation living in areas divided by an east-west oriented mountain vein may have widely different dialects and languages, traditions, living habits, and even religions.

Culturally, rivers running in the south-north direction have proven to be more important than those that run east to west in unifying a country with different ethnic groups and languages. Since people living in the southern and northern sides of a mountain vein tend to have their own languages and cultural traditions, rivers that are south-north bound promote communications, cultural exchange, and mutual understanding between the peoples living in the southern and northern parts of a mountain vein, thus facilitating the political unification and administration of a country. The Grand Canal in China, that runs from Peking in the north to Hanzhou in the south, was artificially hewed in the sixth century, mainly for the purpose of more effectively ruling the country.

No wonder feng shui also pays great attention to the direction and orientation of buildings and tombs. Besides the direction in which mountain ranges and watercourses run, feng shui emphasizes that each residence and grave should have an appropriate frontal exposure that is in accordance with the karma of the owner. Advocates of the Direction school even go so far as to suggest that if the direction of a building is not correct, all auspicious waters and magnificent mountains would be to no avail.

Despite their common point of emphasis on direction, the difference between geomancy and geography in terms of direction is significant. Geography considers direction as a purely spatial issue. In feng shui, however, direction possesses the dimension of both time and space. The issue of direction in feng shui is concerned with the interaction and

harmony between humans and nature, which are a function of both time and space. As has been mentioned before, man is the central pillar in the trinity of heaven-man-earth. This trinity is established and maintained in time as well as in space. Specifically, in the case of residential feng shui, we need to base the choice of direction and frontal exposure of a residence on the birthday of the homeowner, which is a matter of time but overlaps into the domain of space.

The proper layout of a house and how the individual rooms inside are used also depend on the owner's birthday. Because of this, different owners of the same residence may require a different layout and frontal exposure. This is why the same house can bring different luck to different residents. (See chapter 13 on residential feng shui.)

So far as commercial feng shui is concerned, it is the birthday of the business owner that determines the right direction and exposure of a store or office building. That can partly explain why the same business fares with a different degree of success or failure in the hands of different chief executive officers or owners. (See chapter 14 on commercial feng shui.)

Besides the individual birthday of owner, the direction in which mountains and waterways run also count. The answer depends on the point of reference. In feng shui, this reference point is the site of a building or a grave. For example, if a mountain on the left of a house curves toward the right side of the house, the water should preferably flow from the right side of the house toward the left side, as if to merge with the mountain. Such a landscape, where waterways and mountains run in opposite directions and cross each other, represents a merging between yin (left and waters) and yang (right and mountains), a very auspicious sign to have in feng shui. Since the direction of waterways and mountains cannot be easily changed, it is how a site is chosen with reference to water and mountains that requires great skill. For instance, if a river runs away from the front of a site, the site must be chosen so as to directly face the peak of one of the checking mountains downstream (i.e., earthly door or one of the four animals).

Extreme care must be exercised when there are exactly two mountains in the front of a residence or a grave, otherwise, big disasters may follow. A story goes that one day master Liao Jinjing of the Song dynasty and his disciples passed by Leping county in Jiangxi province. They climbed up a huge mountain and found a highly auspicious burial site. Facing this site were two magnificent mountains standing side by side. Liao told his students that who-ever was buried at this site would have one of their descendants become the emperor's son-in-law. His students were excited over the auspicious prophecy and were eager to sell their knowledge for a good price. Several days later when Liao was out of town, a local rich landlord, Mr. Yu, died, and his family was looking for a good burial ground for him. Hearing the news, Liao's students offered to find such a burial site and see to it that the remains were properly buried. Since Liao Jinjing was such a famous geomancer of the time, Yu's family willingly paid a high price for his students' services when they were told that this site was personally chosen by Liao himself.

Upon Liao's return, his students proudly reported to him what had hap-pened several days ago. Liao climbed the mountain to inspect Yu's grave. He found that the grave was dug in the right loca-tion but set to face the wrong direction—directly up to the taller of the two moun-tains in the far front. Apparently, his stu-dents had forgotten his teaching about a site's direction with regard to facing mountains. They thought the more mag-nificent mountain would bring more good luck to the family if used as the wor-shipping mountain. However, this vio-lated a vital feng shui principle that Liao once mentioned to his disciples. The principle states that whenever there are two worshipping mountains in the front, a grave or a residence should face directly to the opening space between the two mountains. In Yu's case, there were only two mountains in front of his grave, so by geomantic principle, his grave should have been set to face the open space between the two mountains. Since the coffin was already buried in the grave, it would be a very inauspicious thing to rebury it. Liao could only regret that he was not present at the time of burial. After reproaching his students for their negligence, Liao left a poem to them as a lesson:

> Set a grave to face a peak while an
> open space it should,
> How can you blame the burial
> ground for not being good?
> Though some descendants will
> become noble through wives,
> The pity is that they will in their
> heydays lose their lives.

Liao meant to leave this poem as a forecast of what would happen in the future as a burial result. What did happen is that two generations down the road, one of Yu's grandchildren did become a son-in-law of the emperor. This sudden good luck turned his head wild, and he became so arrogant and careless that he offended some top governmental officials and committed many crimes. Many officials reported his wrongdoings to his father-in-law. Fearing public opinion and out of consideration for social justice, the emperor had no choice but to order the execution of his own son-in-law.

This lesson of geomantic direction had been taken seriously by Mao's grandfather when he built their house in the province of Hunan where Mao spent his first eighteen years of his life. The Mao family has been handsomely rewarded by this feng shui knowledge. A detailed description and analysis of the feng shui of Mao's old residence is included in appendix 3, "Case Studies."

Another story about the significance of direction in feng shui design is also related to grandmaster Liao Jinjing. The story goes that Liao was once asked to select an auspicious burial ground for a rich man named Liu in Jiangxi province. After considering the appropriate direction, Liao told the Liu family to set the grave in such a way that it would look aslant at a "general's mountain" in the far front of the burial ground. The Liu family did not like the idea of having his grave looking aslant at so auspicious and magnificent a worshipping mountain in the front. After Liao left, the Liu family acted on their own, to the negligence of Liao's advice, and set the grave to face squarely on the frontal side of the mountain. After hearing the news some time later, Liao sighed to his students: "I set the direction in such a way that will bring marquis and noblemen to his family, but they acted on their own and will thus bring ringleaders to the family."

True to Liao's prediction, three ringleaders were found among Liu's grandchildren, who were none other than Liu Hanxi and his brothers. The Liu brothers served Chen Youliang as top generals in his bid for the supreme power in China. Chen's key rival was Zhu Yuanzhang, the founder of the Ming dynasty. As Zhu defeated Chen, he ordered the execution of Liu Hanxi and his two brothers. This is typical in a feudal country like China where the outcome of power struggles determines your political reputation if you are involved in it. Thus, if you win the power struggle, you are a hero. But if you lose the struggle, you will be called a ringleader. Thus, we can see the importance of setting a construction project in an appropriate direction.

However, not all geomancers agree on this theory of direction. Students from the Situation school of feng shui believe that the whole point of direction is to fine-tune an already good site to make sure that all the elements are more balanced. As such, direction theory is at best a complement to situation theory. At

worst, it stands in the way of creative geomantic design.

Furthermore, Situation school students argue that so long as there is a genuine dragon, i.e., lively mountains full of Qi energy, there must be auspicious sites in it. How can we afford to forsake such auspicious sites merely because direction is not right? After all, a good site is primary, direction is secondary. Therefore, we only need to find genuine dragons and lairs.

For instance, there are two mountains facing each other, one in the south and the other in the north. The southern one is ugly but the northern one is magnificent. Under these circumstances, one should set the front of a grave or a house to face the northern mountain, although the south is generally a more preferred frontal exposure than the north, which invites the bitter northern wind. This design is known as "counter-riding a dragon" in the Situation school. By counter-riding a dragon, we offset the malignant effects of the northern wind by use of the magnificent mountain in the north as a shield.

There is another strong argument for southern exposure. According to Chinese tradition, a southern exposure is a royal exposure. Thus, all palaces in China are built with a southern exposure. Almost all important buildings, houses, and tombs for the wealthy and distinguished in China are built with a southern exposure in the front. The famous phrase "facing the south and declaring oneself an emperor" vividly reflects this deep-rooted Chinese belief. This geomantic emphasis on the southern exposure can also be seen by the fact that after the tragic death of Dai Li, one of the most beloved generals of Chiang Kai-shek, Chiang personally investigated the burial ground for Dai and insisted that Dai's grave be given a southern exposure in the front and Dai's coffin be laid along the south-north orientation.

While a southern exposure is generally desired, it is not the only good exposure available. Since different individuals have different birthdays and therefore karmas, different people may have different locations and directions that match with their specific karma. Each building has to be evaluated on a case-by-case basis in the context of its owner's birthday. This is at once a challenge and an opportunity. The challenge lies in that a true feng shui practitioner has to be knowledgeable about the reading of a birthday. The opportunity is that other directions are available to individuals in addition to the southern exposure. Particularly in the United States, where strict regulations are enforced regarding urban development, more choice means more opportunity for house constructors. For example, even if it is geographically feasible and geomantically desirable to have your house exposed to the south, you may not be allowed to do so due to restrictions in urban development. In such cases, geomantic knowledge can give you some room to maneuver and offer you more choices than geographically or legally allowed.

To determine an auspicious exposure for an individual house, two systems have been employed in feng shui: the *ba-gua* system and the eight characters of birth.

Ba-gua System

The ba-gua system is extracted from the eight trigrams in the I-Ching and strictly based on the gender of the homeowner (the legal owner of the property) and the year in which he or she was born. Care, however, must be exercised because the ba-gua system uses the lunar calendar instead of the solar calendar. The lunar year in the Chinese calendar typically starts on the fourth day of February and ends on the third day of February. For example, if you were born on the third of February in 1999, you would still be considered a child of 1998 in the traditional Chinese calendar.

In the ba-gua system, a plane is divided into eight directions or locations with each occupying forty-five degrees, i.e., north or Kan, northeast or Gen, etc. (See Table 9-1, page 99.) These eight

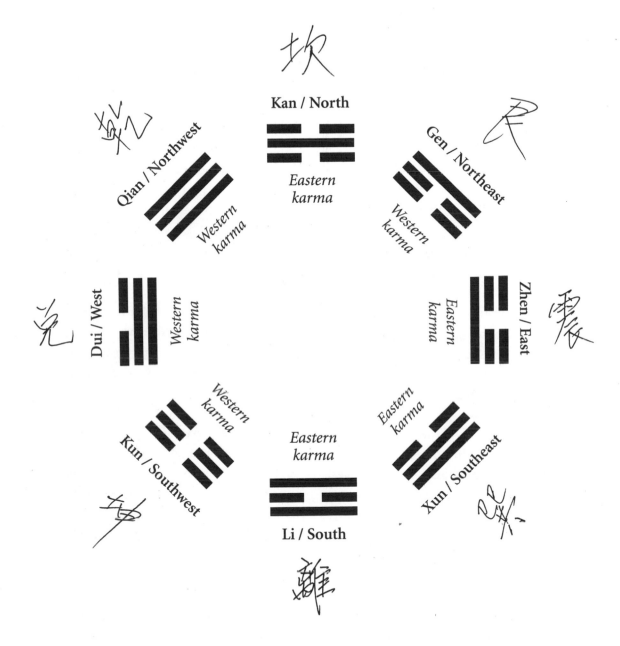

FIGURE 9-1
The eight trigrams and their direction and karma group correspondences

directions are grouped into two categories: the four eastern karmas and the four western karmas.

Four eastern karmas: East (Zhen), north (Kan), southeast (Xun), and south (Li).

Four western karmas: West (Dui), northwest (Qian), southwest (Kun), and northeast (Gen).

All humans are divided into one of these two groups on the basis of their sex and the year in which they were born. For those born under the category of the four eastern karmas, the auspicious directions and locations for them would be east, north, southeast, and south while the remaining four directions are considered inauspicious. Similarly, for those born under the four western karmas, their auspicious directions and locations are the west, northwest, southwest, and northeast, and the remaining directions are unfavorable. Thus, everyone of us has four favorable directions to choose from.

To find which karma group you belong to and your subsequent auspicious directions, refer to Table 9-1. Find your year of birth under the corresponding gender column. Remember that a male and a female may have different karmas even if they were born in the same year. For instance, if a man was born in the lunar year of 1950, his karma is Kun, his original loca-

tion or direction is southwest, and he is in the group of the four west karmas. However, if a female was born in 1950, her karma is Kan or north, and she belongs to the group of the four east karmas.

The time interval between years in the columns is nine years. Based on this, I have found two simple formulae, through which we can find the correspondence between someone's year of birth and geomantic karma. For males, the formula is (2000 − year of birth) / 9; for females, the formula is (year of birth − 1904) / 9.

For instance, a man born in the lunar year of 1962 has the following result: (2000 − 1962) / 9 equals a remainder of 2. A woman born in the same year would have a remainder of 4: (1962 − 1904) / 9.

For both genders, if the remainder of the calculation is 1, the person belongs to Kan karma or north. If the remainder is 2, the person belongs to Kun karma or southwest. If the remainder is 3, the person belongs to Zhen karma or east. If the remainder is 4, the person belongs to Xun karma or southeast. If the remainder is 5, the male belongs to Kun karma or southwest, while the female belongs to Gen karma or northeast. If the remainder is 6, the person belongs to Qian karma or northwest. If the remainder is 7, the person belongs to Dui karma or west. If the remainder is 8, the person belongs to Gen karma or northeast. If it can be divided

Qian		Kun		Zhen		Dui	
Male	Female	Male	Female	Male	Female	Male	Female
1904	1901	1905, 1908	1906	1907	1907	1903	1902
1913	1910	1914, 1917	1915	1916	1916	1912	1911
1922	1919	1923, 1926	1924	1925	1925	1921	1920
1931	1928	1932, 1935	1933	1934	1934	1930	1929
1940	1937	1941, 1944	1942	1943	1943	1939	1938
1949	1946	1950, 1953	1951	1952	1952	1948	1947
1958	1955	1959, 1962	1960	1961	1961	1957	1956
1967	1964	1968, 1971	1969	1970	1970	1966	1965
1976	1973	1977, 1980	1978	1979	1979	1975	1974
1985	1982	1986, 1989	1987	1988	1988	1984	1983
1994	1991	1995, 1998	1996	1997	1997	1993	1992

Kan		Gen		Li		Xun	
Male	Female	Male	Female	Male	Female	Male	Female
1900, 1909	1905	1902	1909, 1912	1901	1904	1906	1908
1918	1914	1911	1918, 1921	1910	1913	1915	1917
1927	1923	1920	1927, 1930	1919	1922	1924	1926
1936	1932	1929	1936, 1939	1928	1931	1933	1935
1945	1941	1938	1945, 1948	1937	1940	1942	1944
1954	1950	1947	1954, 1957	1946	1949	1951	1953
1963	1959	1956	1963, 1966	1955	1958	1960	1962
1972	1968	1965	1972, 1975	1964	1967	1969	1971
1981	1977	1974	1981, 1984	1973	1976	1978	1980
1990	1986	1983	1990, 1993	1982	1985	1987	1989
1999	1995	1992	1999	1991	1994	1996	1998

TABLE 9-1
List of karma groups and their corresponding birth years

exactly by 9, the person belongs to Li karma or south.

Going back to the man and woman born in 1962 in the earlier example, the man with a remainder of 2 belongs to Kun karma, which falls in the group of the four western karmas. His auspicious direction is southwest, with west, northwest, and northeast as his additional auspicious directions. The woman with a remainder of 4 has Xun as her original direction, which is southeast, in the group of the four eastern karmas. East, north, and south are her additional auspicious directions.

This piece of information about the relationship between one's birth year and direction is very valuable to the geomantic design of a house, including the placement of doors and the layout of individual rooms. With the addition of a "center" location to the eight locations already mentioned above, each house has nine locations. As a general feng shui principle, auspicious locations should be reserved for rooms with auspicious purposes, while inauspicious locations should be used for inauspicious purposes. Fathers of feng shui hold that bedrooms, the kitchen, the living room, and the studio are rooms with auspicious purposes for a residence. The bathroom and laundry room are considered inauspicious pur-

poses. These inauspicious uses of a house are, indeed, necessary evils to a modern lifestyle. (See the chapter "Residential Feng Shui.")

Eight Characters of Birth

Another system used by Chinese geomancers in determining the auspicious directions is the eight characters of birth. This system itself is a profound art and one of the most popular methods of divination in Chinese society. But it is also quite complicated. The eight characters of birth consist of the year, month, date, and hour of birth, each of which is represented by two Chinese characters. Each character stands for one of the five elements (water, fire, wood, metal, and earth). Of course, there are duplications of these elements in eight characters. In extreme cases, all eight characters may stand for one and the same element.

Once the birth timing is so recorded, a skillful reader will be able to find out which of the five elements is mostly needed and desired by an individual. This element is known as the "useful spirit" upon which so much of our fate depends. Then since each of the five elements corresponds to a direction, a person's auspicious direction can be determined.

In actual practice, a Chinese fortuneteller would have to evaluate all the eight characters, taking into account not only the season of birth but also the nature of each element and how they are related to each other, before coming up determining what the useful spirit is for a specific client. Generally speaking, if a man was born in the wintertime, mostly likely the useful spirit of his eight characters of birth would be fire, because winter is the season in which fire is most needed. On the other hand, if a man was born in the middle of summer, his useful spirit would most likely be water, because water is most needed in the summertime.

Once an individual's useful spirit (element) is determined, the corresponding direction or location can be found. For example, water corresponds to north, fire to south, wood to east, metal to west, and earth to the center. (Refer to Table 2-1, page 24.) For example, if a person's useful spirit is fire, this corresponds to the south. This means that his house should have a southern exposure. If someone's useful spirit is water, which corresponds to the direction of north, that person's house should have a northern exposure.

Chapter 10

The Bright Hall

Bright hall refers to the area in front of a building or a grave. This is an important point of consideration in the overall feng shui design. Originally, a bright hall referred to the open space in front of a palace where the emperor received his provincial leaders and honored guests. This area was designed to accommodate hundreds of people and was therefore very bright and spacious.

Coincidentally, spaciousness and brightness are also two important geomantic requirements for the space in front of a house, so the term "bright hall" was borrowed. A bright hall in front of a house also symbolizes its traditional use. Just as it was the place where leaders and guests paid their respects to the emperor, the water and mountains that gather in the front of a site seem as if they are paying respect to the land site.

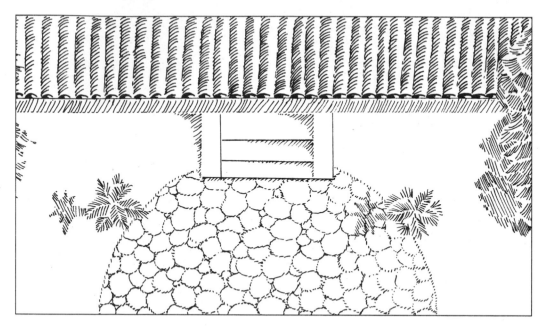

FIGURE 10-1
An example of a basic bright hall for a small residence

Bright halls are divided into inner bright halls and outer bright halls. Inner bright halls refer to the space in the near front of the site (front yard), between the residence and the table hill in the front. Outer bright halls refer to the space between the table hills and the worshipping hills in the front of the house.

Ideally, each residence or grave should have an inner bright hall and an outer bright hall. For the inner bright hall to be auspicious, it should be neither too narrow nor too spacious. Rather, it should be concise, fitting the size of the house exactly, and encircling the site so that the Qi energy in the environment can be conserved and the site can be effectively protected against the attack of winds. If it is too spacious, Qi in it will disperse and the site will be open to the attack of winds. Nor do we want the inner bright hall to be narrow, for this will limit the perspective and future of the residents.

The desirable size of the inner bright hall should be in proportion to the size and purpose of the building itself. Thus, a palace or a commercial building needs a much more spacious inner bright hall than an ordinary residence. Generally, it should not be more than three times the size of the house itself. If less than twice the size of the house, it is considered too narrow.

As for the outer bright hall, it is a different story. An outer bright hall should be wide, open, and magnificent for all kinds of buildings.

While it is a feng shui principle that a site should be well protected against the wind, this does not mean that a site should be pressed on all sides by other objects. While a building should be set close to the black tortoise in the back, and flanked—better still, embraced—on both sides by the green dragon and the white tiger, it should not be located anywhere close to the red phoenix in the front. This means that there must be some open space in the front of a site; if it is pressed on all sides, the benevolent yang-Qi will stagnate and turn into malignant yin-Qi. Using such a site to build a house could lead to bankruptcy, serious health problems, or even violent death for the residents. If it is used as a burial ground, the descendants will suffer from bad luck.

The ideal situation for a site is to have the front open, so that the residents will have a broad, clear view and a bright future. This is because the bright hall symbolizes the way out, the road ahead, the future, and opportunity. Everybody wants to have a bright future, a clear view of the road ahead, lots of room to maneuver, and an abundance of opportunities. Therefore, an ideal bright hall for a building should be open and bright, preferably having some water curving and lingering inside. This theory of feng shui can easily be verified from the standpoint of modern psychology. Just imagine yourself living in a house where the view is blocked by a building or mountains. You cannot see the way ahead, so your prospects are severely limited.

Of course, the bigger a bright hall is does not mean the better it is. The size of a bright hall should be in proportion to the size of the construction lot. The larger the lot, the larger the bright hall, and vice versa. This is a matter of balance, and balance brings about a sense of beauty and harmony.

For a common grave, a bright hall of twelve square feet is considered appropriate. For a medium-sized house, a bright hall of about 500 square feet is considered enough. For a supermarket, a bright hall of about 10,000 square feet is appropriate. For a palace, however, a bright hall would have to be in the neighborhood of 20,000 square feet.

The quality of a bright hall can be greatly enhanced through artistic design.

This is especially the case with residential and commercial buildings in urban areas, where the view is often limited because of the density of construction. To enhance the view, create a small garden, plant a few trees and flowers, dig a pond, or set up a fountain in the bright hall. All these additions help the absorption of heavenly Qi energy into the building, leading to comfortable living and working environments and better luck for the residents or the business. Comfortable living and working environments with nice views can also make us feel at ease and less stressed, boost our spirits, promote our health, and enhance our work efficiency.

Chapter 11

Pinpointing Dragon Lairs

In actual practice, feng shui consists of three major phases. The first phase is to find an auspicious land site. The second phase is to find out the best frontal exposure or orientation of the building and the appropriate color to paint it. The third phase is to construct the building in accordance with geomantic principles, paying special attention to issues such as what shape or appearance the building should have, and where the doors, bedrooms, kitchen, living room, and so on should be located. If it is a business/commercial building, the issues are where to locate the chief executive officer's (CEO's) office, and where specific departments such as accounting and marketing should be located. The first phase can be regarded as the exterior design and the last phase as the interior design.

The most artistic and difficult part of feng shui lies in finding an auspicious land site. Such a site is known as a dragon lair, and the process of finding it is called "pinpointing dragon lairs." Pinpointing a genuine dragon lair is not only the most difficult part in feng shui practice, it is also the most important first step in feng shui design. This step is typically time consuming and often laborious from the viewpoint of geomantic designers. This process often requires that the geomancer climb mountains, wade waters, and spend several days in the open air, as it used to be the case in ancient China.

The reason why pinpointing a dragon lair should be the first step is self-evident. In the absence of a land site, no construction project, be it a house, business, school, or grave, can be carried out. The reason why this is also the most important step in feng shui design is the major point of departure of this book from most feng shui books currently in the American market. The subject of geomancy is primarily concerned with the Qi energy in the earth (geo-), not the architecture above the ground. And a strong reserve of Qi energy is what feng shui is or should be seeking.

This first phase of feng shui design can be regarded as environmental design, which has the macroenvironment as its subject of study, and the finding of genuine dragon lair as its ultimate goal. Typically, this phase involves intensive mental work and extensive physical travel. The more you get to understand feng shui, the more you will realize that good feng shui sites are hard to find. They do not come by easily. Such sites are also limited by nature (i.e., nature only makes so many), a hard fact that gives a political dimension to the practice of feng shui in China.

Geomancers have to exercise their geomantic knowledge and imaginative powers in order to understand the specific significance of individual land sites, with special attention focused on the surrounding mountains and waterways to make sure that enough lively Qi energy exists in the environment. They also must make sure there is no evil Qi (known as *sha*) in the surroundings, and that if there is, there are countermeasures available. The entire process of searching for good feng shui sites is sometimes likened to searching for melons along the vines, where the vines are the mountains and waterways while the melons are the auspicious land sites or dragon lairs. Pinpointing a dragon lair is also like an acupuncturist pinpointing an acupoint for his or her patient.

As mentioned before, the ultimate goal in this phase of geomantic design is to find an auspicious land site for building a house, business, or grave. However, this is not the same as in real estate development. Feng shui is a much more complex concept. In real estate markets, the quality of a residential site is mainly determined by its size, its neighborhood, its distance from commercial and/or educational centers, ease of access to transportation means, and whether or not it has a great view of the mountain or water. In feng shui, a land site should be examined from the following perspectives: how close to a mountain vein the site is situated; the shape, vegetation, and symbolic meaning of the individual hills and mountains nearby; the manner in which rivers or streams come and go away from the site; the terrain of the land; and if the birthday of the homeowner matches the karma of the land.

A site and its surroundings are functions of each other. That is to say, a site is defined in the context of its surroundings, and the surroundings are in turn defined in the context of a specific site. Thus, the same river can have very different geographic features and therefore different geomantic meanings in specific portions of it. For instance, certain portions of a river may be quiet, curving, and flow slowly away, whereas other portions of the same river may be noisy, straight,

and rapid in flow. Thus, the same river possesses different geomantic meanings depending on which portion of it is close to a land site. Similarly, the same mountain can assume different shapes depending on what kind of perspective you have. Thus, from one angle it may look upright and pretty, but from another angle it appears uneven and ugly.

Differences between sites are also reflected in distance. Standing in different sites, we may be closer or farther away from the same mountain or river. An auspicious mountain or waterbody will give more benefit to those who live close to it than those who are far away from it. In very much the same way, the same inauspicious mountain or waterway will have greater damage on those close to it than those far away from it.

To find such a land site, feng shui resorts to imaginative thinking and metaphysical reasoning while drawing heavily on common sense. This is because oftentimes, when confronted with a geographic or topographic situation, common sense can tell us little beyond what is pretty or not, spacious or not, or high or low. It cannot tell us what the mountain or watercourse implies in terms of geomantic meaning. However, by dint of images contained in geographic and topographic forms, a seasoned geomancer will be able to tell good mountains from bad ones, auspicious waterways from inauspicious ones, and eventually genuine dragon lairs from false ones. In fact, the most critical yardstick testing the proficiency and qualification of a geomancer is whether or not he or she is capable of thinking in images. In this sense, good geomancers act like poets who see profound meanings in various images in nature.

One example of this artistic, imaginative thinking of great feng shui masters is found in their generous use of the dragon image. For centuries, the Chinese have a unabated enthusiasm for dragons, because the animal symbolizes so many good things desired in life—power, strength, authority, wealth, security, and adaptability to various environments. You would assume that this is why the dragon image is so widely used in feng shui; surprising enough, it is not. In fact, mountain veins are called dragons because their image is actually similar to that of a dragon—long, extending, flexible, and full of ups and downs.

Of course, the dragon is just one of the numerous members in the huge family of feng shui images. Other family members include the ox, tiger, lion, dog, wolf, bear, deer, eagle, horse, tortoise, phoenix, ape, monkey, crane, rat, snake, and cock. For example, a mountain in the shape of a tiger will bring good luck and money to the residents of a house if it directly faces the house, because the tiger is considered an auspicious animal in Chinese culture, capable of dispelling evil spirits and protecting the household from theft and misfortune.

Feng shui is a product of traditional Chinese culture, and the images used in it are full of cultural connotations. Therefore, these images must be understood in that context. Otherwise, the very image of a dragon itself will carry very different connotations, depending on the geomancer's background or prejudices.

Animals are not the only images employed in feng shui. The human body and inanimate objects are also widely employed to help convey the geomantic meanings of topographic forms. Thus, we find the following images repeatedly showing up in classic feng shui literature: lotus flower, roses, drums, boats, pen, pencil, basket, flag, generals, soldiers, scholars, women, dancers, and so on. Depending on the imaginative power of the individual, topographic forms can assume the image of various objects, animate or inanimate. Indeed, one cannot be too creative when practicing feng shui. Thus, some mountains are called "general mountains," because they look like generals sitting in their headquarters. Others are likened to pens, boats, tables, swords, knives, baskets, bowls, pillars, you name it. Another example is comparing mountains and hills to muskmelon vines. The main peaks of the mountain ranges are considered the roots of the melon vines, while the surrounding hills are thought of as the branches of the vine. The open land and plateau among these hills are similar to leaves in the spreading branches.

The following images are considered auspicious in Chinese culture and in feng shui: dragon, phoenix, tiger, lion, elephant, bear, eagle, drums, rectangular, square, circle, table, and pencil. Images that are considered inauspicious are the dog, wolf, oxen, snake, triangle, monkey, rat, and pig. What really matters are the symbolic meanings behind this cluster of images. In Chinese culture, the dragon symbolizes power, nobility, strength, and resourcefulness, and is therefore linked to wealth and social status. By contrast, the rat is not an auspicious image because it symbolizes thievery and timidity. Nor is a snake an encouraging image, because it signifies cruelty and viciousness.

Thus, feng shui lends itself generously to intuition and imagination. This way of thinking is neither far-fetched nor deliberately mystifying. Rather, it is an essential system of criteria by which the geomantic connotations of geographic features are revealed. It is important, however, to keep in mind that images, no matter how vivid they are, are just tools to the end, which is to understand the geomantic meanings of geographic objects and landforms.

Pinpointing Steps

To make the task of pinpointing a dragon lair easier for the reader, the following steps are outlined below followed by key questions involved in the process. They serve as a road map in our search for genuine dragon lairs.

- Follow the dragons or mountain veins.

- Examine individual hills nearby.

- Study the water in the vicinity.

- Pinpoint dragon lairs or auspicious sites.

Inherent to the above steps are the following questions, which must be answered before one can tell whether or not a genuine dragon lair exists:

- Are the mountains in the region continuous and magnificent?

- Where do they end in the region?

- Do they have good shape and appearance?

- Are there waterways passing by or are waterbodies formed in the area?

- From where does the water come and to where does it go?

- Do the waterways merge or cross each other and, if so, where?

- Do they cross the local mountains and, if they do, in what manner?

- Is the water flow straight or curved, rapid or slow?

- Is the flow of the water checked or stopped somewhere?

- What is the quality of the black tortoise in the back of the site?

- Is this site protected and, better still, embraced by some mountains or hills on both sides?

- What is the quality, height, shape, and appearance of these flanking mountains?

- Does the site have an open, wide bright hall?

- Is the site sloping downward from the back to the front?

In actual practice, especially in trying to answer the first three questions, Chinese feng shui masters find it helpful to move to a high location. From there, they will be able to get a bird's-eye view of the general topography in the area. Then, they will carefully observe the surrounding landforms from all angles. Since the same topography at different times of the day can create different images and impressions upon the same person due to the changes in the light, it is best to examine the surroundings of a site in the late morning. This is because the sun is up high enough, but the sunlight is not too bright, allowing a geomancer to have the most objective view of the topography.

Dragon Lair Elements

Generally speaking, the existence of the following objects is indicative of the existence of genuine dragon lairs:

- The general topography of the land is flat or gently sloping forward.

- A table and a worshipping mountain are in front of the land site.

- There is a green dragon and a white tiger mountain on both sides of a land site, curving, as if to embrace each other.

- There is a bright hall that is open and spacious.

- There are watercourses flowing by that are checked by some hills or mountains.

- Mountains in the environment assume the shape of a banner, a drum, a pen, a horse, a dragon, a tiger, a lion, a seal, or a warehouse.

In this regard of pinpointing dragon lair, *Verses of the Heart of Snow* has the following advice to offer:

> *Mountains normally do not curve, but as they do, Qi energy is cumulated and conserved there. Waters usually do not stop in their flowing, but as they do, mobility becomes stability. . . . Hence we know that the merging point of several mountains must be a genuine dragon site, just like the merging point of watercourses must be a great Bright Hall.*

Ideally, there should at least be four hills or mountains located on four sides of a residential site, i.e., the four black mountains: the black tortoise in the rear, the green dragon on the left side, the white tiger on the right side, and the phoenix in the front. A good site for residential construction is one that is protected in the back and flanked on both sides by good hills and mountains, and has some waterways flowing by; it is better still that these curve and linger. This geomantic principle makes a lot of common sense. For one thing, mountains provide us with rich resources for our livelihoods, from fruit to vegetables, from herbs to logs, from animal protein to various minerals, etc. Water offers us the conveniences of transportation, irrigation, and bathing and washing, in addition to being an indispensable drink in our daily life.

Fathers of feng shui say that genuine dragon lairs are often found at the tail of a dragon, i.e., the end of a mountain range, just like flowers and fruit are found at the end of tree branches. The end of a mountain vein is often bounded by some water, which can be a big lake, a river, or an ocean. Such localities are usually surrounded by mountains and nourished by good waters. This special topography allows Qi energy to build up and condense in such localities.

Generally speaking, a good feng shui site should slope gradually toward the front, and have some mountains in the rear that are higher than the site itself. It should also have hills on both sides, some open space in the front that faces the south, plus some lingering water in the front of the site, as if it is building up momentum before it flows away.

Ideally, the space in front of the construction site should be more spacious than in the rear or on both sides. The idea for more open space in front of a house is to let in and absorb the new Qi energy so

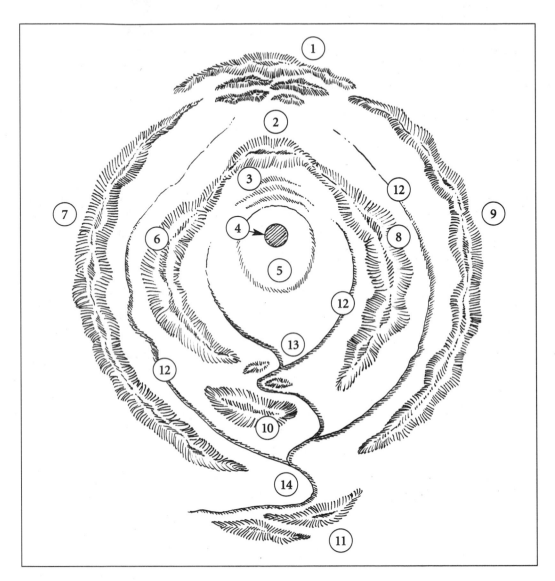

FIGURE 11-1
An ideal dragon lair and its basic environment

1. *Ancestor mountain*   2. *Locating mountain*   3. *Entrance to the dragon lair*
4. *The site (dragon lair)*   5. *Bright hall*   6. *Inner white tiger*   7. *Outer white tiger*
8. *Inner green dragon*   9. *Outer green dragon*   10. *Table hill*   11. *Worshipping mountains*
12. *Curving river*   13. *Inner mouth of the river*   14. *Outer mouth of the river*

that the site can grow in Qi storage and capacity. Such a site, due to its ability to conserve the Qi energy and stay clear of ill winds, is highly recommended because it can bring health, wealth, and prosperity to the people living and working there.

Before dragon lairs can be found, genuine dragons must be identified. If the ancestor mountain is magnificent, extending hundreds of miles and full of rises and falls, this mountain vein must be a genuine dragon containing tremendous Qi energy. Such a dragon must host a lot of dragon lairs or auspicious land sites on its route. A geomancer should also learn to distinguish a "running dragon" from a "resting or stopping dragon." Only when a dragon stops or stays can Qi energy accumulate. While a dragon is still running, Qi is also running with it, so there will be no large reserve of Qi along the running portion of a dragon. Therefore, sophisticated geomancers always look for locations where a lively dragon rests or stops.

The difference between a resting dragon and a stopping dragon lies in the length of the stop. A stopping dragon is one that has come to the end of its trip, as in the case where a mountain meets an ocean or a huge lake. A resting dragon is one that has come to a rest after a long distance before it resumes its trip, as in the case of a valley or a relatively flat land surrounded by mountains and water. Another clue to a resting dragon is when the land is encircled by two rivers that merge in front of the land.

So far as mountain veins are concerned, they should be full of rises and falls (peaks and valleys). When it comes to a rest from its travels and consequently creates a genuine dragon site, it generally shrinks into a narrow area. Such an area is likened to various images, such as the leg of a crane, the waist of a bee, the waist of a beauty, the willow branch, or the branch of a Chinese parasol tree. This is one of the clues to finding where genuine dragons rest and stay.

As for individual mountains and hills, they have been given specific names depending on their geographic relation to a locality. Familiarizing ourselves with these mountains will greatly help our understanding and analysis of mountains. The following is a list of the most relevant mountains (from the back of the site to the front):

- Major ancestor mountain: This is the mountain that is in the far background of a site, usually a big mountain thought to be the origin of small ones in the neighborhood.

- Minor ancestor mountain: This is the mountain or mountains found in the background of a site but smaller and closer to the site than the major ancestor mountain.

- Major hill: This is the highest peak in a mountain range, lying in front of the minor ancestor mountain and in the rear of the site.

- Green dragon: This is the hill lying to the left of the site.

- White tiger: This is the hill lying to the right of the site.

- Protecting hills: These are hills that lie outside of the green dragon and white tiger.

- Table hill: This is the hill lying in the near front of a site.

- Opposing mountains: These are mountains that lie in the far front of a site, facing both the site and the table hill, with a river or stream running between it and the table hill.

- Water mouth hills: These are the two hills lying on both sides of a waterway, as if to stop the water flow. Since water signifies wealth in feng shui, it is highly desirable that a site has such hills protecting the water from flowing away unchecked.

These mountains, when all present, collectively form a landscape that is circular in appearance, with the land site situated at the very center and protected from the wind in all directions by mountains. Naturally, Qi energy will accumulate and linger around the site. This has a lot to do with the circular form itself. Chinese fathers hold that the circle is the best and most lasting geometrical form, because it is the smoothest and most conservative form of all. The sun and moon are circular; they are powerful and everlasting celestial bodies. Even some flowers and plants have annular leaves made to receive sunlight and Qi energy in nature so as to bring about photosynthesis. The reason why flowers are created in a circular form is because this is the best shape to absorb and preserve Qi energy in nature.

The same is true of a circular or semicircular terrain, with mountains and hills standing like soldiers on duty. Such a terrain can effectively absorb, foster, and conserve lively Qi energy in nature. Hence a feng shui proverb says: "A site nestling among the hills and encircled by waters must contain a lot of Qi energy."

Thus, the whole environment surrounding an ideal land site suggests the image of a series of concentric circles. Such an image connotes a high degree of security and conservation of energy in traditional Chinese culture. Indeed, conservation is a motif in both Taoism and Confucianism. Even in the modern world, these connotations of a circle are not lost to us. We call a round moon a full (perfect) moon—the image of perfection, and make many kinds of energy-saving tools and machines in the form of a circle. These are exactly what geomancers are looking for in an auspicious site, i.e., the ability to conserve and preserve as much Qi energy as possible. Such a concentric circular landscape around a land site is just like a city surrounded by walls, or like a stamen or pistil surrounded by petals. Zhu Xi of the Song dynasty made the following comments on such a wonderful landscape: "Layers of mountains encircle and embrace a central site without deficiency, as if to constitute a universe in themselves."

An ideal model of a dragon lair in the mind of Chinese ancients is depicted in Figure 11-1, page 114. In the rear there are three layers of mountains; on both sides there are at least two layers of mountains; and in the front there are no less than two layers of mountains. There are also two courses of water coming to the site from behind, which join forces in the front before flowing away. Downstream there are two soaring mountains standing on the banks as if to stop the flow of water. Thus, the entire landscape surrounding the site looks like a castle.

The following criteria can aid us in pinpointing genuine dragon lairs:

- The ancestor mountains extend over hundreds of miles. In fact, the further away the ancestor mountain starts, the stronger will be the Qi energy it carries. Meanwhile, it should be undulating and continuous, full of ups and downs. Such a mountain vein is called a genuine dragon.

- The two mountains on both sides of a site (the green dragon and the white tiger) should be in such a shape that they seem to embrace the house but do not appear to be pressing. If this is the case, the house and its inhabitants are well protected against the evil winds, which will otherwise blow away the Qi energy.

- The major mountain in the rear of a house (the black tortoise) should be relatively closer to the base of the house and more importantly, should lead itself to the house in a slow, downward slope.

- There should be some waterbodies or waterways in the area, which flow in a slow and curved manner as if to embrace the site. Yang Yun-song tells us that mountains are in charge of population while waters are the controllers of wealth; that a location surrounded by mountains and embraced by waters must contain plenty of Qi energy. According to Yang, the best way for water to embrace an area is to have two separate watercourses running almost parallel from behind the area all the way to its sides, and then merge in the front before the water flows away in a gentle, slow manner.

- In the presence of waterways, there should also be hills downstream on the banks to check the flowing away of water. Since water symbolizes money, we do not want it to flow away freely and unchecked. In fact, the tighter these mountains lie at the water gate down the stream, the better for the financial welfare of the people living upstream. If the area is big, such as a city or a town, there must also be some mountains lying ahead between the area and the water, i.e., the water embraces the area from behind the mountains. In this regard, Zhen Wendi, another father of feng shui and advisor to an emperor of the Tang dynasty, said: "The most valuable are big rocks and mountains standing down the stream, the presence of which gives birth to heroes and millionaires."

- The environment should be pretty and "affectionate" towards the site. Affectionate means that a mountain is in a good shape, covered with trees and grasses, and slightly curved, as if to embrace the site but not seem oppressive. Such a mountain is deemed affectionate toward the site. By contrast, if mountains in the surroundings of a location are of irregular shapes, barren, dotted with strange rocks pointing toward the site, or turn away from the site as if to separate, these mountains are considered not affectionate toward the site; they are inauspicious.

As you can tell, finding a genuine dragon lair is a difficult task. Besides the scarcity of such lairs, our own lack of insight can also cause us to miss some of these rare sites. The following story illustrates how difficult it is to pinpoint a dragon lair.

It is said that grand master Lai Wenjun of the Song dynasty once pinpointed a burial site for Mr. Xu, a wealthy man in Jianxi province. It was a strange site located on a tall, precipitous cliff. Lai metaphorically called the site "a bat on the wall." Most geomancers would have been scared at the precipitous sight, partly because the cliff was largely bare in itself, an image suggesting the shortage of Qi energy. Only someone with Lai's caliber dared to pinpoint such a site, and the Xu family bought it. As a result, two ministers were born into Xu's family two generations later.

Asked by his students the rationale of his choice, Lai replied: "This is a special kind of auspicious site known as 'a bat clinging to the wall.' The cliff symbolizes the wall, and the site we have chosen is like a bat, which clings to the wall. The mountain right behind the site is, though largely bare of forestry, in the shape of a Chinese herbaceous peony, a branch of which intrudes right into the back of the rear mountain of the burial ground. And the burial site that I have pinpointed lies right at the ending point of this peony branch. The worshipping mountain of this site is tall and magnificent. When I stood in the middle of the ground, the worshipping mountain appeared biased. But as I moved to the right corner of the grounds, the same mountain looked upright. Thus, the same worshipping mountain is auspicious if the tomb site is chosen at the right corner of the grounds. But it becomes inauspicious if the tomb site is chosen in the middle of this piece of land, as most geomancers would like to do. Those who have their ancestors buried in the middle of the grounds are bound to go bankrupt shortly afterwards, because the worshipping mountain looks biased. Another reason I chose to set the site to the right corner of the grounds is because there is a small hill on the right side of the major mountain, which serves to protect the site and check the flow of water down the hill."

Of course, not many geomancers are as insightful as Lai. Many of them have failed in this critical step, even though they were situated in a good landscape. To be fair, this is not their fault. For quite a long time, the knack for pinpointing a dragon lair had been kept secret. It was not until the publication of *A Collection of Road-breaking Works* by Li Mozai that a lot of the secrets were revealed.

Dragon Lairs in Flat Lands

According to Li Mozai, the combination of yins and yangs is the key to pinpointing dragon lairs. Whenever a geomancer surveys a site and gets the general impression of the mobility in the landscape, he or she should look for flat areas as the auspicious sites. If there is flat ground in a predominantly "mobile" landscape, then he or she has found a dragon lair. In a "mobile" landscape, you carefully observe the delicate changes between yin and yang, for mountains and hills can be yin and yang, and land sites can be minor yin or minor yang.

According to Li, minor yang refers to slight protrusions (yang) on a vast flat plain, and minor yin means relatively flat, smooth ground (yin) amidst a largely undulating landscape. In terms of protrusions, they should only be three to five feet above the general level of the ground. These protrusions and flat areas are sometimes hard to discern with the naked eye. A lot depends on the insight and experience of the individual geomancer to detect minor yins and minor yangs.

The first clue to the locus of a dragon (i.e., the route a dragon travels) in a flat country is the protrusions in the landscape. This is why Chinese fathers say to look for protrusions in a flat country. A flat country is like a vast expanse of water, and the protrusions in it are like waves in an ocean. Under such circumstances, dragons move under the plain just like whales surging under the water; their movements generates waves. This is similar to dragons moving under the ground. Occasionally, they merge above the land in the form of protrusions. Protrusions in a flat land suggest strong, auspicious Qi energy beneath. They liken such protrusions to submerging dragons lifting their heads above the water so that people can see them. Wherever the land protrudes in a largely flat area, an auspicious site is formed.

Protrusions in the land represent concentrations or reserves of Qi energy, since earthly Qi is carried forward by dragons. (For this reason, looking for auspicious sites in feng shui is alternatively known as finding dragons.) The larger and higher the protrusion, the stronger the earthly Qi energy beneath it, and the bigger a role it can play in the construction project. As a matter of fact, most high lands in China's cities are occupied by those with political power or recent financial strength.

If there are no protrusions in a flat area, a geomancer should then look for water, because water is the dragon in a flat land. Water is sometimes called the "watery dragon." This analogy is very reasonable if you remember that water, like mountains, has the ability to protect the Qi energy of the land from the wind. This is exactly what Yang Yun-song says: "Don't bother about rises and falls when you come to a flat land. Simply look for the curves and encircle of waters, wherein lie genuine dragons." That is to say, a piece of land, no matter how flat and inflexible it is, must be valuable land if it is surrounded by water. Wherever dragons (mountains) stop in their journey, Qi energy gathers and accumulates, and genuine dragon lairs or auspicious land sites are created. Typically, when a big mountain range runs into a waterfront, it spreads itself out as a vast expanse of flat land. Thus, follow the waterways and you will be able to tell where dragons stop and where auspicious construction sites lie.

In terms of a watery dragon, the first thing to observe is the direction in which it flows. Look for conspicuous objects lying downstream. If water comes to a residence from the left side and flows to the right side, attention should be focused on the right side of the residence. In contrast, if water comes from the right side and flows toward the left, attention should shift to the left side of the site. If there are high mountains, huge stones, thick forests, tall buildings, or terraced fields lying to the right of the land, this must be an auspicious site wherein rests the genuine dragon, because the water flow is checked downstream by these natural or man-made objects. These mountains, forests, buildings, stones, and terraced fields are known as "progressive spirits" in Chinese geomancy, the presence of which together with one or more waterways ensures the existence of auspicious land sites. Especially encouraging are locations where water merges or turns around. The area beside merging or turning waters must be excellent sites for construction.

Mountains are static by nature, but their beauty lies in their motion. The word "motion" in feng shui has profound meaning, and the principle of motion is a universal one. A flat land with no motion symbolizes pure yang, which is not very productive. It is written in I-Ching: "Pure yang will not grow." On the other hand, when faced with the situation of a whole bunch of undulating mountains, this is a situation of pure yin, which is not good either. Under such circumstances, a geomancer should look for flatness, because flatness in these circumstances becomes the clue to finding dragon lairs. Thus, if one can find a piece of flat land amid undulating topography, this is certainly a good land site. Hence the importance of a yin-yang balance in the landscape, just like the balance of yin (female) and yang (male) is essential to the continuation of human species.

Another clue to a genuine dragon lair is the presence of an aureole looming and lingering around a site. Sometimes one can dimly see this aureole lingering around a site while standing at a point higher than and near to the site. Such an aureole can assume the form of a heart, a ribbon, an air bladder of fish, a willow leaf, or a wreath. If you see such an aureole, you can be certain that the small area around it must be a very auspicious site, since the aureole itself is a condensation of lively Qi energy in the nature.

While it is highly desirable to have layer after layer of progressive spirits—be it mountains, forests, stones, or terraced fields—lying downstream, these objects are not recommended to occur upstream. The same objects then become "retrogressive spirits," which are bad for feng shui.

What makes this world of difference is the distinction between heavenly doors and earthly doors. Discussed in chapter 7, a heavenly door refers to the direction from which water flows (upstream) while an earthly door refers to the direction toward which water flows away (downstream). Feng shui principle dictates that the heavenly door be left wide open whereas the earthly door be kept tightly closed.

To review, water stands for wealth in feng shui. We all want the source of wealth to be as widely open to us as possible, whereas the use of money should be kept under tight control. Thus, the ideal landscape for an auspicious site is one in which water flowing away from the site is effectively blocked somewhere downstream by "progressive spirits" and preferable forced to turn back for a while before resume its flow. Therefore, we want to see mountains, rocks, forests, terraced fields, or high buildings lying downstream from where we reside but not upstream.

Obviously, the presence of water is very important to a land site. This is even more so when the site is used for residential and commercial purposes. The reason water means more to residential and commercial feng shui than to burial feng shui is because a living man is much more in need of water than a dead man. So long as there is water in the surroundings of a site in a flat land, the site is good for residential construction. The larger an area is, the bigger the waterway is called for. This is not only out of the consideration for balance, but is also due to the fact that the larger a flat area, the more violent the blow of the winds. Therefore, greater watercourses are required to cope with the force of wind in the absence of surrounding mountains.

Dragon Lairs in Mountains

What are the keys to finding genuine dragon sites in the mountains? According to the author of *What Every Son Should Know About Geomancy*, auspicious residential sites in mountainous areas are found in relatively flat grounds, i.e., open, smooth, and spacious lands in the mountains. Ideally, there is water nearby, which is closely guarded by mountains. These grounds, though located in the mountains, give the impression of flat land. The larger the space, the better the site. If the flat area is too small, it is of little value. If you build houses on such small, flat lands, the Qi energy will be drained as a consequence. Worse still, when your children grow up, they are likely to divide the real estate among themselves. Thus, an originally small piece of land is further divided into smaller portions. You are then bound to run into disasters.

Besides being spacious, an auspicious residential site should also have plenty of sunlight. This means that it is located in a relatively high position in the mountains. Otherwise, malignant Qi will gather and concentrate there gradually. A place with no sunlight is called a "yin polar" in feng shui parlance, which is a hiding place for ghosts. A residential site should not be located on low, wet ground, nor should there be a watercourse that runs directly against it, or water nearby that makes a lot of noise. Water running directly against the back of a house will cause them to lose their wealth and ruin the relationships between the residents. Water that makes a lot of noise will invite disaster after disaster for the residents. Evil winds blowing at the site will also produce widows and beggars among the residents.

It is important to note that flat land sites in mountainous areas should come naturally. In other words, these sites are not man-made. A flat ground created artificially is not of the same quality as a natural piece of flat land. Liao Jinjing says: "If a site is originally narrow and you make it spacious, the earthly Qi in the ground may have been damaged. The worst thing to do is to dig into a mountain in a perpendicular way. In so doing, the residents there will come to total bankruptcy."

Besides the overall surroundings of a land site, the site itself determines to a large extent how auspicious it is. This is because different land sites contain different levels of earthly Qi energy. Roughly speaking, genuine dragon sites can be classified into two broad types: trunk sites and branch sites. Here, trunk and branch refer to a mountain range. A trunk site plays the central role in an area, and all other mountains in that area are, so to speak, subordinate and obedient to it, as if the very purpose of their existence is to protect and serve the trunk mountain and trunk site. As such, a trunk site is the best site in a certain area, simply because a trunk is more powerful than its branches. Such a site usually only exists in a long mountain range that has many branches and has traveled over at least a couple of hundred miles from its origin. As a general rule, the longer a mountain range has traveled, the more powerful the Qi storage of the land. According to Chinese fathers, there is no more than one trunk site within miles of a mountain range; others are branch sites at best.

It goes without saying that everybody would like to reside in a trunk site. To find such a site, survey a landscape from some high point in the area, and try to think of the mountains in that area in terms of a pair of scissors. If you can see a group of mountains form themselves into the image of a pair of scissors, the trunk site must be located between the two scissor legs near the vertex. If there is more than one pair of concentric scissors, so much the better. No matter how many pairs of concentric scissors there are, the trunk site is always situated in the innermost pair between the two legs. This key location suggests the image of a head of state surrounded by layers of ministers and bodyguards. This is what Yang Yun-song means: "A dragon is afraid of being lonely and a site is afraid of being isolated."

Since each major mountain range has a number of branch mountains, for every trunk site in an area of mountains, there are many branch sites in its surroundings. Though auspicious, branch sites contain less Qi energy and are therefore less powerful in bringing good luck to their residents than trunk sites. Another major difference between a trunk site and a branch site is this: a trunk site is less dependent on the surrounding mountains for protection than a branch site. A trunk mountain contains in itself strong Qi energy, which will be enough to offset the blow of the winds. Branch sites, on the other hand, are not so powerful in Qi energy, and therefore are more dependent on the protection of mountains. This is similar to human beings exposed to a flu virus;

stronger people are usually much less in need of medical help than weaker, unhealthier ones.

There is an interesting geomantic phenomenon concerning the relationship between a trunk site and its subordinating branch sites. Before a trunk site is used for construction, residents of branch sites can be very prosperous and successful. However, almost as soon as the trunk site is found and used for residential or commercial purposes, residents or businesses in the branch sites begin losing their prosperity. Why? The trunk site behaves like a center of gravity that attracts to itself the Qi energy in its surroundings. Since it is bigger and more powerful than the subordinating branch sites, it prevails in the competition for Qi. This may explain why occasionally businesses in an urban area have been doing well for years until some major building sets up in the area. From then on, they rapid lose their customers and even go bankrupt.

Chinese Art Concepts

In this regard of accurately pinpointing dragon lairs, a basic understanding of aesthetic concepts in the history of Chinese arts can carry you a long way. From such a viewpoint, auspicious land sites share the following topographic features:

Concept of Balance

To the Chinese artists, balance projects beauty. Just think of a good acrobatic performer. How well balanced is his or her body movement, and how beautiful it looks! In feng shui design, balance is mainly reflected in the presence of a line of symmetry. This refers to both the building itself and the topographic environments in which the building is situated. Chinese arts including architecture, project designs are encouraged to yield a clear sense of balance, be it a drawing, painting, a building, a garden, or a palace. If you compare the traditional Chinese building with that of the West, you will notice that one of the outstanding characteristics of the former lies in its symmetry with respect to some central line, thus yielding a clear sense of balance. The urban design of the capital city of Beijing offers a classical example so also does the architectural design of the Forbidden City in it.

This concept of balance has been applied to finding genuine dragon lairs in feng shui. Thus, an ideal land site should have an abscissa and an ordinate. The axis runs a line through the main mountain, the land site, the table hill, and the worshipping mountain. The abscise can be either the line connecting the azure dragon and the white tiger, or a horizontally running watercourse.

Concept of Circle

Chinese fathers hold that a circular form is a beautiful form. Such a geometric configuration gives people a sense of gentleness, coherence, conservation, harmony, and privacy. A land site located at the center of encircling waters or embracing mountains symbolizes a circle, and must therefore be a genuine dragon lair, containing a lot of qi energy and capable of conserving it against the attack of winds.

Concept of Multiple Layers

Traditional Chinese painting emphasizes the beauty of multiple layers. That is to say, a good drawing should be able to create a sense of depth through layers of scenes put together. For instance, a typical Chinese painting will depict a scene with mountains beyond mountains, or waters beyond waters, or buildings beyond buildings. Feng shui masters have drawn inspiration from this long artistic tradition. They want to seek an area surrounded by layers of mountains, one atop the other, from inner circle to outer circle. Such an area, according to them, must possess genuine dragon lairs, because it represents a center of gravity.

As said before, pinpointing dragon lairs is an essential and oftentimes very difficult and creative step in the process of feng shui design. It is a true art that challenges our understanding and imagination. Like any form of art, practice makes perfect. With years of serious practice under the guidance of genuine feng shui knowledge, one can hope to develop an artistic insight into topography and see where a dragon lair lies.

Chapter 12

Different Sites, Different Consequences

After the discussion about the quality of feng shui in the previous chapters, one will naturally be tempted to ask: Where should my family and I reside? Where should I bury my grandparents so that my family will be rich and noble, or more specifically, to have a great diplomat, a great educator, or even a president or first lady born into my family down the road? Ridiculous as these questions may sound, they are totally legitimate questions from the viewpoint of feng shui. Feng shui does have detailed answers for all these questions.

In real estate, the catch phrase is location, location, location. In feng shui, it is site, site, site. The first and foremost concern for a geomancer is to find an auspicious land site to build a house or tomb. It is primarily the location that determines the quality of feng shui for a residence or a grave, which in turn determines what kind of personality will be born into a family line.

Since good feng shui sites are far less in number than poor feng shui sites, the competition for them can be very brutal and political in China. Even in modern Hong Kong and Taiwan, disputes about feng shui are a big feature of politics at local levels. This happens whenever a tall building or a highway is to be built, a pond or lake is to be dug, or even when a large tree is to be cut down in a neighborhood. Such disputes can at times turn into nasty fights among interested parties who may have been close friends or coworkers. That is what gives feng shui a distinct political connotation.

A famous example in China's history is about the dispute between an emperor and his military advisor. The emperor was Zhu Yuanzhang, the founding father of the Ming dynasty, and the military advisor was Liu Ji (A.D. 1311–1375), a great statesman, military strategist, and feng shui master. After they had successfully established the Ming dynasty, Liu was suddenly put into jail by his boss because some of Liu's political enemies accused him of purchasing a piece of burial ground near his hometown for himself in preparation of his death. This burial ground, according to Liu's enemies, was capable of giving birth to an emperor

down Liu's family line. If this was true, it indicated that the Ming dynasty would be replaced by Liu's descendants. Knowing that Liu Ji was a master of feng shui, the extremely cruel and jealous emperor ordered the instant arrest of his mentor.

Feng shui—burial feng shui in particular—is an intangible art rarely supported by hard facts. In the absence of such evidence, the emperor had to release Liu several months later. Shortly afterward, Liu tendered his resignation and returned to his home province of Zhejiang, only to be poisoned to death by the emperor. Before his tragic death, Liu sold the burial ground he purchased earlier. He just dared not own it any more. Knowing that he was predestined to be poisoned to death by the emperor, and that his physical death would still not mean the end of the whole episode, he had secretly selected two burial grounds for himself, one false and the other real. His body was buried in secret on one stormy night.

At the time of Liu's death, Emperor Taizhu himself was very sick. He did not have the energy to further interfere in Liu's private affairs. He did, however, mention to his sons on his deathbed the potential threat posed to his regime by his teacher, who had contributed so much to the establishment of the Ming dynasty and most significantly, knew so much— way too much—about the secrets of the universe. As cruel and jealous as his father, Emperor Yongle of the Ming dynasty eventually sent a group of people to dig Liu's grave. They disappointedly discovered a piece of paper with Liu's handwritten words, which said something to the effect that he knew they were coming to dig his grave. The emperor's men were terrified at these words. They dared not proceed further, but hastily stopped their work and returned to Peking (the new capital of the Ming dynasty) to report to their boss. The emperor was so frightened at Liu's supernatural foresight that he had no choice but to end the whole sabotage scheme.

Listed below are the gems of feng shui knowledge passed down from Chinese fathers. They are result-oriented and distilled in centuries of experience and observation.

Sites of the Wealthy

These are sites that can ensure future wealth and financial success to the people living there or to the descendants of those buried there. To be rich is almost everybody's desire. In fact, money is no longer a dirty word as it used to be. The success of most companies as well as individuals is primarily measured by the amount of money they make.

- The site must be relatively large and slightly protruded like the back of a tortoise or an opened umbrella.

- The site must be protected on all sides by good mountains, ideally with more than one layer of mountains on each side, so that it can hide among these mountains and be free from the attack of ill winds, the same reason why a safe must be put in a safe and private place.

- There must be at least one warehouse mountain located in the rear of the site, i.e., round, large mountains that look like a warehouse.

- There must be two waterways coming toward the site from behind and merge in the front, staying in the bright hall before they resume their trip in a curved, slow manner. For fear that the water will run away too fast, there must be mountains on both sides of the water downstream; ideally there is a small hill or a huge rock standing in the midst of the water. There at least should be some mountains with the appearance of an ox facing the site.

When a site meets these requirements, it will bring great financial success or material wealth to the people residing there. Chinese are a very patient people.

They understand that it took millions of years for the universe to develop into its current state, and therefore are patient enough to wait for the coming of good luck after they have moved into an auspicious feng shui area. However, you can be sure that in no later than two generations, wealth will come to those who have lived in such a site, no matter what occupation they are in.

Sites of Dignitaries

In traditional China, as it still is in modern China, nobility often comes before wealth. If money can buy power in capitalist nations, power can earn money in China and other Asian countries.

Dignitaries here refer to people in general who hold great political or military power. Such people include heads of state, premiers, chancellors, generals, and so on. Therefore, this is a general description of the characteristics of sites which are conducive to people of social importance.

From the descriptions given by Chinese fathers, the following are essential features for such a site:

- A construction site should be situated at a relatively higher position than its neighboring land. This is suggestive of the higher social position one holds as compared with ordinary people.

- A land site must be situated on the forward-moving side of a dragon mountain. This refers to the side that slopes forward so that the rear of any construction project on the site is protected by the mountain, which stands above most buildings in the area.

- It is flanked by mountains that assume the appearance of banners, warehouses, drums, pens, tigers, lions, or oxen.

- It is the shape of the mountains in the rear and on the sides of a site that determines what kind of powerful figures will be created. Thus, if one of the flanking mountains look like a pen, high-ranking civil officials will be born there. However, if the mountains look like banners, drums, tigers, or lions, great soldiers will be created there.

- There must be a spacious and open area in the front of the site (bright hall).

- There should be a waterway running from behind the site and slowing down as it approaches the site. Preferably, this waterway will curve or stall in the front of the site, near or far, before it continues downstream. Since water symbolizes wealth and most dignitaries are rich, it is therefore important that water be in the area.

It must be pointed out that any land site, like a human being, always has a limited amount of Qi energy in reserve, no matter how auspicious it is. As humans, we need to rest and eat food to replenish our energy when we are running short of energy. It is the same with Qi energy. A generation of dignitaries in an area means a reduction of precious Qi energy of that area. Indeed, the greater a personality is created, the more Qi energy is lost. The more dignitaries that are created in an area at the same time, the more Qi energy is consumed. Qi energy of all kinds in the universe takes time to replenish. This then determines the number and level of dignitaries that can be born in the site.

The temporal length of the cycle in which a new generation of great personalities will be created in the same area depends mainly on three factors: the inherent Qi reserve in that area; the greatness of personality that has been born into it; and the number of dignitaries that have been born into the area. All three factors boil down to the issue of Qi energy, for it is the Qi that should be credited with the birth of dignitaries. It stands to reason that the more abundant the Qi reserve in an area, the greater and more dignitaries will be created in the area. The greater the personality, the more Qi reserve will be consumed, thus draining the Qi reserves of the locality and prolonging the process of creating another great personality.

In extreme cases, as in the birth of a founding emperor of a dynasty, the entire area may suffer from famine or flood due to the enormous drainage in the Qi energy. This is the price that residents pay for the honor of living in the same town as the emperor. Personally, I know a village in my hometown known as the "Village of Generals," thanks to the birth of more than a dozen generals in the People's Liberation Army. Ironically, the villagers remain poor to this day.

Sites of Heads of State

As has been mentioned before, one of the basic principles in feng shui is that of the trinity among heaven, man, and earth. Most people with some knowledge of feng shui know that the geomantic qualities and feng shui properties of a site correspond to the karma of specific people related to the site. Few, however, are aware that such qualities and properties also reflect themselves in the astronomy of the skies. This is especially conspicuous in the cases of great leaders, simply because they carry more importance than ordinary citizens. They are traditionally referred to as "Sons of the Heaven" in China. Yuan Tiangan of the Sui dynasty and Liu Ji of the Ming dynasty were two such people who were able to directly relate astrology to geomancy.

Chinese fathers of feng shui tell us that there are three possible configurations of stars corresponding to sites for a head of state. They are Ziwei layout, Taiwei layout, and Tianshi layout. Ziwei, Taiwei, and Tianshi are lucky stars in Chinese astrology. If any of the three layouts shows up in the sky at night, there must be a site beneath it that will create a head of state.

This is exactly how Yuan Tiangan found Li Shimin, the founding emperor of the Tang dynasty. At the time, Yuan was a high-ranking official in the Sui dynasty, which was eventually overthrown by Li Shimin. Knowing that some new emperor was to show up in the political landscape of China based on his astrological knowledge, Yuan quit his job in the Sui dynasty and went to serve the future emperor. You may blame Yuan for his treason, but the Chinese believe that whoever understands and follows the situation is a hero.

Similarly, Liu Ji (1311–1375) successfully discovered Zhu Yuanzhang, the founder of the Ming dynasty, based on astrology. Liu devoted his rare talents to Zhu and helped him establish a new empire. Although Liu later died a tragic death at the hand of Zhu, he had no regrets and Liu saw his mission completed—to help Zhu establish the Mandate of Heaven and drive out the Mongolians from China.

Apart from the astrological signs (signs of the zodiac) for a head of state, there are some more tangible geographic features that can help us recognize land sites with such a promise.

- On both sides of the site, there should be high mountains resembling a banner, drum, pen, tortoise, or a horse. This is because a head of state must be aided and protected by officials and generals in his administration. Since banners and drums were the commanding tools in the hands of generals in ancient times, these images stand for great soldiers. In ancient China, the banner of an army always bore the name of its commanding officer. In similar token, pens and pencils stand for an outstanding civil career in Chinese tradition, and therefore they have come to symbolize premiers and ministers.

- There must be a high, magnificent mountain behind the site to offer a strong back for the ground and the building. This mountain provides strong protection.

- There must be at least two waterways running by, joining forces in the front of the site and encircling it. These waterways also must have made at least 100 turns before they reach the site. Since water stands for wealth, and a head of state tends to be rich, it is little wonder that such a site must be encircled by water.

- In the front of the site, especially downstream, there must be layers of mountains, preferably with one of them standing right in the middle of the stream (seal hill). This ensures the preservation of wealth.

- Somewhere high in the major mountain range along which the specific site is located, there is a pond or lake. Such a pond is known as a heavenly pond. The water springs out of the ground and flows forever. It is said that the Tian Mountains in northern China boasts of such ponds, and ancestors of Chin emperors were buried close to some of the heavenly ponds in the Tians. That is the geomantic reason for their mandate to rule China for 200 years.

- There must be at least 100 peaks in the major dragon within 100 miles behind the site. In other words, the major mountain vein must be full of significant rises and falls, creating plenty of magnificent peaks before it reaches the site.

When a site meets all six geomantic conditions, the chances are great that some heads of state will be born in the area, no matter what title he or she may assume—an emperor or empress, a king or queen, a chairman or a president.

Sites of Queens and First Ladies

A queen or a first lady occupies a unique position in a country. Due to her special relationship with the head of state, she can exert significant influence on national policies that affect the welfare of the people. If she is wise and kind, people can benefit a lot from her or her influence over her husband. Even in traditional China where women were strongly discouraged from entering politics, empresses often exerted strong influence over the administration, largely because the emperors liked to listen to "words from the pillow side." It is said that Emperor Zhu Yuanzhang would have killed many more of his own loyal people if not for the objection made by his kind wife.

Virtuous or not, queens and first ladies are the most respected women in a country. The sheer scarcity of such dignitaries at any time in any nation suggests that there must be a strong influence from feng shui on their birthplace or an ancestor's burial ground.

The characteristic features for a land site to "produce" female dignitaries include:

- A mountain in the shape of a dressing table somewhere in the near distance of the site along the major mountain range at which the site is located.

- A mountain resembling delicate eyebrows located in the front of a site.

- Some water lingering in the front of the site or flowing slowly by in a curving manner.

Fathers of feng shui say that the combination of such mountains and water can ensure the birth of a female dignitary.

Sites of Premiers, Chancellors, or Secretaries of State

A premier, chancellor, or secretary of state is one of the most powerful officials directly responsible to the head of state. As a high-ranking official, a premier, chancellor, or secretary of state must possess both wealth and nobility. The authority and responsibility of such a personality cross the border between military and civil affairs of the country. Therefore, such a person should be well versed in both "polite letters and martial arts," so to speak. But ability alone is far from enough to ensure the acquisition of this much vied-for position. Feng shui also plays a large role in the making of a premier.

According to feng shui fathers, the following five geographic features must be present in a site in order for it to create a premier:

- High mountains in the shape of banners, drums, or pens. The banner and drum symbolize military talents and authority, while a pen stands for talents and authority in civil administration.

- A curving, gently moving waterway encircling the site and running away from it in the front.

- The existence of magnificent mountains at the earthly door or water gate downstream, or the presence of a small, beautiful hill or rock in the midst of the stream in the front of the site.

- The major dragon, or the mountain range in which the burial ground or the house is located, must be magnificent and full of ups and downs, forming a lot of peaks in its journey.

- The space in the front of the site (bright hall) should be spacious and bright, indicating good prospects and a bright future.

Sites of Senators and Members of Congress

Senators and congressional members are the legislators of a nation. Disregarding whether a nation is democratic or not, similar positions exist in almost all nations around the world, although the titles may vary. They are highly respected representatives of a nation. As legislators, they are responsible for drafting, revising, and reviewing the laws of the country, approving administrative programs including key personnel appointments and the annual budget. In addition, they are given the authority to declare war in time of emergency. Thus, their ability and personality exert a significant impact on all aspects of a nation's life and future. For this reason, it is essential that senators and members of congress are people of superb ability and upright personality. They should be well versed in the subjects of politics, history, and current events of their own country as well as that of the world.

From the geomantic theories have been passed down, residential and burial sites must satisfy the following two geomantic requirements:

- There must be mountains with the shape of a seal in the vicinity of the site, preferably in the middle of a watercourse in the front of the site.

A seal stands for power and authority in ancient China, so therefore senators and congressional members have power and authority.

- There must be at least one mountain facing the site in the front that assumes the appearance of a pen. As explained before, such a mountain symbolizes a successful civil career and a high-ranking official, which a senator or a congressman is. It signifies an upright personality.

Sites of Secretaries of Education and Great Educators

Although of a lower caliber and power than heads of state, secretaries of education and other top education officials exert significant influence over national education policies, which are widely regarded as part of the foundation of a nation.

The idea that education constitutes the foundation of a nation is not hard to understand. What deserves the greatest credit for the economic and commercial success and overall greatness of a nation is not the natural resources but the people, especially their intelligence and skills that make the difference. In the final analysis, it is the minds, not the mines, that mainly account for a nation's prosperity and development. Education is the food for great minds. A good educational system creates a pool of talent, which in turn creates cutting-edge technology and competitive industry. There is a popular saying in China: "It takes ten years to raise a tree, but it takes 100 years to raise a talent." A nation short of talent must be in a weak economic and strategic position.

If education is important to a country, so must also be the position of the minister of education. It is his or her responsibility to draft a comprehensive, strategic plan for the nation's educational system, including the securing of sufficient funds; efficient and wise allocation of these funds such as the training of qualified teachers, and the acquisition of the best teachers, teaching facilities, and materials; the design of optimal teaching methods and materials for the country in light of its national objectives and the trends in the world.

Expectedly, so vital a dignitary to a nation should have some special geomantic causes for his or her birth. From the teachings of feng shui fathers, the following two geographic features for residential and burial sites can lead to the creation of education ministers and great educators:

- It is stated in feng shui classics that "A seal floating in the water bodes well for great literary talents." Here, the "seal" refers to the hill or huge rock that stands in the middle of a water body, assuming the appearance of a seal. The seal is the symbol of power and authority in China. A minister of education must be a literary person with power and authority.

- There must be quite a few mountains on both sides of the site for protection. Among these mountains, there should be one peak in the shape of a pen standing out against the others, just like a long pen standing out from a pen container. Again, the pen is symbolic of successful literary and civil careers, so it makes sense that such a geomantic feature is conducive to the creation of great educators and educational officials.

Sites of Secretaries of Defense

The duties and abilities of a secretary of defense are intimately tied to the security of a nation. A competent defense minister will see to it that adequate funding is secured for the acquisition of military equipment, and for the training and hiring of talented and qualified military personnel; that capable people are assigned to important positions and given the command of a troop; that soldiers are well trained and prepared for any emergency; that the command, control, and communication system is well maintained and updated; and that the entire military machine of the country is kept at a high level of readiness for action. Obviously, it takes extraordinary talent and a superb energy level to satisfactorily carry out these duties. A defense minister must also possess a remarkable level of courage, both morally and physically.

The following geographic features are required:

- There must be magnificent hills and mountains in the shape of banners or drums positioned on the sides or front of the site. This is because banners and drums are necessary command and communication tools used by generals in ancient China. Thus, mountains with these images symbolize the power and authority of great generals.

- There must be some curving waterways passing by the site and encircling it. Such waterways represent the walls and moats that protected a city in ancient times. Since it is the duty of a general to protect a city, the presence of such water, together with the appearance of banner and drum mountains, symbolizes the creation of defense ministers.

Sites of Secretaries of Transportation

The importance of the infrastructure in the modern world speaks for the significance of the position of ministers of transportation. Rather, it should be understood from a long-range, strategic standpoint. In fact, the selection of ministers of communications has always been a serious issue for countries, an issue that is often finally determined by the leader of the country.

In 1975, when the name of Wan Li (meaning literally "ten thousand miles" in Chinese) was presented to Mao Tse-tung among others competing for the position of Minister of Railways, Mao was very pleased with the name. "Ten thousand miles of railway run unimpeded," exclaimed Mao. "What an excellent name!" Wan was thus offered the position, and he did as excellent a job as his name suggests. From then on, his political career took a giant leap forward, until he eventually occupied the seat of China's Speaker of the House before his retirement in 1996.

The residential or burial site should possess the following features:

- The site must be located on the back of a progressive dragon or a living dragon. A progressive dragon is a mountain range that is moving toward the front of a site. It extends into a multiple of branches and smaller hills, all spreading themselves out like a communication system. The forward-moving image symbolizes a smooth, unimpeded transportation system as well as the future of those holding the position of ministers of transportation.

- A living dragon refers to a group of undulating mountains full of peaks and valleys. Such a mountain vein signifies strong Qi energy and the ability of the transportation system to surmount geographic obstacles.

Sites of Diplomats

Diplomats such as foreign ministers and ambassadors are high-ranking officials. They are some of the most visible dignitaries in the international arena with the exception of premiers and heads of states because they make frequent trips abroad in representation of their own countries. In fact, many of them continuously visit foreign lands in the interests of their own government.

It is easily understood that foreign ministers and ambassadors tend to be attractive people if only because they represent their country around the world. The first three foreign ministers of People's Republic of China—Chou Enlai, Chen Yi, and Qiao Guanhua—were widely considered handsome men at home and abroad.

Since not many people can qualify for these positions, there must be some geomantic causes for the making of great diplomats. According to feng shui principles, we can imagine that land sites that lead to the generation of great diplomats share the following characteristics:

- The site must be located on a progressive dragon—on a side of a mountain range that moves forward. Progression is typical of the career of a foreign minister or an ambassador. He or she needs to progress not only at home, but also abroad.

- There must be high hills or mountains in the shape of horses located either on the same progressive dragon or in front of a site. In China, a horse is symbolic of travel and diplomats often had to travel on horseback from country to country.

- There should be a small hill standing above the horse mountain, completing an image of someone riding on a horse. This is a sure sign of a great diplomatic career, most likely the one belonging to a foreign minister.

Sites of Finance and Economic Officials

High-ranking finance or economic officials are in charge of a nation's fiscal and economic policies and affairs. At a time when money speaks louder than ever and the state of the economy dominates national policy, the position of a finance or economic official carries great importance, authority, and respect. Much of a nation's development and success in today's world economy depends on the ability and integrity of its finance and economic officials.

A capable person holding this position will see to it that more revenues are generated than expenditures; that financial resources are adequately allocated; and that there are feasible strategic and tactical blueprints for the nation's economic and fiscal issues. Without a doubt, the satisfactory fulfillment of these responsibilities requires both profound academic knowledge and superb administrative skills. This can be a hard combination to find in an individual.

With a population pool as large as China's, its senior leader Deng Xiaoping lamented that few people inside the Communist Party, which boasts more than sixty million members, have a deep understanding of economics, and that Zhu Rongji was one of those very few members. Simply because Zhu is superbly versed in economic and financial affairs of the nation, he had been put in charge of the entire government as China's premier.

Obviously, special geomantic properties in residential and burial sites are required to give birth to such talents. After a careful look at the topographic situation surrounding Zhu's old residence and that of a Ming Tomb (Zhu is said to be the descendent of Zhu Yuanzhang, founder of the Ming dynasty), the following are believed to be the two essential geographic features conducive to the birth of great ministers of finance or economics:

- There must be mountains that look like warehouses along the major dragon. A warehouse symbolizes money and wealth.

- There must be curving watercourses flowing by the site and merging in the front of the site. Water signifies wealth, and curving and lingering water indicate the accumulation of wealth, personally or nationally.

Sites of Chief Justices, Supreme Court Justices, and Attorneys General

People who hold these positions are some of the most authoritative interpreters of a nation's laws and regulations. As such, they must be highly versed in many fields of knowledge, including law, history, and politics. They are expected to not only apply the existing laws, but also draft new laws in accordance with a nation's changing social and political climate.

In a democratic country ruled by law, it is easy to understand why these dignitaries are held in high esteem and accorded lofty honors. Actually, quite a few American presidents have had a background in law. No wonder a lot of brilliant young people flock to the field of law in hope of extraordinary political and financial rewards.

The following are the most important geomantic features of such a residential or burial site:

- A site must first be a noble one (see "Sites of Dignitaries"), because these positions are noble occupations and are treated as such by society.

- A site must occupy a relatively conspicuous position in the area, signifying that a chief justice or similar personality stands out above the others in terms of authority.

- The mountains facing the site in the front must be straight and well balanced, symbolizing the moral and ethical behavior of a person.

- There must be a curving, slow-flowing, waterway passing by the site. The water must be clear, which signifies integrity and clarity of mind.

Sites of Geniuses and Prodigies

The Chinese are very education-oriented people. For them, an intelligent and successful child is worth more than a chest full of gold. Such a child is a fountain of comfort, happiness, and pride for the entire family, hence the popular saying: "I don't want to be wealthy; I just want every one of my children to be clever and able."

While most skills can be learned through conscious effort, to be outstanding in any profession seems to require something more than mere diligence. That something is intelligence, which comes with birth to a large extent. While most people would want his or her child to be a genius or a prodigy, few actually are. For one thing, not all land sites for a residence or tomb possess the kind of feng shui capable of creating such a personality.

Generally speaking, a land site that is conducive to the creation of a genius has the following features:

- There must be some mountains or hills looking like pens or pencils in the surroundings.

- There must be some water curving in the front of the site.

- There must be some hills standing on both sides of the water downstream, or some huge hills or rocks sitting in the middle of the stream to slow its flow.

Sites of Nobel Prize Winners

Nobel Prizes are annual awards given to individuals or institutions that have conferred some of the greatest benefits on humankind in any one of six fields: chemistry, medicine, literature, physics, diplomacy (peace), and economics. They are the highest international honors in academic fields.

The equivalent of a Nobel Prize winner in traditional China is the so-called Number One Scholar, a title conferred directly by the emperor on those who placed first in the highest imperial examinations held every three years. The person who won such an honor often ended up becoming the son-in-law of the emperor, and invariably became a high-ranking official in the nation.

Many people have spent most of their lives in laboratories and libraries trying to earn a Nobel Prize, but to no avail. The rarity of such honors suggests that fate has a big role to play in it. It is told that Yang Zhennin and Li Zhendao, two Chinese physicists and Nobel Prize winners, went to "throw I-Ching" to seek an answer as to whether they would win this high academic honor. The answer they received was very positive, and they eventually won. This story clearly shows that diligence and intelligence combined are not enough to claim such supreme honors. Feng shui should be given due credit.

Residential and burial sites conducive to the generation of Nobel Prize laureates or Number One Scholars share the following geomantic features:

- There are soaring, magnificent mountains on both sides of the site, protecting the Qi energy of the site and ensuring high social positions for the inhabitants.

- There must be a curving waterway flowing from behind the site. The more curves it has, the more auspicious the site is (i. e., the more curves, the slower it flows). Such a watercourse can bring a lot of Qi to the site yet carry little Qi away. If nine curves are visible from the site, the honor of a Nobel Prize is guaranteed. A lake in front of the site enhances the financial prospects of the inhabitants. Since Nobel Prize winners and academicians are all rewarded in monetary terms, it makes sense to have water present at a site, especially in the front, for water stands for wealth.

- If the waterway is a river, there must be at least one hill located downstream. This hill must assume the shape of a bird or a pen, for these images are associated with literary talent and excellence. If such a hill stands in the midst of the water flow, so much the better.

Sites for Longevity

Most people would like to live a long and healthy life. However, health and longevity are two separate issues. In fact, being healthy cannot guarantee a long life. There are just too many ways in which one's life can be cut short: car accident, plane crash, fire, or flood. Obviously, the issue of longevity goes far beyond the control of medical science and health care. The traditional Chinese belief is that it is primarily a matter of fate, which in turn is a function of feng shui.

Some land sites can ensure longevity for those living on it. Such land sites most likely possess the following geomantic feature:

- There should be some high, if not soaring, mountains behind the site.

As you can tell, the requirement for a longevity site is much less demanding than those for noble and wealthy sites. This seems to indicate that longevity is much more accessible than wealth. In fact, there are more people who are able to live a long life than the number who are wealthy and noble combined.

What, then, are the geographic features of a bad land site? What will entail from such a site? These are questions that will be answered next.

Sites to Avoid

Sites of the Poor

Houses or graves built on such sites will bring about poverty and disgrace not only to the current generation, but to the descendants as well.

- Isolation of the land site.

- Lack of mountain protection in all directions.

- Mountains in the vicinity are slim, ugly, rocky, and bare of forestry.

- Lack of water in the surroundings.

- The presence of dirty water or straight-flowing water against or away from a site.

- A narrow, small bright hall.

More specifically, if a mountain by the site assumes the appearance of someone carrying a basket, the site will give birth to a number of beggars. This is because in China, beggars always carried a basket wherever they went to keep the food they have received. Thus, baskets became a symbol of beggars. Here, one should be careful not to confuse "mountains of baskets" with other similar shapes. They may look the same, but they carry widely different geomantic significance. Therefore, a keen eye sharpened by geomantic practice is needed to correctly identify various mountain shapes.

Sites of Prostitutes

It is said that prostitution is one of the oldest professions in human society, and there are various reasons why some people are caught up in the profession. Whatever the reason, there are some geomantic causes behind it. Fathers of feng shui tell us that the presence of any of the following properties in the vicinity of a residential site or a burial ground will lead to prostitution:

- There are mountains in the front of a site resembling a woman pulling up her skirt.

- Flanking the site, there are pointed hills that turn outward, away from the site. As mentioned above, the mountains on both sides of a site must turn in toward each other as if embracing and protecting the site. If they turn outward, away from the site, the ground is left vulnerable to the attack of ill winds—a very inauspicious feature.

- There are two hills leaning against each other, as if a couple were embracing each other.

Sites of the Short-lived

While most of us want to live a long, healthy life, there are quite a few among us not born with this fate. The feng shui of their birthplace, or that of the burial ground of their ancestors, determines whether they will live a long or a short life. The presence of any two of the following features at a land site can lead to the birth of people destined to live a short life:

- The site is low and isolated in that it is depressed in topography (such as a valley), and open to wind from all sides.

- The black tortoise, i.e., the protective mountain in the rear, is short, bare, and narrow.

- The site is located on a retreating dragon or a weak dragon. A retreating dragon is a mountain that slopes toward the back of a house or a grave built on it. A weak dragon is a group of small, low, lean, and bare mountains that scatter around like individual rocks with no relation to each other whatsoever.

- There is a waterway that runs straight toward the site in the front.

- There is a waterfall in the neighborhood that is noisy and loud.

Chapter 13

Residential Feng Shui

Residential feng shui has become a popular topic in America. Most people want to own a house, and want the residence to contribute to their health, wealth, relationships, and overall happiness. Most Americans believe residential feng shui is the entire subject of feng shui, but that is not so. Traditionally, residential feng shui is only one branch in the ancient tree of Chinese feng shui. It belongs to the so-called "yang-house feng shui" category while the "yin-house feng shui" is another name for burial feng shui. They are so named because Chinese fathers regard the living as yang creatures and the deceased as yin creatures. As such, all kinds of facilities designed to be used by the living—be it residential, commercial, or public—are considered yang houses, whereas tombs and cemeteries are considered yin houses.

It must be pointed out that residential feng shui in the classical Chinese sense has a wider scope than what is currently practiced in the West.

The practice of residential feng shui preceded that of burial feng shui. One of the reasons for this is because it is much easier for the living to experience and feel the feng shui effects. It is common knowledge that the environment has a lot to do with our health, and therefore our happiness and success. Thus, a clean, quiet living environment is conducive to better rest and health, whereas a noisy, dirty living environment can cause various mental and physical ailments such as insomnia and hypertension. This common sense approach has been successfully incorporated into the art of feng shui. Of course, feng shui does not stop there. It goes much deeper into metaphysical factors such as the location, structure, color, direction, and even the birthdays of those who live there. These factors have made feng shui a very complicated subject, of which most people are not aware of or trained in.

Another reason why residential feng shui was developed prior to burial feng shui is that we all care, by nature, more about our own living places than those of our deceased ancestors. After all, residential feng shui is much more easily verified than burial feng shui, which studies how the location and position of an ancestor's grave can impact a descendant for generations to come. For this reason, burial feng shui must base itself on a set of abstract theories or imagination on the part of geomancers. That is why the practice of burial feng shui came at a much later time than that of residential feng shui. Together, they form the complete body of feng shui as it stands today.

Yin house or yang house, the basic principles of feng shui remain the same. In residential feng shui, as in burial feng shui, the first and most vital task is to make sure that the land site possesses auspicious feng shui. This is to make sure that our residence is located in a Qi-strong land, as Qi energy, both earthly and heavenly, is largely beyond our limited power to add or subtract. Unless there is enough lively Qi energy in and around the construction site in the first place, no amount of internal design or color choice can go very far. Location is the foundation; house layout is the structure. A house with good structure but poor foundation will not last long, nor will a fancy residence built on inauspicious land bring good luck to its residents.

Thus, the first and single most essential step in feng shui design is to survey the land in order to find an auspicious site. In this regard, there are a lot of similarities as well as some differences between burial feng shui and residential feng shui. Again, as it is with burial feng shui, the practice of residential feng shui should start with the essential steps of finding genuine dragons and pinpointing dragon lairs or auspicious land sites. Yao Ting-Luan says in his *An Epitome of Residential Feng Shui*:

> *Residential buildings should start with the selection of construction sites. Ideally, these sites should have water in the front and hills at the back. Hills in the rear should be links in some mountain veins that have traveled a long distance before reaching these sites, and the water should curve around the sites. Besides, the space in the front of a residential building should be open and wide. There should also be hills down the stream of water so that the water flowing away from the site can be checked.*

This is exactly the case with burial feng shui. What we should know is that different landscapes have different geomantic requirements and emphasis. In mountain areas, for instance, the pinpointing of dragon lairs should stress the shapes, vegetation, and distance of mountains in the surroundings. In urban areas, especially in a flat country, however, emphasis should be shifted to the presence of waterways as well as the frontal exposure of a house. Also, there are usually few mountains to speak of, but the concepts of the "four animals" remain intact, albeit assuming different forms in different topographic situations. Thus, the streets on the side of a residential building are likened to waterways, while houses or buildings in the neighborhood play the roles of the black tortoise, green dragon, white tiger, and red phoenix.

Since we have talked a lot about land surveillance and the way to pinpoint dragon lairs or auspicious land sites, we will just focus on differences rather than similarities in our current discussion.

Residential grounds should be relatively large, spacious, and open. People need space to move around and develop. The larger the space, the stronger the Qi reserves underground, and the greater a role the ground can play for residential and political purposes. Thus, a land with the size of about 1,000 square miles can be the site of a national capital. Those with a size between 500 and 1,000 square miles are good candidates for big cities. Those with an area of 300 to 500 square miles are good for medium-sized cities. A normal house will also need an area of no less than 1,000 square feet. Moreover, for a land site that serves as political or commercial center, the major dragon should preferably be long and large, with huge watercourses flowing by in the surroundings, with facing mountains far away from its center.

While Qi is the central concern for both residential and burial feng shui, it becomes more complicated when it comes to residential feng shui. This is because it has to consider not only earthly Qi that is embodied in the location of a house, but also the heavenly Qi that flows in the air. As mentioned before, earthly Qi travels underground and is carried forward by mountains, which Chinese fathers called dragons. Heavenly Qi flows in the air and is affected by traffic, water, and buildings in the environment. Earthly Qi effects come from underground, and therefore its influence is slow, profound, and permanent. Heavenly Qi moves more freely and exists in the air, and therefore its influence is faster and more changeable. Both kinds of Qi are needed to nourish a residential building. In fact, the more of both, the better it will be for the house and its residents.

The selection of auspicious land sites is regarded as "taking advantage of the earthly Qi," whereas the process of introducing heavenly Qi into a house is known as "absorbing the heavenly Qi." With the finding of an auspicious location for a house, the task of taking advantage of earthly Qi is completed, and actually more than half of the job is done. If the house happens to be situated close to some good waterways, all the better. If not, do not worry. Major urban areas tend to be resting places of long, huge dragons and therefore contain powerful earthly Qi. In fact, the larger the urban area, the more powerful the earthly Qi energy. Therefore, every house in it will have its share of that strong Qi energy.

What remains to be done is to absorb the heavenly Qi into the house. In a sense, every house can absorb heavenly Qi because Qi flows in the air. However, there can be huge differences in the quantity and quality being absorbed by individual houses. This is partly what makes one residence differ from the other. To absorb heavenly Qi into a house, there are a number of factors to consider. These factors range from streets in the neighborhood, other buildings in the vicinity, the internal layout of the house, the location of doors and stairs, and the frontal exposure of the house.

According to Wei Qingjiang, the author of *Essential Guides to Residential Feng Shui*, the key to absorbing heavenly Qi is to build a residence in the right location surrounded by a good landscape. This includes aligning the residence with water (if there is some present), and placing the front door in the right direction in accordance with the yin-yang principle. The front door is essential because heavenly Qi enters a residence through the main front entrance. Alignment and direction of the front door are important because heavenly Qi interacts with the eight trigrams, or eight karma's, and the five basic elements (water, fire, wood, metal, and earth). You want to make sure that heavenly Qi enters your residence through the right direction (karma), defined by your birthday, as well as the productive direction in terms of the five elements. Thus, if a woman was born in 1977, the front door of her residence should be located on the north side, the south side, the east side, or the southeast side. North corresponds to the element of water, so the direction of north (water) and east (wood that is produced by water) are her best bets for locating the front door.

Another major contribution made by Wei Qingjiang to residential feng shui lies in his creative interpretation of the Four Animals in an urban environment. According to him, buildings in the surroundings of a residence represent the green dragon, white tiger, red phoenix, and black tortoise. Thus, a tall building to the right of your residence is a green dragon, which helps prevent the dissipa-

tion of heavenly Qi in the environment and causes it to return to your residence. This is an auspicious sign and therefore desirable for the residence. Thus, even in urban areas without mountains, there still are green dragons, white tigers, red phoenixes, and black tortoises. They are just made of different materials.

This creative application of a feng shui principle by Wei is a significant development in the theory of feng shui. Once more it demonstrates that feng shui is not a set of fixed rules. Instead, it is a body of principles, which willingly lend itself to creative interpretation and application by its students.

As Wei wrote, heavenly Qi enters a residence through the front door. In other words, heavenly Qi enters the house the same way humans do. That is exactly why Wei Qingjiang called heavenly Qi as "door Qi." Many things determine the quantity and quality of heavenly Qi that enters a specific house. First of all, it depends on the quality of the main entrance to the residence. The quality of a door is a function of its relative location to other parts or rooms of the house. Different houses may require different frontal exposures in accordance with the specific birthday of the homeowner.

Chinese fathers alternatively call residential feng shui "residential appearance." As the term implies, the analogy is between a human face and the appearance of a residence. This analogy is also helpful to the understanding of some of the general rules governing the design and examination of a residential building. Chinese fathers regard the analysis of houses as something similar to the analysis of human faces.

Thus, if protruding eyes, broken-up eyebrows, a crooked nose, and dim complexion signify an unlucky person, how can a residence be auspicious if it is slanted and irregular in structure? A residence should have good light and be clean, spacious, and well ventilated. An auspicious house, from whatever viewpoint, simply cannot be dark, dirty, irregular, disorderly, and smelly.

The investment of time and money in the maintenance of our residence is one of the best investments we can ever make. Our health, our sleep, the efficiency of our work, and the happiness of our family all depend to a large extent on the quality of the houses in which we live. It takes little imagination to tell that a dark house with a smoky kitchen, messy bathrooms, leaking water pipes, broken lamps, dirty walls, and laundry scattered around like garbage contributes nothing to the good luck of the family. If people do not want to enter such a house, will the god of fortune be willing to enter it?

On the other hand, a clean, orderly, well laid out, well-lit, and well-ventilated house with flowers strategically planted can enhance the spirit and efficiency of work for the residents, promote unity and happiness in the family, and bring good luck and success to family members.

Let us take a closer look at the two major considerations of residential feng shui: how to find a good site so that we can get the highest amount of earthly Qi possible, and how to design the house to absorb the maximum amount of heavenly Qi.

Selecting an Auspicious Site

To determine if a location is a genuine reservoir of earthly Qi energy or a genuine dragon lair, look at the major mountain veins in the area. The mountain vein or dragon should have traveled a long distance from its origin, at least hundreds of miles, before it comes to stop at a location that is relatively flat and spacious. Indeed, the longer the mountain vein has traveled before it comes to a stop, the more powerful the Qi energy is at the stopping site. Traveling means the continuous extension of the mountain vein.

For major residential sites, the surrounding mountains and hills are generally located far away in the suburbs. Even so, buildings in urban areas are not without protection. For one thing, Qi reserves of major residential sites are powerful enough to offset the negative impact of evil winds blowing against these sites.

Major residential sites generally have large waterways in the area that also help to protect the local Qi from being lost to the wind. Most metropolitan areas usually have more than one water body in the surroundings, such as oceans, rivers, or large lakes.

In terms of Qi energy, many geomancers are of the opinion that the most essential feature of a residential site is the presence of water. They hold that the more water there is in the area, the more auspicious will be the land site. In fact, some authoritative geomancers even go so far as to suggest that only in the presence of water can good residential sites exist.

Xu Shanji and his brother, for instance, are of this opinion. They said in *What Every Son Should Know About Geomancy*:

Almost all major cities are embraced by big waterways or water bodies. Even small cities are often built on the bank of major rivers, providing the convenience of transportation. Thus, we can see that great residential sites are found where waters merge and curve. Sometimes, such sites are found in the middle of two large waterways. Sometimes, they are located down the stream of two waterways that have joined forces. Sometimes, one side of the land site borders on a big river or ocean while the other side witnesses the merge of smaller waterways. Sometimes it is completely encircled by waters. Sometimes, it is semi-encircled by some big water. Waters come by different ways, and they assume various shapes, but they must be present. This is one of the major differences between burial sites and residential sites.

Another strong advocator for the emphasis of water in residential feng shui is Wei Qingjiang, who says the following in his *Essential Guide to Residential Feng Shui*:

The largest residential sites are metropolises where waters curve, merge or overlap with the mountains. These residential sites are densely populated, culturally sophisticated, and have a long history of prosperity. They are brilliant models of residential feng shui, providing us with situational examples for understanding the art of residential feng shui. In order to understand metropolitan situations, one has to feel the pulses of the landscape. Zhu Tse once said: There will be some watercourses lying between two mountain veins, and there are bound to be mountains between two watercourses. Waters flow on the sides, while mountains run in the middle. Waters surrounding a city often flow on its sides and sometimes reverse their courses. Big waters can be located in the far distance of the metropolis, but you know in your heart that they are there even if you cannot see them. If you are ignorant of the existence of big waters, you may not be clear about the meanings of small waters, which may be in the city.

From what has been said by Chinese fathers, we can sum up the desirable qualities for an auspicious residential site in these four important factors:

- A site should be wide and spacious with an auspicious bright hall.

- The house should occupy one-half to two-thirds of the entire lot.

- A site should either be flat or gradually sloping toward the front of the house.

- The shape of the lot should be square or rectangular.

First, a residential site should be wide and spacious with a bright hall in the front. To be considered auspicious, the residence should strike a balance between its micro- and macroenvironments in order to benefit from the Qi energy in the environment. To strike such a balance, feng shui masters pay special attention to the bright hall in front of a residence. They hold that the bright hall should be appropriate in size, neither too large nor too small. If it is too large, Qi energy cannot stay. If it is too small, it will exert pressure on the house and limit the sight and future of its residents. The appropriate size of the bright hall depends on the size of the house itself. A rule of thumb is that the bright hall should be approximately the same size as the house itself, or a little bigger.

Second, the house itself should occupy one-half to two-thirds of the entire lot on which it is built. If the house is too small as compared to the lot, the Qi energy in the lot will easily be blown away by winds. On the other hand, if the house is too big for the lot, people living in it will feel pressed and lack room to maneuver. As such, their eyesight as well as their future will be blocked, especially when there are taller buildings on all sides. This issue of proportion between the house and its lot is a principle of balance and harmony. A well-proportioned house gives the impression and feeling of harmony, and harmony is one of the key considerations in feng shui.

Third, a residential site should either be flat or gradually sloping toward the front of the house (the land is lower in the front than in the rear). However, if a residence is built on a land site which makes the residence higher in the back than in the front, it offers the residents a commanding point, a bright outlook, and a secure rear.

Since the southern exposure is generally considered the most desirable exposure, then if a land must slope, it is best to slope towards the south. The worst case is a site that slopes back toward the rear, where the land is higher in the front. Such a topography creates a feeling of insecurity, as if the house and the residents in it are going to fall backward at any moment, or as if there is no escape in the rear. Nor is it auspicious for the land to lean toward either side, out of the same consideration for stability.

Fourth, the shape of the residential lot should be square or rectangular. If the lot is longer on the left than on the right, female family members will suffer the most misfortune. This is because left is the male side while right is the female side. A longer left side means deficiency for the right side, i.e., females. For the same reason, if a lot is longer on its right than on its left, the male members of the family will most likely bear the brunt of any misfortune. Only a square or rectangular lot can avoid both undesirable situations.

In addition to these principles, Chinese fathers also want us to keep in mind the following points when analyzing the landscape of a residence:

- A house should not be located at the dead end of a road, nor should it be located beside a highway or a fast-flowing watercourse.

- A road that runs straight against a residential building from the front can cause a lot of trouble for the residents of the building, including accidents and life-threatening events.

- There should be some open space to the south of the house.

- It would be an ideal environment for a house to have a watercourse to its east, a road to its west, a mountain to its north, and an open land to its south.

- It is good to have a small pond in the front of a house.

- It is better to have a small house with many residents than a big house with few residents.

- If buying a used house, inquire into the history of the house and ask these vital questions: How many owners have lived in the house? Who were they? What were their professions? Were they successful or unhappy? Were they in good or poor health? Did they have happy families?

Designing the House

This is as much an architectural issue as a geomantic one. Since residential houses are built on earth surface, they are directly influenced by heavenly Qi flowing in the air in addition to the earthly Qi running beneath them. Both kinds of Qi energy are desired for a residence. Once a construction lot is determined, earthly Qi becomes a set factor for the residence. But the heavenly Qi still remains a variable until the house itself is finally built and every aspect of it is taken care of. This means there is still plenty of room to maneuver after a site has been chosen.

The absorption of heavenly Qi into a residence involves almost every aspect of the house design. The following are key considerations to help absorb the maximum amount of heavenly Qi into a house.

House Shape

So far as building shape is concerned, residential buildings in a square or rectangular form are best. Houses in these shapes are thought to be in the most advantageous position to absorb heavenly Qi energy, because such geometric forms give a better sense of harmony and balance with the environment and are therefore best positioned to benefit from heavenly Qi. You can argue that round or cir-cular is another harmonious shape, but in feng shui, it is mainly recommended for commercial and religious purposes. This is because roundness, though a harmonious shape in itself, lacks a distinct sense of orientation and exposure. And the direction of a building is an important factor in the overall consideration of the feng shui of a residential house. Each owner of a house has his or her own optimal direction, determined by his or her birthday. A round house will leave its owner at a loss as to where to face. This causes a lot of confusion.

For commercial and religious facilities, a round or circular shape is all right. Such facilities are for public purposes; numerous people come into and go away from them everyday. They all stay there temporarily, typically for a short time, as contrasted with residential buildings in which family members spend the better half of their time everyday. Thus, the sense of ownership becomes much overshadowed for such facilities. In other words, customers and clients are more important to the success than the ownership itself. This is particularly the case with big malls and temples, the ownership of which is most likely in the hands of many people, rather than a single individual as in the case of residences. The number of people coming in and going out of a business or religious entity is the major mark of its success.

If square and rectangle are auspicious shapes for a residence, triangular, ladder-shaped, or irregular houses are considered inauspicious. Buildings in such shapes lack a sense of balance and harmony, and the points in the angles create conflict with their environments. This entails the spoiling or destruction of heavenly Qi, leading to disease, divorce, conflict, and accidents for the residents.

Geomantic evaluation of the shape of a building should also include the shape of its roof. Fathers of feng shui tell us that the roof of a house should not be pointed toward heaven. A pointed roof symbolizes confrontation with heaven and therefore destroys heavenly Qi. From the standpoint of feng shui, a good roof is one that is either flat, round, or gradually sloping toward the eaves.

Frontal Exposure

The frontal exposure is the face of the house. Feng shui requires that special attention be paid to the selection and design of the front of a house, just like we pay attention to our face. At issue is the question: To which direction should the front of a house be exposed? While a southern exposure is generally preferred, this is not the only choice. The principle is that the frontal orientation of a house

should match the auspicious directions of individual homeowners. For instance, if a homeowner was born in the lunar year of 1950, the house should have a frontal orientation of south, north, east, or southeast. Thus, frontal exposure of a residence is a personal matter, depending on who the homeowner is and the birthday of this homeowner. (For individual karma and auspicious orientations, refer to chapter 9.)

Front Door

The front door is the main entrance to the house. It is also the gateway to the family's private life—the link between the family and the outside world. Most significantly, it is the place where heavenly Qi enters the residence. As such, it affects the health, career, prosperity, and happiness of family members. For this reason, the front door has a significant impact.

Wei Qingjiang has some valuable messages for us:

Of particular importance is the door in your residence that opens to the main street, because heavenly Qi flows with the traffic and pedestrians in the street. Whenever the door opens, Qi enters the residence. It does not matter whether it is the front door, the side door, or the back door. So long as it opens to the main street, it becomes a particularly significant door due to the powerful movement of Qi along the street. Again, if this door is opened to your auspicious direction, your family will have good luck. However, if it is opened to your inauspicious directions, all kinds of ill luck will hit you and your family.

A well-designed front door serves as a powerful guard for the safety and happiness of the family.

Independent of architectural and aesthetic principles, feng shui has its own criteria for how the front door of a house should be designed. The following are the most important considerations for the design of a front door:

- The front door must open to face one of the auspicious directions as determined by the homeowner's karma. This ensures that the maximum amount of heavenly Qi will be introduced into the residence, promoting the luck of its residents.

- The size of the front door should be in proportion to the overall size of the house. In other words, it should be neither too big nor too small. Again, this is a matter of balance and harmony, which is an important principle in feng shui. Too large or too small a front door is a sign of imbalance, and imbalance entails bad luck and discord in relations among family members. While there is no hard and fast rules as to what is too big or too small, it is safer to err on the larger side than on the smaller side.

- The front door should not line up in a straight line with the door of the fence, if there is one. This is out of fear that ill winds will come directly through the fence door into the deep of the house unchecked. Such a design would greatly reduce the privacy of the house, because outsiders could easily look into the house. If the two doors are directly lined up, it also means wind could go straight through them, and this should be avoided by all means, especially if the house does not have a southern exposure.

- The front door should not line up directly with the back door of the house. Otherwise, the house will have a very hard time keeping the heavenly Qi that comes into the house.

- The front door should not be in a straight line with the stairs.

- The front door should not directly face a large tree or a telephone pole in the front. These are considered "killers" in feng shui, capable of bringing misfortune to the household.

- The front door should not directly face the pointed corner of another building. This is because another building's pointed corner represents a dagger hanging in front of one's head. Obviously, this is a very inauspicious image, and should be avoided. Otherwise, bad luck will visit down the road.

- There should not be a road heading in a straight line to the front door. This symbolizes a sharp dagger pointing at the heart of the residents.

- The front door should not directly face a church or a temple. This is because the Chinese hold a church or temple carries strong Qi of the yin nature, which is not desirable for a residential building.

Back Door

It is out of consideration for both the balance and the security of the residence that a house should have a back door in addition to a front door. In terms of balance, the back door and the front door make a couple. In terms of security, it is always desirable to have more than one exit in case of an emergency. As has been pointed out, the back door should not line up directly with the front door, even if there is something between the two (such as a wall). Otherwise, the Qi energy that comes into the house through the front door would otherwise easily run out through the back door.

Once we have taken care of the exterior design of the house in terms of the frontal exposure and the basic shape of the house, its front door and back door, we can now move inward and make sure that the interior design of the house is also in accordance with feng shui principles so that the maximum amount of heavenly Qi can be attracted into the residence and flow freely inside it. The central concern of interior design includes the location and layout of individual rooms inside the house. Both the environment and structure of a house are visible aspects of feng shui.

Feng shui is a combination of man and his environment. As such, the factor of man plays a key role in the overall design of feng shui. This helps explain why the same house can have dramatically different impacts on different people owning and living in it. Perhaps it is not too farfetched to use the example of foods. Using the same healthy food, some people become stronger and healthier, while others feel sick. Milk is one of these foods. Fresh milk is a nutritious and healthy food. However, when taken by some people, it can cause allergic reactions.

Exactly the same argument can be made for houses. Personally, I have known several houses that have changed owners in the past decades. For instance, one of my clients contacted me for feng shui service five years ago. Upon visiting her house and reading her birthday, I told her that this house was not set in the right direction for her and was bound to bring her lots of bad luck. She regretfully agreed to my statement and asked what was to be done. I told her bluntly that the best solution was for her to move to another house, if she could not pull down the current one and rebuild another house on the lot.

Living Room

The living room is the gathering place for the entire family, and the place in which the family entertains friends and guests. In it, family members and guests chat, relax, and discuss issues of interest to them. As such, it symbolizes unity inside the family and the connection between the family and the outside world. Therefore, the living room should be located in a strategically logical place, giving people a sense of convenience, comfort, peace, and unity without interfering with the privacy of the family. The following feng shui rules are tailored toward designing such an auspicious living room:

- The living room should be located at the very front of the house, right behind the main entrance so that as soon as people enter the house, they are in the living room. Just imagine yourself as a guest being introduced into a house. If you have to go through the smoky and oily kitchen, or pass by bedrooms or the laundry room, or even worse, the bathroom before you come to sit down in the living room, how would you feel? The Chinese used to say: "The onlooker sees the game best." If guests feel comfortable with your house and would like to come again, it shows that the house must possess some good feng shui.

- A living room must be kept clean, bright, well ventilated, spacious, and comfortable. The living room is the least private part of a house and is supposed to be shared with friends and visitors. A bright, spacious, and beautifully decorated living room creates a sense of comfort, joy, togetherness, and a "home away from home" for guests.

- The living room should be bigger than any other room in the house, because it is by definition the gathering place for the entire family where everybody can relax.

- The living room should be well lit and well ventilated, and have enough room for a passageway. The number and size of furniture pieces should be in proportion to the size of the room. Too few pieces yield the impression of coolness, while too much furniture creates a sense of congestion. Neither situation is desirable from a feng shui point of view.

- The living room should be appropriately decorated. Decorations and furniture do not have to be expensive, but they should be clean and in good taste. By good taste I mean being appropriate to the professional and social status of the homeowner. Furniture should be arranged in an orderly way, leaving enough space for movement. These days it is a common practice for people to decorate their living room with various pictures, but different pictures have different connotations. Thus, a picture of a tiger can expel evil spirits and protect the household from potential danger; a dragon can bring about good luck and wealth to the family; a sword and an ox horn have some protective effects and are fit for those engaged in highly competitive businesses; a peacock can bring prosperity to the family; a pine tree can promote longevity to family members; and water and mountains can create peace of mind.

Another thing to keep in mind while decorating the living room is that lamps should be round and bright. Roundness is a symbol of completion and amity, while brightness contributes to the generation of yang-Qi in the house.

- The ceiling should not be designed too high or too low. Too high of a ceiling reduces the sense of safety while too low of a ceiling generates a sense of oppression. (Generally, a ceiling that is more than ten feet high can be considered too high, while less than eight feet can be considered too low.)

- There should not be any beams showing across the ceiling of the living room. A visible crossbeam above the living room is a great taboo in feng shui. Such a beam signifies threat from above, which is the least preventable and, therefore, the most dangerous. We give little thought of what is going on on top of us. A crossbeam above us threatens to fall down upon us without our notice.

Stairways

In terms of stairways, feng shui has the following advice to offer:

- There should be no more than one stairway in a house. Otherwise, confusion will result within the family.

- The stairway should not be placed at the center of a house. Otherwise, the family's financial and social position will decline over time. The center of a house is the most important and valuable place. Such a place should be kept private, quiet, and stable. A stairway located in such a place disturbs this stability and privacy.

- The stairway should have no more than one turn for each floor. Otherwise, objectives set by the family will be hard to achieve.

- The stair should not be so narrow as to give people the feeling of oppression or fear of falling down the stairs. Nor should it be so broad as to occupy too much space in the house. A rule of thumb is that the width of a stairway should be no more than one-fourth of the floor space in which it is located.

- The stairway should not be immediately visible from the front door. That is to say, the stair should not be located right behind the front door, as is the case with modern tri-level houses. Otherwise, residents will suffer from hesitation when coming to important decisions.

Bedrooms

Humans spend an average of eight hours each day sleeping and relaxing, about one-third of our lives. This impressive amount of time spent on sleeping speaks to the special importance of bedrooms. Besides the biological need for sleep, a bedroom is also the place in which we share our most intimate feelings with spouses, and the place where new lives are created. This is especially the case with a master bedroom, which has a direct impact on the fortune of the entire family, the size of the family, the health of parents and children, as well as the children's ability to successfully continue their parents' business.

For a bedroom to successfully carry out its functions of sleeping, intimacy, and procreation, follow these suggestions:

- The master bedroom should ideally be located at the center of a house. This central location is also the center of heavenly Qi energy that enters the house. Since the master bedroom is the single most important room in a house, it makes a lot of sense to reserve the central location for it.

- In the absence of a central location, the master bedroom should be situated in one of the four auspicious locations in the house as determined by the homeowner's karma or year of birth. This location should have a high degree of privacy, preferably far from the front door. A master bedroom situated at one of the auspicious locations will improve the relationship between husband and wife, and between the parents and the children. However, if the master bedroom is situated in the unfavorable locations, relations between the spouses and between the parents and children will be strained or turn sour.

- A bedroom should not be connected to a bathroom, as is often the case nowadays with a master bedroom. In feng shui, a bedroom with a bathroom in it is known as "hitting the emperor's seat"—a very inauspicious situation.

- The bedroom for the elderly in the family should be located close to the bathroom. This is mainly for physical convenience.

- No bedroom in the house should be larger than the living room.

- No bedroom should have its door open directly to the bathroom, kitchen, the front door, or the door of another bedroom. The bathroom carries Qi of the yin nature, which is incompatible with the general feng

shui principle. The kitchen is a noisy and dirty place that can disturb the quietness of the bedroom. The reason why the door of a bedroom should not face directly to the front door is self-evident. Who would like outsiders to see through to the activities going on in one's bedroom?

- The same consideration of privacy demands that no two bedrooms should have their doors facing directly across from each other. Chinese observation holds that if the door of a child's bedroom is face-to-face against the door of the parents' bedroom, children will grow up with little respect for their parents.

- Bedrooms should be well ventilated and have good exposure to sunlight.

- The bed should not face a mirror or the bedroom door. Mirrors can disturb our peace of mind, while the open door reduces the sense of privacy and security. A television or a computer should not be in the bedroom. They all have a negative impact on peace of mind.

- There should not be a lamp or a skylight directly above the bed, nor should there be a beam hanging above the bed. These symbolize danger and threat. In a master bedroom, such danger can come in the form of discord and conflict or divorce.

- The light in the bedroom should not be too strong as to disturb the peace of mind and the atmosphere of privacy in the room. If the light is too strong, it can cause insomnia and nightmares in some people. A gentle light is preferable.

- The bed should be put against the wall, in an auspicious location and heading toward an appropriate direction in the bedroom.

- Babies should not sleep in the same bedroom as the elderly. This is because human Qi is of a different nature for the young than the old. The elderly can have a negative impact on the children.

Kitchen and Dining Room

The kitchen is another most essential unit in a house. We need food to survive as much as we need sleep, so the kitchen is as important as the master bedroom. Just as Mencius said: "Man's appetite for food and sex comes from nature, wherein lie the greatest desires of human beings." The kitchen is the place where food is prepared and stored, and therefore, symbolizes the livelihood of a household.

Feng shui has several rules governing the design of a kitchen:

- The kitchen should be situated in an auspicious location that is based on the homeowner's birthday. A kitchen so located can improve the appetite, digestion, and livelihood of the residents. (Food is a traditional Chinese symbol of livelihood.) If, however, the kitchen is placed in an inauspicious location at odds with the birthday of the homeowner, health problems will develop among the residents, including but not limited to indigestion, malnutrition, and diarrhea.

- There should be no more than one kitchen under the same roof. Traditionally in China, a kitchen stands for a separate social entity. Thus, a house with more than one kitchen is a house divided against itself. Serious conflict will occur among family members, which threatens to tear the very house down.

- The kitchen should not be placed adjacent to a bedroom, nor should it face the door of a bedroom or a bathroom. The reason why we do not want the kitchen to face a bedroom is out of consideration of the peace, cleanliness, and safety (for fear that fire will catch residents sleeping and unprepared) of the bedroom. The kitchen is normally full of noise and smells of food, and we do not want noises and smells to enter the bedroom. The kitchen also contains fire, which can (if only symbolically) threaten the safety of the bedroom. The kitchen should not face a bathroom out of hygienic considerations. The kitchen is where food is prepared to eat, whereas the bathroom takes the wastes away from our body. The two totally different functions and nature of Qi should not be mingled.

- The kitchen should not line up directly with the front door or the back door. Otherwise, the livelihood of the family may be lost to competitors outside the family (i.e., visitors).

- The kitchen should not be used as a dining room at the same time. While closely related to each other, they perform different functions. The preparation of food can be very hectic and "fiery," but the enjoyment and digestion of food should be done in a peaceful, slow, and enjoyable manner. Therefore, the two should be kept separate, at least symbolically, by use of a screen or a counter between the two.

- The kitchen should be located in a well-ventilated place, so that greasy dirt generated there will not flow into the other rooms.

Studio

A studio is the same as the den or the library. It represents the careers of the family members. It should be situated in one of the auspicious locations inside the house. This will enhance the intelligence of the residents and improve their academic performance. Family members will show increased interest in knowledge and study. However, if the studio is placed in an inauspicious location, the memory and intelligence of the residents will decline, as will their academic interests and performance. In an age in which knowledge and education are critical to career success, the feng shui of a studio cannot be underestimated.

Bathroom

There are two kinds of Qi energy in a residence: yang-Qi and yin-Qi. The task of residential feng shui is to promote yang-Qi while minimizing yin-Qi. This is because yang-Qi is auspicious, and can bring about happiness and good luck, whereas yin-Qi is malignant and can cause misfortune of all kinds. A house is not all yang-Qi; the Qi coming out of the bathroom is of the yin nature. Some houses in China do not have bathrooms but use public bathrooms and bathhouses instead. While this may reduce the yin-Qi in the house, the drawback is the great inconvenience—too great for most people to bear nowadays. To minimize the yin-Qi from the bathroom, follow these suggestions:

- Bathrooms should be placed in inauspicious locations. In no case should they be placed in the center of a house. For a bathroom to occupy an auspicious location is a terrible waste of the very limited space inside a house. If this is the case, then some rooms meant for favorable purposes, such as bedrooms and the kitchen, would have to be situated in inauspicious locations, feeding a vicious cycle of bad luck.

- A bathroom should not be readily visible from the main entrance. There are two main reasons for this. First, the less readily visible a bathroom is from the view of guests and visitors, the harder it is for the yin-Qi to come out and permeate the house. Second, the less visible a bathroom is, the more privacy the family will have.

- Bathrooms should be located in the back of a house in concealed places so that privacy can be ensured.

- The bathroom door should not directly face a bedroom, the front door, or the kitchen.

- The door of the bathroom should be closed at all times, or the yin-Qi will get out and affect other parts of the house.

- The door of the bathroom should not have the same orientation as the front side of the residence. That is to say, the front door and the bathroom door should not face the same direction. Otherwise, misfortune will visit the family.

- To further reduce the negative impact of a bathroom, it should be well lit and well ventilated, and have a working sewer system.

Garage

The garage represents a modern challenge to the ancient Chinese art of feng shui. While automobiles were unheard of in ancient China, Chinese fathers did have the luxury of horses and carts if they were rich. Horses and carts were placed in the backyard at a considerable distance from the house. Nowadays, we are confronted with a totally new situation where automobiles drive directly "into a house" and stay there for a good part of the day. This situation is totally unknown to the Chinese fathers of feng shui. An unconnected garage is preferred, but if you have no choice but to connect the garage to your house, place the garage in an inauspicious location.

Enclosure

An enclosure is the buffer between a residence and the outside world such as a fence. The existence of such a buffer is highly important and desirable, because it can bear the brunt of evil attacks from the environment (natural or human), and protect the privacy, security, and tranquility of the family. It offers additional room for geomantic maneuvers such as planting flowers and placing auspicious objects in it to enhance the quality of the residence. Traditional residential buildings in China always have enclosures. More and more, this is being replaced by a fence or a circle of shrubs planted around the house. Materials differ, but the feng shui significance remains the same. In this regard, the following important rules should be kept in mind:

- No enclosure should be constructed prior to the completion of the house. Otherwise, the future prospects of the residents will be limited. Meanwhile, laying down an enclosure before the house is completed will severely affect the efficiency of construction, because materials have to go through it.

- The enclosure should not be located too close to the house, especially in the rear and in the front. Otherwise, it will create a physical and mental sense of pressure on the residents.

- The enclosure should not be too high. Otherwise, the residents will be too isolated from the outside world, ending in poor interpersonal skills and bad reputations. Generally, an enclosure should not be taller than six feet.

- The enclosure door should be placed on the left side when viewed from inside the enclosure.

- The enclosure door should not line up directly with the main entrance of the house, if privacy of the residence is desired.

- The enclosure door should not open directly to a big tree, an electric pole, or the pointed corner of another building.

- The best form for an enclosure is one that is arched in the front but square in the back, generating a sense of harmony and regularity in people's minds. Such an enclosure shape can bring good luck and harmony to the family.

Yard

A house should have both a front yard and a back yard. Yards provide a safety buffer as well as a room to maneuver (for feng shui purposes). For these reasons, yards should be of considerable size. Feng shui requires that both yards combined should be approximately one-third to one-half the size of the house.

Yards are places where one can implement a lot of geomantic ingenuity and creativity. Typically, the Chinese will use yards to plant trees and flowers. This is a commonly used geomantic means aimed at enhancing the feng shui of the residence. These trees and flowers serve several purposes. First, they help bring out the earthly Qi of the site so that people living there can maximize the benefit of Qi energy inherent beneath. Trees and flowers tell us whether a location is full of Qi or short of Qi. Thus, if a place has a lush growth of trees and flowers, it must be permeated with Qi energy. If, however, a place is barren of plants and cannot even support the growth of grass, it must be short of Qi energy. This is because trees and flowers draw upon the Qi and nutrition in the soil for their growth. So the more lush the trees and flowers, the stronger the Qi reserve in a location, and vice versa.

Second, trees and flowers planted on a site give people a sense of comfort, relaxation, and beauty. It is pleasing to both the eye and the mind to look at the green trees and fresh flowers around the house. Such a view can ease fatigue and depression and enhance our spirit. Since our mental state has a direct impact on physi-cal health and therefore our happiness and success in the world, and happiness and success are exactly what feng shui is seeking to achieve, it makes a lot of sense to strategically plant trees and flowers around a house.

Third, trees and flowers, including shrubs, planted around a house serve as walls protecting the house from the merciless blow of ill winds. This is particularly the case when there are few mountains or hills in the surroundings.

However, no large trees should be planted in the yards, especially in the northeastern and southwestern corners. The belief is that large trees in the yard will invite evil spirits to the house, and the southwestern and northeastern corners become "devil's doors" if there are trees planted there. Feng shui has its own rules as to what kinds of trees can be planted and at which corner of the yard. For instance, the best trees to be planted in the eastern corner of a lot are peach, poplar, and cypress trees; in the southern corner of the lot, plum, jujube (date), and willow trees; in the western corner of the lot, elm, pomegranate, and Chinese scholar (locust) trees; and in the northern corner, apricot trees.

Apartment Buildings

Apartment buildings are a modern variation of residential houses. For an apartment building, not only does the shape (square or rectangular) and direction of the building count, so do the individual units.

- For a unit to be auspicious, it should not be located next to an elevator or a stairway, nor should a corridor lead directly to the unit.

Once such a unit is found, follow the procedures for residential houses to make it a really auspicious living place. Obviously, there is less flexibility and complexity in laying out an apartment than a house. Reduced flexibility is due to the fact that the unit is not owned by you and cannot be remodeled. Therefore, you do not have the right to remodel it even if you know how to. This setback is compensated by the reduction in complexity, since an apartment unit is simpler than a house in structure and facilities. For example, there is usually only one door into the unit and no attached garage. Obviously, living in apartments can have its pros and cons.

So much for our discussion of residential feng shui. Let's turn to commercial feng shui.

Sample Residential Layouts

Figure 13-1

(See page 169.) Several things stand out in this layout. First, the fence (enclosure) door and the front door are not directly aligned with one another in a straight line. Second, the living room is located right after the front door, giving those entering the house a sense of comfort. Third, the kitchen is separated from the dining room. Fourth, all the bedrooms are situated in the middle of the house, giving a sense of security and privacy. Fifth, there is not only a front door, but also a back door. Moreover, these two doors do not line up in a straight line.

Figure 13-2

(See page 170.) This layout shows a curved front enclosure and has the same auspicious features listed in Figure 13-1. For example, the fence door and the front door are not directly aligned, and the living room is located right after the front door. All the bedrooms are again situated in the middle of the house and both bathrooms are located at the back of the house.

Figure 13-3

(See page 171.) The front door is located on the side of the house, instead of the front as is typically the case. Such a design is often found when there is a deficiency in the front of the house. The good thing about such a layout is that you can turn the deficient part of the house into a small garden in front of the front door. This helps make up for the deficiency.

There is both a front door and a back door and they do not line up in a straight line, which is good. Fourth, three bedrooms are on the same side of the house. This can be a desirable layout if the other side of the house faces a busy street.

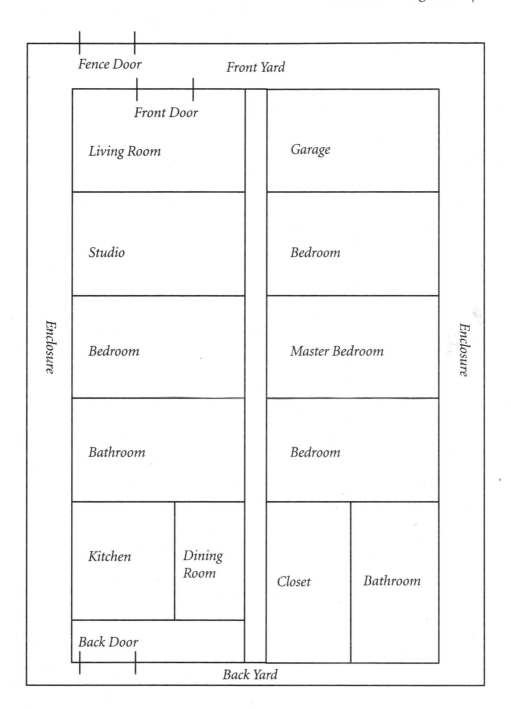

FIGURE 13-1
Sample residential layout

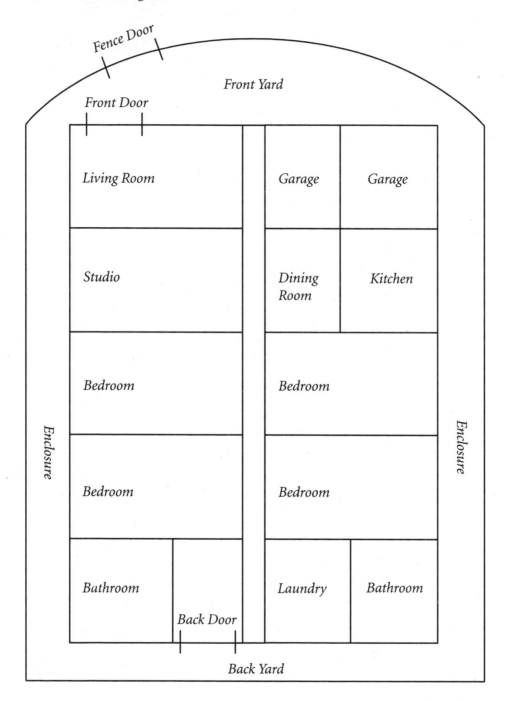

FIGURE 13-2
Sample residential layout

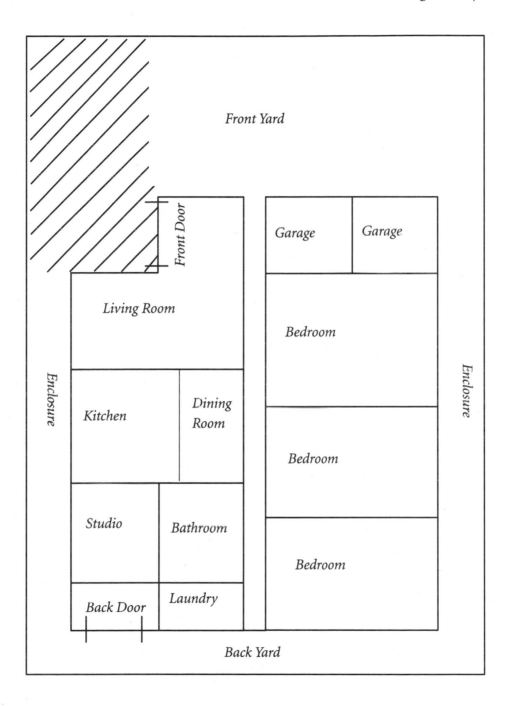

FIGURE 13-3
Sample residential layout

Chapter 14

Commercial Feng Shui

Commercial feng shui is another branch in the yang-house category of feng shui. Since both residential and commercial feng shui fall under this same category, it is little wonder that most of the principles governing residential feng shui also apply to commercial feng shui.

Commercial facilities include stores and corporate office buildings. The objectives of commercial feng shui are to site a business and configure its environment so that it can benefit from both earthly and heavenly Qi in the area, and eventually attract the maximum number of customers and, therefore, success. While residential feng shui has peace and privacy among its goals, this is the opposite of what commercial feng shui wants. Granted, the success of a business depends on many factors including product quality, customer service, marketing skills, as well as pricing strategy. But all these boil down to the issue of profit. For any commercial business, profit is the ultimate goal and criterion of success, and profit is created by customers. The more customers there are, the more profitable will be the business.

From a geomantic viewpoint, the degree of success in which a commercial entity can attract customers relies on many elements. These include the business' location and surroundings, the decoration of the building in terms of color and wall hangings, the design of the front door, the allocation of the treasury or safe, the layout of the CEO's office, the location of the various departments, and other details related to the interior design of the building where the business is located. Let us go through some of these aspects.

Location and Surroundings

As with residential buildings, commercial buildings should take into account the landscape around where they are located. A commercial building should be situated at or slightly above street level in the front, so that rain does not flow into the store. However, it should not be too much above street level, or people will have difficulty accessing it because of too many steps. It should not be located in a landscape that slopes backward, from the rear of the building. Nor is it auspicious to be located on a lot that slopes toward either side. A commercial building should not be constructed on a lot that is triangular, or irregular with deficiencies (forms other than square or rectangular). Moreover, it is considered inauspicious to have a commercial building located on a dead-end street.

To help improve the environmental landscape in order to solicit and attract customers, a store or commercial building should plant some bamboo, evergreens, or flowers around the building. These plants generate comfortable feelings and a good impression, and can attract heavenly Qi energy to the business. This results in more and more customers coming into the business.

Another effective way to beautify the landscape and enhance the feng shui around a commercial building is to create a spring pool in the front of the building. Since water symbolizes money, and money is what businesses strive for, it makes sense to have water near the business. This ancient Chinese wisdom has been followed by more and more modern businesses in the West; many have something similar to a water pool in the front of their building. Some of them even create a garden inside. All these designs serve the function of not only beautifying the environment, but also accumulating the Qi energy and consequently boosting business.

Front Door

The most crucial aspect of a store's design is the front door or main entrance. The front door is not only the outer appearance of a business, it is also the way through which customers and, subsequently, wealth enter the store. Therefore, special care must be exercised in the design of the front door so that it is in accordance with feng shui principles.

The following are essential considerations regarding the front door:

- The front door of a business should normally be larger than a residential door, even if the store and the house are the same size. Privacy is the dominant consideration for a residence. For a business, however, the more people that come to visit the store, the better. Thus, convenience of movement becomes the dominant consideration for the design of the front door of a business.

- The environment in the immediate front of the main entrance of a store should be pleasing to the eye. Such an environment can easily be created by putting pairs of green plants or potted flowers on both sides of the door. A pair of stone lions is also good. These objects are considered promoters of good luck in feng shui. Lions also symbolize wealth and security in traditional Chinese culture.

- The glass used for the front window of a store should be clear so that people can see through it easily and know what products are sold in the store. If, however, the glass is hard to see through from the outside, customers will most likely walk away from the store because of a lack of information.

- As with houses, the main entrance to a store should avoid directly facing a large tree, an electric pole, or the pointed corner of another building. Nor should the front door directly line up with the bathroom or garbage bins outside the store. These are considered evil forces in feng shui that have a dampening effect on the business.

- If the business is a restaurant, the front door should not directly face the kitchen. Customers should not be able to see the kitchen when standing in the doorway, otherwise, the restaurant runs the risk of being burned down in the future.

- Sewer pipes should not be allowed to flow beneath the store or through the front door. Violation of this will lead to financial and legal trouble.

- A business should have two doors to it, one in the front and one in the back. The back door is used for replenishing the stock and taking away the garbage, while the front door is used for doing business. Make sure that these two doors do not line up in a straight line, lest wealth coming in from the front door will be lost through the back door.

- In case the first floor of a building is used for commercial purposes while the second floor is used as a residence, the bathroom should not be located directly above the front door .

Treasury (Safe)

The second most crucial consideration is the location and concealment of the treasury. The treasury refers to the safe. While there is no set rule regarding where the safe should be located, feng shui considers a secure, less visible part of the building appropriate, such as the back of an office in the corner, or better still, in a separate room with a safety devise and lock. This is out of the general Chinese consideration that money should be kept out of the sight of outsiders.

Besides the appropriate location, the treasury should be appropriately concealed to have the highest degree of privacy and security surrounding it. Usually, this is achieved by surrounding the treasury with counters and placing it against a wall. For the same reason, the treasury should be placed against a wall so there is no access to the back of the treasury, nor should there be windows right behind it. If there is a window behind the treasury, the window should be covered and closed permanently, for fear that wealth will "escape through the window."

As for the counter surrounding the treasury, it should be curved, symbolizing smoothness and harmony with the customers. Also, the counter surrounding the treasury should not be too high or too low. It should be at a height that most customers can easily and comfortably rest their arms on without overextending. If it is too high, it tends to push customers away. If it is too low, the privacy and security of the treasury will be compromised.

This area should only be used for the purpose of collecting money from the customers. It should not be used for other purposes such as brewing coffee. To further enhance the feng shui around the treasury, consider placing a potted flower or an ox horn on the counter. Also, a bathroom should not be located directly above the treasury counter.

CEO's Office

If it is a corporate office building, there must be an office for the chief executive officer (CEO) inside the building. Since the CEO is the head of the company and directly responsible for its success or failure, the environment in which he or she works daily bears heavily on the welfare of the company. Therefore, a CEO's office must provide him or her with a comfortable, secure, peaceful, and private working environment. This often means that the best location inside a building be allocated for the CEO's office, just like the best location in a house should be reserved for the homeowner's bedroom. A quiet, comfortable, and private working environment is needed for the promotion of the CEO's decision-making process and to enhance the CEO's prestige. To this end, it is advisable to keep in mind the following geomantic principles when designing a CEO's office:

- A CEO must have his or her own private office in the company.

- The office should have an even, basically square shape.

- The office should be located in the back of the building, not directly visible from the front door. If there is a receptionist in the building, "the back" can be defined as the furthest point from the receptionist. In a high rise building, this point becomes unnecessary, because the height itself provides an additional degree of privacy.

- The door to the office should not face a bathroom.

- The desk in the office should be placed on the right side of the room, when viewed from inside the door, i.e., parallel to the walls, with the CEO's chair facing toward the door.

- All furniture in the office should be aligned parallel to one of the walls.

- The size of the desk should be appropriate so that there is enough space around the desk for movement.

- It is advisable to put a potted plant on the desk.

- There should be no passageway behind the CEO's chair. To ensure that nobody can walk behind the CEO in his office, the desk should be placed close to the wall.

- There should be no windows or doors behind the chair of the CEO.

- The windows should be made of glass that only allows people to look out but not in.

- There should not be a mirror directly in front of or behind the desk.

- While seated in the office, the CEO should face an auspicious direction as determined by his or her birthday.

- A bathroom should not be located directly above the CEO's office.

- The office should be well lit and well ventilated.

- There should be no crossbeams visible along the ceiling in the office.

Individual Departments

Most medium-sized and all large companies also have offices for individual vice presidents, in addition to individual departments such as accounting, finance, marketing, engineering, personnel, information systems/data processing, etc.

In terms of importance to the company, vice presidents are second only to the CEO. Since they are collectively responsible for making major decisions for the company, and communication between them requires a higher level of privacy, the offices for the vice presidents should be located at the back of the building, close to the CEO.

Accounting department should generally be put close to the front, because it handles billing, money collection and other customer services. Such a front position helps customer relations and makes the cash flow easy for the company. This is also true of the marketing department, which is responsible for marketing company's products or services to the customers, and should therefore be located close to all potential customers. However, this is not the case with finance, especially the treasury, department, if there is one, because the finance/treasury department does not have direct customer service responsibilities, and their functions in the company are more "internal," and therefore "private," than the accounting and marketing departments. They should then be located in the middle of the floor. This is also the case with the personnel department, which handles employee issues, benefits, as well as interviewing and hiring issues. By nature, these functions are considered credential, and therefore personnel department should be situated in the middle of the company layout.

The functions of the information systems/data processing department are also credential to the company. The department handles all kinds of information which are considered essential to the company's operation and to the decision making process of the top management. A lot of the information processed here is considered private to the company. For these reasons, information / data processing department should be located further back in the company layout, close to the offices of the CEO and VP's. This helps both guarding the internal information from being lost, and aiding the top management in making strategic and tactical decisions."

Color

Color is yet another consideration in commercial feng shui. The auspicious color for a house is one that is compatible with the useful spirit of the homeowner. In commercial feng shui, the auspicious color of the building is determined by the nature of the business and which of the five elements it corresponds to—water, fire, wood, metal, or earth.

For instance, if a business is of a fire nature, such as a restaurant or a bakery, then red or pink are auspicious colors for the business because they are the color of fire. Green, the color of wood, would also be auspicious because wood promotes fire. If a business is of a wood nature, such as a furniture store, green becomes its basic auspicious color, with black also being an auspicious color because black stands for water, and water nourishes wood. If the business is of a water nature, such as a fishery or a cleaning business, the auspicious colors are black and white, since black is the basic color of water while white stands for metal, which generates water. As for a metal-nature business, such as a hardware store or a jewelers, the best colors are white and yellow; white is the basic auspicious color of metal while yellow is the basic color for earth, which can generate metal. For a business that is earth in nature, such as a real estate company, the best choices are yellow and red, since yellow is the native color of earth while red is the basic color of fire, which promotes earth.

The following is a list of common businesses and their classifications under the system of the five elements. (Also refer to Table 2-1, page 24.)

Wood-nature businesses: These include paper manufacturers, horticulture/ gardening businesses, sawmills and timber mills, furniture stores, advertising and packaging companies, stationery stores, bookstores, publishing houses, hospitals, newspapers, and carpenters.

Fire-nature businesses: These include restaurants, department stores, beauty salons and barbershops, clothing stores, and optical shops.

Earth-nature businesses: These include agricultural stores, farms and farming equipment, cement plants, pawnshops, antique shops, employment services, dating services, accounting services, financial services, legal firms, crematoriums, construction firms, real estate companies, and architecture firms.

Water-nature businesses: These include banks, insurance companies, stockbrokers, aquatic products and stores, and cleaning businesses.

Metal-nature businesses: These include goldsmiths and jewelry stores, electronic stores, computer firms and stores, engineering firms, mining plants, hardware factories and stores, metal fabrication, machinery (manufacture of or retail), auto manufacturers, car rentals, notary public, and martial arts schools.

Unless it also owns the ground floor, a business should avoid being located on the second floor. A store should offer its customers direct access rather than asking them to walk upstairs. This is especially the case with the weak and handicapped.

Sample Commercial Layouts

Figure 14-1

(See page 182.) This commercial layout has several feng shui points to note. First, there are potted plants flanking the front door. This serves to attract the lively Qi energy in the environment as well as customers to the business. Second, a potted planted is put inside the reception room, giving guests and customers a sense of relaxation. Third, the parking lot is located in the front of the building. This design makes it easier for the business owner to observe the coming people and what happens in the environment --a matter of security. It also makes it easier for customers to get into the building--a matter of convenience for the business. Fourth, the marketing department is located in the front right after the receptionist, so that it can respond to customer's questions quick. Fifth, the offices of the CEO and VP's are located at the back of the building, creating a sense of importance and privacy for the key figures in the company. The sense of importance is created when guests are led to see them, they have to go through a series of offices before they finally come to the offices of the CEO and VP's. Finally, there are both the front door and the back door to the building, and the two doors are not lined up in a straight line toward each other. This enhances the sense of security for the business, especially so when you think that the back door is close to the offices of the key company figures.

Figure 14-2

(See page 183.) This layout has several feng shui points to note. First, on both sides of the front door, there are potted plants flanking it. This serves to attract the lively Qi energy in the environment as well as customers to the business, while creates a comfortable atmosphere for people coming in and out of the building. Second, the parking lot is located in the front of the building. This design makes it easier for the business owner to observe the coming people and what happens in the environment—a matter of security. It also makes it easier for customers to get

into the building—a matter of convenience for the business. Third, the marketing and accounting departments are located in the front, a good location for providing customer services. Fourth, the offices of the CEO and VP's are located at the back of the building, creating a sense of importance and privacy for the key figures in the company. The sense of importance is created when guests are led to see them, they have to go through a series of offices before they finally come to the offices of the CEO and VP's. Last but not least, there are both the front door and the back door to the building, and the two doors are not lined up in a straight line toward each other. This enhances the sense of security for the business, especially so when you think that the back door is close to the offices of the key company figures.

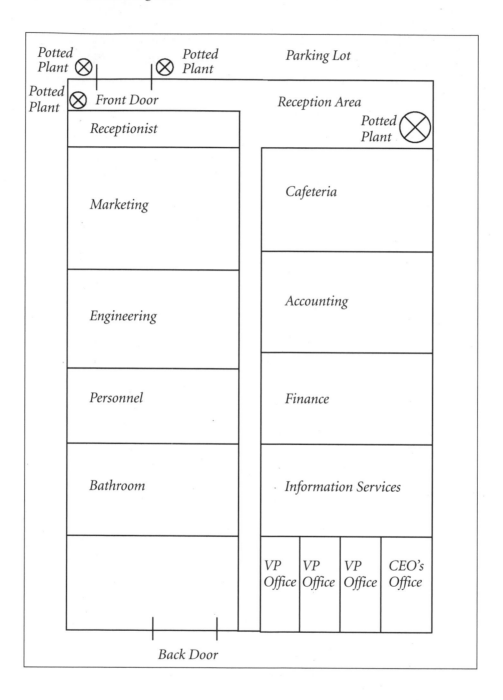

FIGURE 14-1
Sample commercial layout

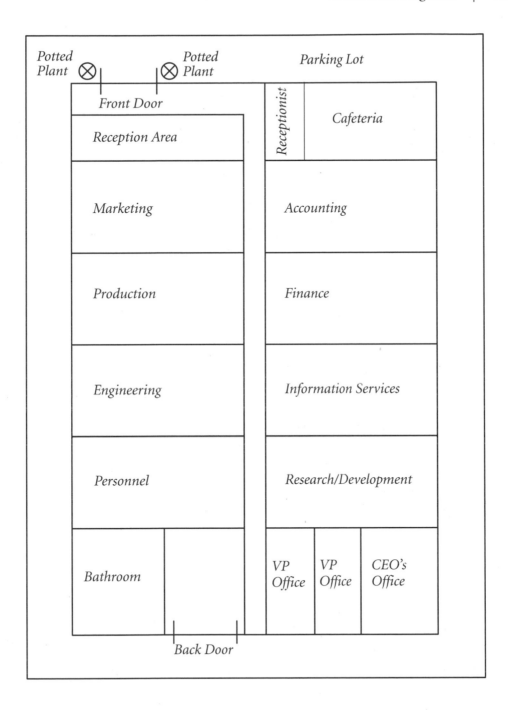

FIGURE 14-2
Sample commercial layout

Chapter 15

Extensions and Deficiencies

While a regular shape (square or rectangular) is highly recommended for a residential building, not all irregularities are necessarily bad. This includes extensions and deficiencies. An extension is defined as a protrusion on any side of a building, given that the width of the protrusion is less than one-third of the entire width of the building, and the length of the protrusion is less than one-fourth of the entire length.

A deficiency is defined as a depression or indentation on the side of a building. The width of this depression should be less than one-third of the width of the entire building and the length should be less than one-fourth of the length of the entire building.

If the measures of a protrusion exceed those defined above, it cannot be regarded as a protrusion. Instead, it may be the main part of the house with an opposite feature—a deficiency. Similarly, if the measure of the depression exceeds those defined above, it may be an extension instead.

An extension is generally preferred to a deficiency. For one thing, extensions are symbolic of growth, development, prosperity, and strength, while deficiencies suggest frustration, unhappiness, failure, and imperfection. Of course, not all extensions are good things. For instance, if there is an extension in the middle front of the house, the house is vulnerable to fire, theft, and loss of money. Such a house is known as a "cold-shoulder house" in feng shui, because both sides (shoulders) of the house are depressed.

All deficiencies generally mean that a family's health will be poor. Depending on the direction the deficiency faces, certain health problems will afflict the family. For example, a deficiency on the east side of a house bodes badly for the health of the liver in the family, since east corresponds to the liver organ, based on the theory of the five elements (see chapter 2). A deficiency on the south side of a house means the family will have heart problems. A deficiency on the north side signifies kidney problems, and a deficiency on the west side generally means lungs problems.

Therefore, when analyzing extensions or deficiencies, we need to know where the extension or deficiency is located on the house, since different directions have different meanings.

East or Zhen

This direction bears on the physiological, psychological, and spiritual health and vitality of the residents. It is also related to their drive, diligence, creativity, and ability to study.

An extension on the east side of the house bodes well for the family's health. The family atmosphere is characterized by harmony and affection. It also bodes well for marriage, children, and prosperity of the family business. In particular, children are diligent and intelligent, ambitious but law-abiding, have developed good interpersonal skills, and enjoy a wide circle of friends. They are welcome in the community and can get support from others. They will also be successful in their careers, and are particularly suited for academic professions that may bring wealth, fame, and good social positions to them.

A deficiency on the east side or east corner of the house bodes ill for the health of the family members. They are especially susceptible to liver disease, rheumatism, arthritis, eye problems, and neurasthenia. They are easily contented, tending to drag out an ignoble existence. They deliberately avoid social events because of their poor interpersonal skills. A lack of stamina and courage will lead to failure in business and a decline in the family fortune. There is apparent disharmony and conflict within the family, with the children being rebellious, showing little respect for their parents.

West or Dui

This direction affects the family's achievements, wealth, reputation, and ability to recover from loss or ill health.

An extension on the west side or corner of the house bodes well for the family's health, appetite (digestive system), and material enjoyment. The family can be very affluent, a fact that contributes to the stability and fulfillment of their spiritual life. They are intelligent and helpful to each other and possess good interpersonal skills. Full of drive and energy, the parents enjoy a happy marriage and the children are good and love and respect their parents. They tend to become the focus of the community they live in.

A deficiency on the west side or corner of the house bodes ill for the family's health. They are especially susceptible to the flu, colds, sinusitis, asthma, pneumonia, stomach diseases, and female-related ailments. There is strong discord in the family. Members are prone to romantic scandals that often result in separation and divorce. They are opportunistic and given to drinking and sexual indulgence. Family members violate laws and are not welcome or respected by the community they live in.

South or Li

This direction has influence over the family's intelligence, determination, confidence, courage, reputation, and social position.

An extension on the south side or south corner of a house bodes well for the family's health, energy, and life expectancy. They are intelligent and have imaginative power and ability. They are diligent, ambitious, and full of self-esteem. The children will have happy marriages and outstanding achievements in the arts or science. They will bring wealth and honor to the family. The family tends to be active in the community and is respected by others.

A deficiency on the south side or corner bodes ill for the family's health. Members are susceptible to insomnia, constipation, neurasthenia, hypertension, and heart disease. They are oversensitive, often experiencing a sense of inferiority. The atmosphere in the family is dull, characterized by discord, impatience, suspicion, and conflict among the members, as well as a lack of careful planning. They tend to act on impulse and jump before they look. The children cause a lot of headaches for the parents. They do not show much respect nor do they listen to the advice given by their parents. They are also frustrated in their careers, oftentimes finding themselves in financial and legal troubles. Isolated, with few friends, they have poor credit and reputations.

North or Kan

This direction affects the family's peace, comfort, stability, leisure, depression, loss, and death.

An extension on the north side or north corner of a house bodes well for the family in physical and mental health. Members of the family are rarely affected by disease. There is stability, love, and harmony among them. The children are excellent. They have good credit and reputations in society, enjoying a wide circle of friends. Careers are stable and progressive so wealth keeps coming into the family.

A deficiency on the north side or north corner of the house bodes ill for the family's health. They are particularly susceptible to insomnia, neurasthenia, infertility, kidney disease, diabetes, impotence, menstrual disorders, and venereal disease. Family members tend to be irresponsible,

engaging in dishonest work and behavior. Children are more of a problem due to their poor interpersonal skills. Family life tends to be dominated by discord and instability with a lot of frustration and setbacks in their careers, largely due to their personalities.

Southeast or Xun

This direction is related to the family's health, energy, ambition, stamina, intelligence, courage, social status, romance, and marriage.

An extension on the southeast side or southeast corner bodes well for the health of the family members. Besides enjoying good physical and mental health, family members are composed and well organized. There is lots of affection and care for each other. The children are smart and active, with good interpersonal skills. They are trusted by colleagues and successful in their careers.

A deficiency on the southeast side or southeast corner of the house bodes ill for the family's health. Particularly, they are susceptible to colds, flu, arthritis, rheumatism, and female-related diseases. Family life is characterized by coolness, separation, and lack of organization. They will be cheated and betrayed by their friends. Female members of the family are likely to get tangled in romantic trouble. Their careers will be full of frustrations, and their lives overshadowed by worries and financial strains.

Northeast or Gen

This direction is related to the family's passiveness, loss, instability, unrest, and abandonment.

An extension on the northeast side or corner bodes well for the health of the family. They are strong and energetic, rarely affected by disease. Although they are conservative, there is no lack of harmony and affection among the family members. It is a quiet but happy family. In society, they will think twice before speaking or acting. They are not very good at taking advantage of opportunities, still less at creating opportunities, but they are well trusted by others. They will be able to climb the ladder of success in their chosen careers, slowly but steadily.

A deficiency on the northeast side or corner of the house means family members will have poor health. Particularly, they need to watch out for hypertension, stroke, constipation, rheumatism, arthritis, and even cancer. Family life is characterized by disharmony, conflict, and a lack of trust. Some of them will have endless romantic and sexual troubles. Typically, daughters in the family will have a hard time finding husbands. Members of the family tend to have sour relations with their colleagues and bosses at work, and are not welcome and trusted in their community. This contributes to failure in their careers in the end.

Southwest or Kun

This direction is related to the family's management, obedience, determination, consideration of each other, as well as the health of their digestive systems.

An extension on the southwest side or corner of the house bodes well for the family's health. Family life is well organized, comfortable, and affectionate. The wife deserves a lot of the credit in this regard. Intelligent, patient, and capable, she is the role model for the entire family and is conducive to their good luck. As a result, family members will be successful in their careers.

A deficiency on the southwest side or corner means family members will not be healthy. They tend to overeat and consequently suffer from indigestion, ulcers, and other stomach diseases. Family life is tempestuous, full of arguments and conflicts. The marriage is not a happy one. Children are not well managed nor educated. They lack the determination and perseverance to see things through. In the end, they will accomplish little in terms of career and academic achievements.

Northwest or Qian

This direction is related to a family's efficiency, achievements, development, financial savings, preparation, defense, and avarice.

An extension on the northwest side or corner of the house bodes well for the health and happiness of the family members. Although seriousness is a trademark of the family life, they are nonetheless happy and affectionate. All members are responsible and considerate, caring for each other, both inside and outside the family. They are well trusted in society. This is part of the reason why they succeed in their work, wealth, and social status. There is a good chance that they will become leaders in their community.

A deficiency on the northwest side or corner of the house is a bad sign for the family. Family members have poor health, especially susceptible to pneumonia, neurasthenia, constipation, and cancer. Female members are susceptible to miscarriages and infertility. The family also has many accidents over their lifetime. Family life is full of instability, disorganization, discord, separation, and even divorce. Very possibly, the children of the family will lead a loose life, indulging in drink and sex. Since they are selfish and arrogant, they are not welcome in society and will be isolated by others.

Example of a Deficiency

Figure 15-1

The depression found on the left side of the front of the house is a deficiency, because its width is less than one-third of the width of the house, and the length is also less than one-third of the length of the house. Assuming that the house has a southeastern frontal exposure, this deficiency is located on the east side. A deficiency found in this direction signifies that the family is susceptible to liver diseases, rheumatism, arthritis, eye diseases, and neurasthenia. Their interpersonal skills are poor, and there is apparent disharmony in the family.

For a remedy, plant a group of trees or flowers in the deficient part of the house, so that the entire house will look more rectangular, reducing the negative impacts of the deficiency.

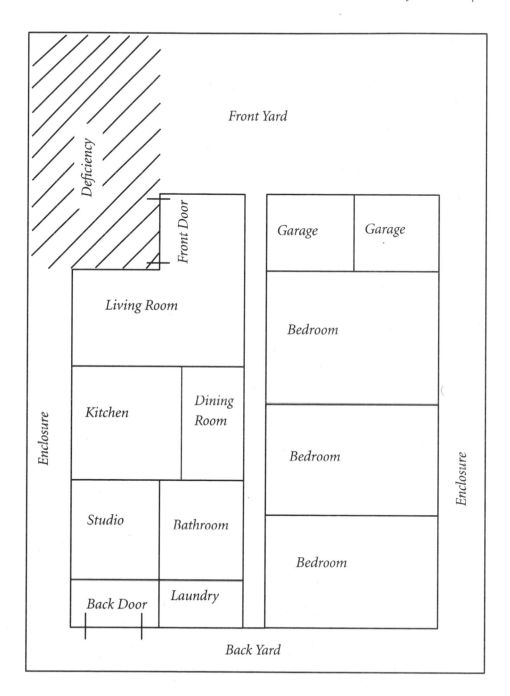

FIGURE 15-1
Example of a deficiency in a residence

Chapter 16

Feng Shui Remedies

Few locations on earth can be considered perfect from a geomantic viewpoint. More or less, a land site or a house leaves something to be desired, due either to geographic deficiencies or to structural problems. While a perfect location or house is hard to come by, most geomantic problems have a remedy or cure in feng shui. The search for such remedies has made feng shui a full-fledged art.

In his *A Collection of Road-breaking Works in Geomancy*, Li Mozai says: "Heaven cannot be balanced without man; earth cannot be successful without man. In a word, man's effort is indispensable to geomancy."

Cai Yuanding, another master of feng shui, also says some similar things in his *Expounding the Profound Truths of Geomancy*:

Geomancy is, in the beginning, just a body of knowledge and intuition, but in the end it can challenge the power of the supernatural and modify human fates. This is different from what is naturally existent. . . . Thus, if there is an excess of soil on a site, feel free to remove the redundant part whenever you feel necessary; if there is deficiency in the ground, feel free to make it up whenever necessary.

Feng shui relies heavily on human intuition and effort to not only recognize what is deficient in nature and in buildings, but to then make up for the deficiency. Basically, remedies are done in two ways: improving the land site where a building is located and modifying the building structure.

In terms of a land site, various measures can be taken to improve its feng shui, depending on the nature of the deficiency. For example, if the land is too low or depressed, add more soil or stone to it. If a construction lot is triangular, expand one or two sides to make it look more square or rectangular. Similarly, if there is an ugly (in shape or image), stone-dotted hill facing a house close by, build a wall or plant a row of trees between the house and the hill to create a shield from the malignant effects of the hill. If hills on both sides of the land site are too barren, plant trees, grasses, and other plants on the hills. If there is a watercourse that runs rapidly away from a residential land site, build the house behind some taller buildings downstream so that you cannot directly see the water running away from the house. The tall buildings in front of the house serve as checks against the water. Another solution is to plant some trees downstream on the banks of the water. Depending on the actual topographic situation and environmental circumstances, a number of solutions are available to make the location of a residence a better place for living.

In history, master geomancers had demonstrated great ingenuity and originality in remedying a deficient land site. For instance, Li Mozai had selected his own gravesite located in the tortoise mountain of Canton in southern China. Seeing that the tortoise mountain was too steep in the center to be auspicious, he chose the two small areas on both sides of the mountain as the burial grounds—one for himself and the other for his grandparents. In so doing, he deliberately avoided using the central ground, which is generally considered desirable because it strikes a balance between yin and yang. Li proudly called these twin graves "a pair of eyeglasses." The steepness of the tortoise mountain was thus avoided and a yin-yang balance was reestablished with the two graves, which were in symmetry to the central ground. In addition, Li ordered a small man-made hill to be built immediately in front of the site, thus making up for the lack of a table hill on the site. With all these masterful maneuvers, Li had brought a lot of wealth and honor to his descendants.

While not everybody can have the same degree of ingenuity and creativity as displayed by Li Mozai, a number of remedies are available to shield us from the inauspicious effects in the environment and improve the structure of our residence. Listed below are some of the easy-to-implement, useful countermeasures widely used in feng shui practice. They are designed for specific situations in real life.

Improving the Land Site

- As a general rule, plant small trees and flowers around the house to enhance the Qi quality of the environment in which you live.

- If there is a large tree (ten feet or higher) or an electric pole in front of the building, plant a row of small trees or green shrubs between the building and the large tree or pole. This line of trees or shrubs serves as a buffer against the malignant effects created by the tree or pole.

- If there is a road running straight toward your house, this is known as "an arrow shooting at your heart." This is a very inauspicious sign for your residence that is capable of causing various disasters. To remedy this situation, first, hang a large convex mirror (about half the size of the door) in front of your house, better still a geomantic mirror with eight trigrams in it. Second, put a large, tall stone in front of the house, right in front of the oncoming road. Third, build a wall or a fence or plant a row of shrubs in front of the house to intercept this "shooting arrow" before it reaches the house. To be effective, such a wall, fence, or row should be tall enough to visually separate the road and the house. Fourth, enhance the front door of your house by building a series of steps that lead to the front door, so that the front door will not be in direct contact with the ground. Fifth, you can place a pair of stone lions on both sides of your front door or set up a water fountain in the front yard to repel any bad effects. In the worst-case scenario, if the road runs straight toward your front entrance, consider relocating the front entrance.

- If there is a temple or church located right across the street in front of your house, you can do one of several things to protect your house from unfavorable effects. First, hang a convex mirror on the front of your house by the front door (size does not matter). Again, a geomantic mirror is highly recommended. Second, place a large stone in front of the house. Third, tie together a series of bronze coins or bells (from seven to twelve) with a red thread, and hang the bundle on the front of your house. Fourth, place a pair of stone lions on both sides of your front door to repel any negative impact.

- If the pointed corner of a building across the street is directed at your house, this is also considered an arrow shooting at you. You can either build a wall or plant a row of shrubs in the front of your house. Or, you can hang a talisman on your house directly facing the pointed corner. (See page 198 for info on talismans.) Hanging a convex mirror on the wall of your house will also help.

- If the soil of the land on which you want to build your house is too soft, too wet, or too dry, you can dig several feet into the ground, remove the original soil and replace it with soil of better quality taken from elsewhere.

Compact the soil for a solid foundation and level it out before you construct the house.

- If the land on which a house is to be built is full of small stones, pebbles, or tree roots, or used to be the site of a rubbish heap, dig three feet into the ground and remove that layer of soil. Then fill with new soil taken from a better quality site.

- If the construction lot used to have a pond or a water well, you should wait about three years after you have filled the pond or well with soil until natural settling has taken place before you start the construction of the house.

- If you have no choice but to build on a lot that used to be the site of a temple, church, or graveyard, dig three feet into the ground, remove the soil, and fill with soil taken from a better location that is mixed with some lime and sulfur.

- If the lot is an irregular or triangular form, plant a row of shrubs on each angle, parallel to the house, so that the angles will be artificially cut off and the lot will appear to be more rectangular or square.

- If the lot has been the site of a massacre, fire, or another type of violence and destruction in the past, place a statue of Kuan-yin, the great Goddess of Compassion, in the house. This can dispel the evil spirits lingering around the lot.

- If there is an ugly-looking hill near a residential area, construct a pagoda on the top of the hill. A pagoda can subdue the evil effects the hill has on the environment. Or, place a pair of stone lions on both sides of your front door to repel the bad effects.

- If there is a bare hill in front of the house, display in the front door some auspicious paintings containing the image of a dragon, tiger, phoenix, or goldfish. This will help dispel the bad impact of the hill and direct good luck into the house.

- If there is a rapid watercourse running through a residential or commercial area, build some piers in the middle of the water to minimize the bad effects.

- If there is a huge, metal-shaped object pointing at your house (such as the corner of a monument made of metal or an antenna made of metal), paint the house red as a countermeasure. Red symbolizes fire, which can conquer metal, thus subduing the harmful effects of the metal-shaped object.

- If the house faces north and there are no protective objects in front to shield it from the wind, place a water tank or dig a pond in the front of the house as a buffer. Water is a natural countermeasure to the wind and preserves the Qi of a location.

- If the lot slopes toward the back of the house, make the back of the house the front, using the back door as the main entrance. Or, plant some tall trees in back of the house to help make up for the land depression.

- If there is a major deficiency or depression at the corner of a building (see chapter 15), build a circular iron grid and use it as the roof of the depression. This covers up the deficiency from above.

Improving the Building Design

- If the front door lies in a straight line with the kitchen, put a screen between the front door and the kitchen to physically separate them.

- If the front door is placed in one of your inauspicious locations, build a new front door in one of your auspicious locations and close the old door permanently. (See chapter 9 to find your auspicious directions.)

- If a bathroom is located in the center of the house and it cannot be relocated, place a bowl of salt in the bathroom and renew the salt everyday. This will help absorb the bad effects that the bathroom will have on the house.

- If the stairway is located in the center of the house and cannot be relocated, hang a long mirror on the wall directly opposite the stairway, so that it is completely reflected in the mirror.

- If there is a crossbeam exposed overhead inside your house, cover it up with paper or, better still, some art design. Also, attach a piece of hollow bamboo tied with red ribbon to reduce the negative impact of the beam.

- If there are more bedrooms than family members, which is not an auspicious sign, consider renting some of the rooms to tenants.

- If a bedroom faces a bathroom or the front door, this is a violation of residential feng shui. Either change the location of one of the doors or put a screen between the bedroom and the opposing door.

- If the kitchen directly faces the bedroom door, hang a glass crystal on the bedroom door. The idea is to balance fire with water—a kitchen symbolizes fire while glass crystals are associated with water. A balance between water and fire will lead to better health and harmonious relations between the couple.

Talismans

Talismans are an integral part of the remedy system in feng shui. In a sense, they are the last resort when all other countermeasures are either too complicated or costly to implement. The beauty of talismans is that they are inexpensive and convenient (just hang on a wall), within the reach of everyone. They can be powerful countermeasures against inauspicious impacts from the environment. See pages 199–202 for the author's drawings of some of the powerful talismans commonly used in China for geomantic remedies. They are equally good and serve the same purposes.

FIGURE 16-1
Example of a talisman

FIGURE 16-2
Example of a talisman

FIGURE 16-3
Example of a talisman

FIGURE 16-4
Example of a talisman

Chapter 17

Summary

Feng shui is an ancient Chinese art of architectural placement and environmental design that covers the placement and design of tombs, residential houses, commercial entities, and towns and cities. Feng shui seeks to explore all interrelationships and interactions among nature, humans, time, and space. It tries to reveal the innermost secrets regarding the relations among heaven, man, and earth, aimed at helping people live harmoniously with nature so as to benefit from, rather than be hurt by, nature.

In its long history of development, feng shui has evolved into a highly sophisticated subject that permeates the social, cultural, and everyday life of the Chinese. It connotes geographical and philosophical, architectural and environmental, physical and metaphysical, and scientific and artistic aspects of ancient Chinese civilizations.

Since feng shui is preoccupied with the well-being and happiness of people, it has been exerting profound influence on the material and spiritual lives of people in China and other East Asian countries. Those interested in and practicing feng shui in that part of the world run the gamut from ordinary people to heads of state. Recently, feng shui has taken the Western world by storm. This is especially the case in the United States. This is evidence of some of the universal truths contained in feng shui, and a clear indication that more and more people in this modern age have come to the realization that the pursuit of happiness has metaphysical as well as physical dimensions.

As a product of ancient Chinese civilization, feng shui draws heavily upon basic principles of traditional Chinese thinking. These principles include the balance of yin and yang, the productive and destructive relationships among the five basic elements, the meanings of the eight trigrams, the triad of heaven-man-earth, the importance of natural harmony and balance, and the astrological and geomantic significance of timing. Anyone serious about learning and practicing feng shui is strongly encouraged to familiarize him or herself with these basic theories. The time and effort spent will handsomely pay off.

Chinese fathers were very intuitive and imaginative in bringing feng shui to life. For instance, they view the entire earth as a vast field of energy, as something similar to the human body, with its own veins and arteries. Just as the energy of a human is carried through the body via veins and arteries, with concentrated places known as acupoints, the energies of the earth are carried from location to location through earthly veins and arteries, and concentrate in locations known as dragon lairs. Since feng shui is preoccupied with the acquisition of earthly energy, the task of a feng shui practitioner lies first and foremost in locating these geomantic veins and arteries and finding these dragon lairs where earthly Qi energy concentrates.

Feng shui normally follows this series of steps:

1. Survey the general topography and environment of the land site, so as to find the Qi energy flow.

2. Locate a dragon lair—a land site full of Qi energy.

3. Improve the lot, if necessary, before construction.

4. Design the building in light of feng shui principles (residential or commercial), taking into account all the visible objects in the environment as

well as the birthdate of the home-owner, making sure that the building has appropriate overall configuration as well as color.

5. Correctly design each room and stair-way inside the building based on its function and the homeowner's birth-date, paying special attention to the placement of the front and back doors, bedrooms, bathrooms, the kitchen, and the living room.

6. Design the enclosure and front and back yards for the building, strategi-cally placing artificial objects that will help enhance Qi energy in the lot and shield the building from inauspicious forces in the environment, while mak-ing sure that the space left open around the building per se is in good proportion to the size of the building itself, and the height of the enclosure is appropriate with regard to the building.

7. Choose the right decorations for each room, and carefully arrange the furni-ture so that there is enough room for passageways in each room, so that Qi energy can flow freely inside the house.

In an already existing building, there is less room for the creative work of feng shui. Since the location and lot are already set, there is no need to pinpoint dragon lairs. Instead, most of the work will first go into judging whether or not the building is situated on an auspicious lot and surrounded by a favorable envi-ronment. The building and lot should have the following:

- The lot has a regular square or rectan-gular shape.

- The lot is level or slopes down toward the front.

- There is good quality soil.

- The lot has not been a burial ground or has not had a history of violence.

- There is no major, irremovable threat in the surroundings, such as inauspi-cious waterways, bare or stony hills close by, a huge roof or a corner of another building pointing directly at the house, or a major road that runs straight toward the building.

If any of these qualities are missing, forget about the building and look else-where until you find one that offers posi-tive answers to all of these questions.

If the answers to these questions are positive, the next step is to decide if the building possesses a favorable configura-tion, which in most cases means a basi-cally regular shape, be it square or rectan-gular. If it is, go to the next step and find out more information about the building. If it is not a regular shape, ask yourself if the configuration can be changed without costing too much money and time or causing damage to the building. If this is not possible, it is best to look for a different building.

The next question to ask is if the building is oriented in one of the owner's auspicious directions (karma). This is based on the owner's year of birth. (See chapter 9.) Keep in mind that feng shui is a combined study of the relationships between man and his living environment. If you are going to be the owner of the house, you want to make sure that the house faces a direction that is in line with your specific karma. Everybody has four appropriate directions to choose from. For instance, if you are a woman born in the year 1950, you want to live in a house with a frontal exposure to the south, north, east, or southeast. However, if you are a man born in the same year, you want to live in a house with a frontal exposure to the west, northeast, northwest, or southwest. Unless you can easily change the frontal exposure of a house to fit your karma, it is generally not advisable to live in the house.

When you have positive answers to all of the above questions, you can be sure that the residence will bring good luck to you and your family. Even so, there is bound to be some modification and improvement done both inside and outside the building. Remember that no building is perfect for everyone from a feng shui point of view.

At this point, most of the hardest obstacles have been overcome. Any problems that come up after this usually have a remedy that is reasonable. For instance, you may find that the master bedroom of the house is situated in an inauspicious location. Simply find another bedroom that is located in an appropriate place and make it the master bedroom. If there is a big tree in the yard, or the house is not painted the right color, there are simple remedies for these: consider cutting the tree down or simply paint the house another color. There is usually a remedy or countermeasure for most geomantic problems. (Refer to the chapter "Feng Shui Remedies" for more information.)

From everything that has been covered in this book, there should be no doubt that feng shui is both a science and an art. Indeed, it is more an art than a science. Like any science, feng shui has developed a set of general laws to be applied to specific circumstances. However, feng shui recognizes that constant change is one of the motifs of nature and human society, and therefore there can be no hard and fast answers to all geomantic situations. Authentic feng shui is simply not a body of fixed rules and regulations about how and where to arrange furniture and place things in the house. Instead, it is primarily an art of recognizing the existence and movement of Qi energy in the environment, as embodied in various geographic and architectural objects such as mountains, watercourses, and neighboring buildings.

The movement of Qi energy alone is intangible enough. To detect it and relate it to various objects and individual humans becomes even more metaphysical. Obviously, scientific understanding of geomantic rules alone is not enough for the correct practice of feng shui. Feng shui relies heavily on the intuition and imagination of individual practitioners. This is especially true when it comes to pinpointing dragon lairs—selecting a land site full of live energy for the purpose of architectural construction. And the selection of an auspicious construction site is what gen-

uine feng shui is primarily about. Since all kinds of land sites exist on earth and there are a wide variety of topographic features, no single rule can encompass all situations or be expected to work in all circumstances. Therefore, each area and land site must be studied on a case-by-case basis.

While some people are born with stronger intuition and sharper imagination than others, the good news is that the kind of intuition and imagination needed for feng shui can be cultivated and enhanced in anyone so long as he or she is willing to learn and has the good luck to learn it under the guidance of authentic masters.

Here, as anywhere in the domain of arts, experience counts and practice makes perfect. In this regard, it will be very helpful to study the geomantic features of the residences of successful people in history. It is through practice and observation of different environments and situations that intuition and imaginative judgment are sharpened.

Appendix 1

The Art of Moving House

America is the single most mobile country on earth. Mobility is the keynote character of American life. Other people in the world are surprised with the frequency and enthusiasm with which Americans move to a new home. This may be a sign of greater freedom enjoyed by Americans, which can be envied by people elsewhere around the world. However, this advantage of freedom can be a disadvantage if we are ignorant of the feng shui principles concerning the art of "moving house."

In China and other Asian countries, moving house is a very serious topic. It typically requires detailed preparation on the part of family members, and intense consultation with feng shui masters, such as information about appropriate ways to clean the house being moved into, auspicious days for moving into the new house, the order of items to be moved into the new house, and, strangely enough, which family members are to be physically involved in the moving process. These are deemed essential considerations for moving into a new house.

The following is a list of considerations to keep in mind before moving into a new residence:

- The day a family moves into a new house should not conflict with the head of the household's year of birth. This is based on the eight characters of birth theory (see chapter 9). If it is an office building, it is the CEO's birthday that counts.

- Those who are not members of the family should remove belongings from the old house. But, family members should move them into the new house.

- After cleaning the new house, open all the windows for at least two days before actually moving in. At the same time, place some evergreen plants inside the house to help cleanse the house and attract Qi energy into it.

- Family members should not enter the new house empty-handed. Everybody should carry something into the new house.

- The new homeowner should walk into the house first, followed by the other family members.

- The first items to be moved into the new house should be the most precious belongings of the family. These can be jewelry, computers, or anything that is of high value to your family (financial or sentimental value). This is to ensure that wealth will come to your household later on.

- Ideally, the whole moving process should be done in the morning and completed by noontime. If at all possible, avoid moving in the evening. This is because the evening is permeated with yin energy, and not very auspicious for moving into a house. Try to complete the move in the same day rather than continue it to the next day, so that there is a sense of continuity and completion.

- Those who were born in the lunar years of the tiger, such as the years 1950, 1962, 1974, and 1986, should stay away from the actual moving, even if they are family members. (The Chinese believe that a moving tiger will hurt people.) Pregnant women should also not participate in the moving process.

- Those born in the lunar years of the chicken and dragon, such as 1952, 1957, 1964, 1969, are the best candidates to do the actual moving. The chicken in the Chinese horoscope symbolizes the phoenix, which is a very auspicious bird. The dragon is also an auspicious symbol. If no one in the family was born during one of these years, hang a painting of a dragon or a phoenix on the wall of the new house.

Appendix 2

Geomantic Compass

A geomantic compass is first and foremost a compass. It must be able to perform the primary function of any compass—to take bearings and find directions. Feng shui design takes into account the orientation and alignment of a building project—burial, residential, or commercial—because they have a significant impact on the fortune of the residents. In geomancy, this means finding the right direction and optimal line with which a building ought to be aligned.

Finding the direction and orientation is more complicated than merely knowing which direction a house is facing, mainly because we are dealing with geomantic directions, not the familiar cardinal directions. Therefore, simply knowing where north, south, east, or west is cannot solve geomantic problems.

Geomantic factors include the birthday, or karma, of the owner, the relationship between a specific site and the mountains, waterways, roads, and other buildings in the surroundings, the relationship between a specific location and the major constellations, and even the time of year a project is undertaken.

Obviously, it is a tremendous task to incorporate all these factors. For one thing, it is hardly possible for the naked eye to accurately locate a specific direction, let alone accurately pinpoint to, say, 165 degrees on a plane. While most of us have some sense of direction, this sense can vary widely in acuteness from person to person. Thus, when people say "to your left" or "to your right," we know what they are referring to. But we may be quite at a loss as to which cardinal direction our right or left is. Even more difficult is the task of relating a specific locality with the waters and mountains in the surroundings, let alone stars in the heavens. All of these present a difficult challenge for those interested in feng shui.

To reduce the level of difficulty and enhance the efficiency and accuracy of a geomancer's work, Chinese ancients invented the geomantic compass, a powerful device alternatively known as a Lo-pan or Lo-jing.

A geomantic compass or Lo-pan contains one (sometimes two) magnetic needle, which is aligned to the north-south direction. This needle is about one-inch long and moves freely on a pivot covered by a glass piece. All geomantic compasses are circular devices made of lacquered wood, with a glass disk in the center containing the magnetic needles. Most compasses are about five inches in diameter.

On the compass are several concentric circles where important geomantic, astrological, and philosophical information relevant to feng shui is inscribed: the 360 degrees of a plane; the eight trigrams; the sixty-four hexagrams; the five basic elements; the twenty-four divisions of the year known as "*jie* and Qi" in the Chinese lunar calendar; the twenty-eight heavenly constellations known as *xiu* in Chinese astronomy; the nine palaces; the ten heavenly stems and twelve earthly branches; and the sixty binary combinations of these stems and branches widely used in both Chinese divination and the Chinese calendar.

These factors are numerical and divination tools in Chinese culture. Combined, they are able to encompass the cosmic environment surrounding and influencing a specific land site, revealing its geomantic information. Thus, a geomantic compass is truly a four-dimensional (spatial plus temporal), intensely informational device that relates man and a specific site with the macroenvironments in the surroundings, offering an invaluable, powerful aid to those who know how to use it.

There are two kinds of geomantic compasses in use in China. One is called Yang-pan or Yang's geomantic compass, and the other is called Jiang-pan or Jiang's geomantic compass. They are named after their creators, grand master Yang Yun-song of the Song dynasty, and grand master Jiang Dahong of the Qing dynasty, respectively. The major difference between these two compasses is that while the Yang compass emphasizes the relationship between a specific locality and its surrounding topography, the Jiang compass stresses the relationship between a specific locality and the nine stars and eight trigrams. This is the major point of departure between the Situation school and the Direction school of feng shui.

Compass Layers

Most geomantic compasses have more than a dozen concentric circles or layers and some have up to forty. A basic compass has sixteen layers. Each of these layers are defined as follows.

At the innermost layer in the very center of the compass lies a magnetic needle. This layer is called the Heavenly Pool, symbolizing taiji, or the Great Ultimate, which is assumed to be the mother of yin

and yang as well as the origin of everything in the universe. In some compasses, there are two needles, each pointing to a slightly different direction, which may cause confusion for beginners. This is due to the geographic fact that there are two meridians in the earth: the magnetic meridian and the geographic meridian. The difference between the two meridians and therefore the two needles is less than ten degrees. This shows that the Chinese have known for a long time the distinction between magnetic north and geographic north.

The second innermost layer contains the eight trigrams of I-Ching, which is a significant concept and tool used in feng shui for determining the appropriate locations for each room in a house. It is also a way of relating a specific location with objects in its surroundings, such as mountains and waterways.

The third layer divides the compass into twenty-four points of direction, each of which is assigned one of the five basic elements (water, fire, wood, metal, or earth). For example, north is assigned the element water, south the element fire, east the element wood, west the element metal, and the center the element earth. This layer corresponds with the eighth layer in the compass that contains the twenty-four divisions of the year in the Chinese lunar calendar. Some geomancers in China use this information to tell if the timing is right in building or moving into a new house. Ideally, the timing of construction or moving house should coincide with one of the twenty-four subdivisions of the year.

The fourth layer gives alternative combinations of the five elements such as water-fire, water-metal, water-earth, and so on.

The fifth layer combines the impact of the constellations with the points shown on the third and fourth layers. The names of the constellations are listed here, showing their relationships with the five elements as well as with the earthly directions listed on the third layer.

The sixth and seventh layers are similar to the third layer in that all the twenty-four divisions in these layers are made up of one of the five elements. However, there are some differences. While the third layer is made up of a combination of elements from the heavenly stems and earthly branches, the sixth layer only consists of elements coming from the heavenly stems, and the seventh layer is only made up of elements from the earthly branches. This is because some geomancers think that the heavenly stems are representative of heavenly Qi energy, the earthly branches for earthly Qi energy, and the combination of the heavenly

stems and earthly branches is an attempt to bring these two kinds of Qi together.

The eighth layer contains the twenty-four divisions of the year in the Chinese lunar calendar (each division comprises fifteen days and each solar season has six divisions), indicating the appropriate time of year for a house or a grave to be constructed. (This calendar system is also indispensable to the eight characters of birth system, which is one of the most popular forms of Chinese divination.) The divisions of the year are the Beginning of Spring, Rain Water, Waking of Insects, the Sprint Equinox, Pure Brightness, Grain Rain, Beginning of Summer, Grain Full, Grain in Ear, the Summer Solstice, Slight Heat, Great Heat, Beginning of Autumn, the Limit of Heat, White Dew, the Autumnal Equinox, Cold Dew, Frost's Descent, the Beginning of Winter, Slight Snow, Great Snow, the Winter Solstice, Slight Cold, and Great Cold.

The ninth layer contains the nine stars (specific names of constellations written on the compass), which correlate not only with the eight trigrams and five elements, but also with the earthly branches and the twelve stages of life: conception, nourishing, birth, baby's first bath, youth, middle age, heyday, decline, retirement, death, tomb, and extinction, represented by the twelve earthly branches. These stages of life determine the relative strength of the five elements during the year and their subsequent bearings on a person and a site. Generally speaking, the stronger a relevant element is, the more auspicious will be the site. Since the stages of life are primarily a temporal concept, location and time are once more found to merge in the compass for a comprehensive evaluation of a land site. The twelve earthly branches are Zi (rat), Chou (ox), Ying (tiger), Mao (rabbit), Chen (dragon), Si (snake), Whu (horse), Wei (ram), Sen (monkey), You (chicken), Xu (dog), and Hai (pig).

The tenth layer contains the nine palaces. (They are the eight trigrams, plus the palace at the center.) These indicate the positions of hills, mountains, and waterways in terms of yin and yang.

The eleventh layer shows the twenty-eight heavenly stars, which depict stars in the heavens and their symbols. These stars are the same as the zodiac symbols of astrology.

The twelfth layer is the earthly plate, containing the twenty-four directions marking the demarcation between earth and heaven. The layer is a significant one. It divides the compass into sixty sectors. Each sector is assigned one of the sixty permutations made of the ten heavenly stems and twelve earthly branches. Since all the stems and branches are classified

by the five elements and each element corresponds to a constellation, this layer is used to tell the influence of the elements and constellations upon a specific land site, and the relationships between adjacent locations and objects.

For instance, if a site occupies a position of the earth element, but is directly aligned with a constellation of wood, this site cannot be considered auspicious since wood destroys earth. However, if the same locality is aligned with the constellation of fire, it will be a lucky site because fire generates earth—a productive relationship.

The thirteenth and fourteenth layers show the division of the compass into 360 degrees.

This is followed by the fifteenth layer of the seventy-two dragons, based on the relationship between various heavenly stems, earthly branches, and the eight trigrams. This system of dragons is used specifically for evaluating the quality of mountains from the viewpoint of the five elements.

The sixteenth layer, the outermost layer, divides the twenty-four directions of the compass into twelve "divisions of the field," each corresponding to an area in China proper governed by a corresponding constellation.

Such a complicated device is aimed at identifying the four-dimensional relationship between a land site and the topography of the surroundings, the stars in the sky, the time of the year, and the birthday of the owner. For such a complex relationship to be auspicious, elements in it should be productive toward each other, or at least compatible. Since there are so many factors involved, it is inevitable that conflicts and confusion will occur. Thus, a site may have beautiful mountains and water in the surroundings, but it may run counter to certain constellations, compromising or even overwhelming the auspicious nature of the site. How all these discrepancies are reconciled is a personal choice of the geomancer involved. It largely depends on which school of feng shui the geomancer follows: the Situation school or the Direction school.

The geomantic compass is deliberately complex to ensure that few outside the field can understand how to use it, thus securing the steady income of a few feng shui masters. Due to the extreme complexity and high density of the information involved, a geomantic compass is viewed by most people with reverential awe. Not all professional geomancers even know how to use it, especially how to reconcile and coordinate this huge body of numerical and divination information. Not surprisingly, it has been misused by some greedy but ignorant people. It takes more than this book to explain in detail how all this information is related and how it all bears on the feng shui of a land site.

At this point, it is not necessary to become concerned with learning how to use a geomantic compass. It will only confuse beginners and cause them to lose sight of the significant issues, such as discerning auspicious topographic situations and the Qi energy created by them. However, anyone interested in learning more about using the geomantic compass is advised to check out specialized books on the subject, such as *A Complete Illustration of the Geomantic Compass* by Wang Daoheng (Peking, China: Classics Press, 1926).

Appendix 3

Case Studies

Case #1. Mao Tse-tung's Residence

On December 26, 1893, one of the most influential people in China was born in a village called Shao-shan-chong in Xiangtang County in Hunan province in southern China. He was none other than Mao Tse-tung, the late leader of the most populous country on earth. The village name, broken down, describes the landscape. Literally, "Shao-shan" means "Mount Shaoshan," a famous series of mountains in southern Hunan. "Chong" refers to a stretch of flatland in a hilly area, encircled by hills on three sides, with only one side—the front side—being relatively open and spacious. These are some of the topographic features of Mao's birthplace, with the hilly area mentioned surrounded by Mount Shaoshan.

Mount Shaoshan is one of the most beautiful and major veins of Heng Mountains. This mountain vein stretches over 100 miles and is covered with lush forestry and dotted with magnificent peaks. The peaks of Mount Shaoshan are often shrouded in a sea of mist. In the center of Mount Shaoshan, there is a spring falling into a huge hole in the mountain. This is the famous "Water-dropping Hole." It is recorded in a Chinese geography book that about 4,000 years ago, the sage Emperor Sun of China toured the Mount Shaoshan area with his two concubines. At that time, the emperor was already 110 years of age. They were so fascinated by the beautiful scenes in the area that they spent quite some time there, up to the end of the Emperor's life. The two concubines were so sad over his death that they cried day and night. Their touching tears dropped on the bamboo on the ground, which were thus turned into mottled colors.

On the outer edges of Mao's birthplace, there is the magnificent Xiang River encircling Mount Shaoshan. There are two clear streams slowly flowing by the village of Shao-shan-chong. The entire landscape of the village and its surroundings offers an ideal model for a village site, with the presence of favorable mountains and water in the environment, and the village proper occupying the central position in the entire landscape. Mao's old residence is situated at the foot of a hill in the rear, which is full of green trees and bamboo, and offers strong protection in the back.

The structure of the house itself is designed in strict accordance with feng shui principles. The center of the house is flanked on both sides by extensions, which are less than half the length of the central portion. The side extensions were apparently designed with the concepts of the green dragon and the white tiger in mind. While there is an actual green dragon and white tiger on both sides of the residence, this architectural enhancement further strengthens the protection of the main residence and ensures that Qi energy will be conserved there. In the far rear of the house, there is a huge hill that leads to the residence in a slowly descending slope. The hill has lots of trees and grass. In front of the residence, the house boasts an open, spacious bright hall.

Mao's grandfather, apparently under the advice of an experienced geomancer, had a large pond dug in front of the residence, about thirty feet from the house, thus artificially creating a topography with water gathering in the bright hall, adding luster to the streams embracing the entire village in the outer environment. The pond itself is about 10,000 square feet in size. Mao later told people that he liked to swim in the pond as a child, almost all year round (the temperature is fairly warm in the southern province of Hunan). This developed into a lifetime interest in swimming and also of feng shui. He carried his inclination for swimming all the way to his palace in Beijing and into his old age. After he became ruler, Mao had a luxurious swimming pool built in front of each of his palaces, including the Forbidden City. Mao's belief in feng shui is further confirmed by the fact that wherever he slept, he insisted that his head be pointed toward the east (his name "tung" means "east" in Chinese). This is also because wood was the desired spirit in his horoscope, and wood occupies the direction of east.

Perhaps the greatest geomantic craftsmanship of Mao's residence is shown in the design of the main entrance. Several years ago, while I was touring the village, I stood in the doorway of the main entrance and looked ahead into the distance. I was surprised to find that the front door was directly lined up with the opening between the two worshipping mountains in the far distance. In feng shui, this opening between two mountains is called "the mouth of Qi," which can greatly improve the feng shui of a res-

idence or a tomb. Obviously, Mao's grandfather was keenly aware of the feng shui principle that whenever there are two worshipping mountains in the front, a construction project should face directly up to the opening space between the two mountains.

It is also told that when Mao's mother was pregnant with him, she and her husband simultaneously saw a strange ray of red light in the eastern corner of the house. One day when Mao was only four years old, his mother—a devoted Buddhist—took him to the biggest temple in Xiangtang County near his residence. As Mao was taken into the main hall of the temple by his mother, the Four Big Warrior Attendants of Buddha "backed up" a few steps at the sight of Mao. All Buddha and warrior attendants in the temple were made of earth, but apparently they did move. This strange phenomenon was observed by only two people—the abbot and the young Mao. Mao was so frightened that he burst into a loud cry. His mother was at a loss, assuming that Mao was just too young and shy to see the ugly faces of the four warrior attendants, but the abbot knew better. He stepped down from his seat and came over to the mother. Patting Mao on the head, he told his mother: "This son of yours is going to be great."

Based on all this information, there should be little doubt that the making of Mao Tse-tung as one of the greatest leaders in the modern world was not a coincidence. The extraordinarily auspicious feng shui of his old residence in Hunan had well prepared his coming into the world in that specific village of Shao-shan-chong.

Case #2. Xikou—Hometown of Chiang Kai-shek

Chiang Kai-shek, the late president of the Republic of China (1926–1975), was a descendent of the celebrated Duke of the Zhou dynasty in the twelfth century B.C. The Duke was held in high esteem as a Confucian sage and a model premier in Chinese culture. In the thirteenth century A.D., some members of the Duke's family left the old capital city of Loyang along the banks of the Yellow River, and emigrated to Zejiang province on China's southeastern coast. They assumed the surname of Chiang. About 400 years later, one branch of the Chiang family settled in Xikou, a town in the county of Fenghua in Zejiang province along China's eastern coast. It was in this town that Chiang Kai-shek was born on October 31, 1887.

From a geomantic standpoint, it is by no means a coincidence that Chiang was born in Xikou. Xikou is a place with royal feng shui that was bound to give birth to a head of state—actually two, if we count Chiang's son, Chiang Jin-guo, who succeeded his father as president of the Republic of China in Taiwan. A geomantic analysis will reveal the interesting cause and effect of this.

The town of Xikou is located in a hilly terrain. To the southwest, the river of Yenxi curves along the twisty foot of the bluff toward Xikou. To the north, magnificent mountains with lush forests project their undulating outline against the sky. Nearby, there is Mount Xuedu, famous both for its Buddhist temple and picturesque scenery. To the west, the river Jinxi flows from deep in the mountains toward Xikou, and merges with the river Yenxi in the outskirts of Xikou. Combined, they flow away from Xikou toward Mount Wulin and are blocked on their way downstream by five hills. This forces the waterway to return a bit and form into a huge lake in front of Xikou.

Xikou is surrounded by clear waters and green, magnificent mountains. Particularly significant from a geomantic perspective is the Yenxi River, which is full of twists and turns. In one portion of it, the river manifests nine turns or curves, earning it the reputation of "the river of Yenxi with nine turns." Li Bai and Du Fu, two great poets in China's history, both thought very highly of the river. Li remarked: "The water and stone in the river of Yenxi are very clear and wonderful." Du also said: "The river of Yenxi is extraordinarily beautiful."

Equally beautiful are the mountains surrounding Xikou. These mountains belong to the mountain vein of Shimin, which runs for almost 800 miles and lies between the Jinjiang River and Yongjiang River. The mountain vein of Shimin boasts 280 mountains, of which seventy are located inside the county of Fenghua. Mount Xuedu is the most magnificent of these seventy mountains. As if all this were not enough, a lake was created high on Mount Xuedu, which is made of two small mountain brooks. This lake is known as Mirror Pond.

From this geographic sketch, we can tell that Xikou is really an ideal residential location with extraordinarily auspicious geomantic features. For instance, Mirror Pond is a heavenly pond, the existence of which almost ensures the birth of a head of state in its vicinity. In addition, there is more than one curving river near or passing by Xikou. The Yenxi River with nine turns adds to the promise of giving birth to at least one head of state. Equally significant is that the water flowing away from Xikou is effectively blocked by five hills, including Mount Wulin, which force

the water to turn around and stay in the front of the village of Xikou. These mountains form mighty guards, acting as an earthly door, powerfully guarding the wealth, and reserving the Qi energy in Xikou. The entire town is situated amid magnificent hills and is therefore protected on all sides from the blow of evil winds. The entire topographic landscape of Xikou suggests the image of a center of gravity amid the protection of layer after layer of mountains. In addition, the long, continuous mountain vein of Shimin adds to the luster of the feng shui, ensuring the continuation of the Chiang empire for more than one generation.

Case #3. Seattle — The Emerald City

Seattle is called the Emerald City for its beautiful landscape. It is the largest city in the State of Washington in the northwest United States. A major port for decades, the city is booming again from high-tech industry and trade with Pacific Rim/Asian nations. Increasingly, it is becoming a trend-setting city at home and abroad, in terms of economic development, city planning, and scenic landscape. Seattle's solid success as a trade and manufacturing center, and its leading position in some of the key technological fields, plus its beautiful surroundings, has made the metropolitan area one of the fastest growing in the United States in terms of both economy and population. Today, Seattle has the largest number of homeowners of any major American city, and is the base for big brand names such as Microsoft, Boeing, and Starbucks.

How much credit does the feng shui of Seattle deserve for all its success? To answer this question, we have to take a closer look at the geographic features of the city and their geomantic significances.

There are two outstanding geographic features in the city that contributes geomantically to the economic and technological successes of Seattle. The first and most outstanding feature is the dominance of water. Water, water, water—it is almost everywhere in Seattle. Seattle has the Pacific Ocean as its western border. This great ocean has also never been violent to Seattle; the Pacific is truly accommodating in this part of the world. War or violent weather is not heard of here. Indeed, all is quiet on its western front.

In addition to the vast expanse of water on its western border, the Seattle area boasts of seven freshwater lakes. Lake Washington, a huge freshwater mountain lake extending twenty-two miles from north to south, borders the city in the east. In between the Puget Sound and

Lake Washington is Lake Union, which lies to the immediate north of downtown Seattle. The other lakes are Green Lake, Haller Lake, and Bitter Lakes in the north end, the Duwamish Lake lies in the south, and Lake Sammamish in the east. All these lakes and the ocean convey a sense that water is omnipresent and always close at hand.

Since water stands for wealth in feng shui, it should come as no surprise that Seattle has been so successful economically, with the city enjoying the highest bond rating (AAA) in the country, and also being the home to the richest man in the twenty-first century (Bill Gates). Besides money, water also signifies intelligence. This could be why Seattle has been able to attract a huge number of well-educated, highly intelligent people to it, making Seattle a leader in many key areas of modern technology, including computer science, aerospace technology, biotechnology, and telecommunications. With this in mind, we can better understand why such big names as Microsoft and Boeing are based in the Seattle area.

The second outstanding geographic feature that contributes geomantically to the success and growth of Seattle lies in the beautiful mountains in and surrounding it. One hundred miles west of Seattle, along the coast, is Quillayute.

Between there and Seattle rise the Olympic Mountains. These undulating, snow-capped mountains create a land formation that intrudes into the Pacific Ocean through Seattle and rise out of the west across the deep blue waters of Puget Sound. Marching south and east of the city are the massive peaks of the Cascade volcanoes, with Mount Rainier taking up half the horizon. To the north, Mount Baker stands with its snow-clad, glittering peaks. Inside the city proper, we have Queen Anne Hill, First Hill, Capitol Hill, and Beacon Hill.

Thus, Seattle has both water and mountains—the two most desirable features in feng shui. Geomantically, mountains stand for population growth. It is only natural that Seattle area has been one of the most attractive places for immigrants, both in America and around the world.

Glossary

Ba-gua system: A system based on I-ching, the Book of Change. The system has eight (*ba*) sectors (*gua*), each of which points to a specific direction and corresponds with some specific years.

Doctrine of the Middle Way: One of the key values in the Confucian value system, this doctrine advocates that we should adhere to the Middle Way in our behavior and conduct. The Middle Way is interpreted as lack of bias, prejudice, and excess. For, as Confucius maintains, too much is as bad as too little, neither of which will last long because both will cause harm and damage, not only to others, but also to oneself. Only the Middle Way, which is the compromise of two extremes, can long endure.

Twelve earthly branches: As contrasted with the ten heavenly stems, these are the twelve Chinese characters arranged in the following order: Zi, Chou, Ying, Mao, Chen, Si, Whu, Wei, Shen, You, Xu, and Hai. Again, these branches are classified in terms of the five elements and yin and yang. Thus, Zi is yang water, Chou is yin earth, Ying is yang wood, Mao is yin wood, Chen is Yang earth, Si is yin fire, Whu is yang fire, Wei is yin earth, Shen is yang metal, You is yin metal, Xu is yang earth, and Hai is yin water. Each element has two representatives in the branches except earth, which has four representatives. Together with the ten heavenly stems, the twelve earthly branches are used to indicate lunar years. The twelve branches are the basis of Chinese astrology and the zodiac, with each of the elements standing for one unique animal. Thus, Zi is identified with rat, Chou with ox, Ying with tiger, Mao with rabbit, Chen with dragon, Si with snake, Whu with horse, Wei with ram, Shen with monkey, You with cock, Xu with dog, and Hai with pig. The system of the twelve earthly branches is in itself a representation of years in the Chinese calendar. Thus, 1999 is the year of rabbit, and 2000 is the year of dragon.

Eight characters of birth: This is a divination method used in China. The eight characters of birth refer to the year, the month, the date, and the hour in which one was born. Each element is assigned two Chinese characters. Together, they make up eight characters. By analyzing the complex relationships among these eight characters, a skilled fortune-teller is able to come up with a detailed picture about one's fate.

Five elements: The five elements in Chinese culture refer to water, fire, wood, metal, and earth. These are considered the very basic materials by means of which everything in the universe is created. Together, they form a philosophical system, a system of thinking characteristic of Chinese fathers. Each element represents a host of objects and phenomena in the universe. For instance, kidneys correspond to water, heart to fire, liver to wood, lungs to metal, and spleen to earth. There is a dual relation among these elements: mutual creation and mutual destruction. The relation of mutual creation works this way: water creates wood, wood creates fire, fire creates earth, earth creates metal, and metal creates water, thus completing the cycle of mutual creation. The relation of mutual destruction works this way: water quenches fire, fire melts metal, metal cuts wood, wood looses earth, and earth stops water flow, thus completing the cycle of mutual destruction. Feng shui uses this system in three main ways. One is to classify mountains in terms of the five elements, another is to group different businesses by means of the five elements, yet another is to decode one's birthday by means of the five elements to find out the auspicious orientation and location for each individual.

Feng shui: Alternatively known as kun-yu and geomancy, feng shui is a unique product of Chinese culture that has a history of three thousand years. Literally meaning "wind" and "water," feng shui seeks to first select land sites for construction that contain the maximum Qi energy in the universe, and then to design buildings and graves in a way that will harmonize a construction project with its environments in an attempt to create a productive trinity among heaven, earth, and humans, so that humans will be benefited by the Qi energy in the universe and enjoy good luck in their lives. Feng shui is an involved, complex subject which draws heavily upon the Taoist theories of yin-yang,

the five-element system, and the eight characters of birth. In practice, it simultaneously takes into consideration interrelations among the macroenvironment (heaven), the microenvironment (earth), and the resident's birthday (humans). A special compass is designed to help people with the task of alignment and orientation.

I-Ching: One of the oldest and most significant ancient Chinese classics dates back to twelfth century B.C. It consists of a set of symbols and texts for divination, and is regarded as the source of traditional Chinese culture. It explains in detail the theory and implications of yin and yang, the trigrams, as well as the origin of the universe and how man is related to the universe. Its original purpose was to aid in fortunetelling, for both individuals and the entire nation. But later generations have applied the principles of the book to many fields of human endeavor, from medicine to geomancy, from warfare to politics, from astronomy to business. Its application in geomancy mainly comes from the principle of yin and yang, as well as the division of a plane into eight locations.

Karma: This means the correspondence of one's birth year and the eight gua's in the ba-gua system . The Chinese ancients believe that each individual belongs to one of the eight gua's or sectors as specified in the ba-gua system, and this individual relationship with a specific sector is called karma, which is determined by the birth year of the individual.

Liu Ji: (1311–1375) A great Chinese statesman, military strategist, writer, and feng shui master during the Ming dynasty. Most of his life, he served as a military and astrological advisor to the founding emperor of the Ming dynasty. He was significantly responsible for the establishment of the empire, and was revered by the emperor as "old teacher." He knew things past, present, and in the future. When persistently asked by his emperor, he wrote *Songs of Cakes*, a collection of poems which ambiguously depict the major political events in China for the next 1,000 years. He also wrote a couple of books on military strategy and tactics, as well as geomancy and divination.

Nine palaces: This is very much the same as the ba-gua system for determining the appropriate directions for individuals. The only difference is the addition of the Attraction Palace located at the very center. The nine palaces consist of New Luo Palace (Northwest), Mysterious Palace (Southwest), Warehouse Palace (East), Fruit Palace (West), Hibernation Palace (North), Heavenly Palace (South), Yin Luo Palace (Southeast), Reserve Palace (Northeast) and Attraction Palace (Center).

Qi: Qi is an encompassing concept in Chinese medicine, philosophy, and indeed, the entire traditional Chinese culture. The operation of the human body as well as the universe depends on Qi. Any disturbance, disharmony, and deficiency of Qi will cause disease and natural calamities. Broadly, Qi can be defined as life energy; our lives and the universe depend on it. Chinese fathers hold that the stronger the Qi one possesses, the stronger will be one's immune system, the healthier one will be. Meanwhile, Qi determines the brightness of the celestial objects such as the sun and stars, and the weather patterns. As such, the conservation, promotion, and circulation of Qi become one of the central themes in traditional Chinese natural health care and medicine, as well as feng shui. In fact, the whole subject of feng shui pivots around the concept of Qi and has the preservation and creation of Qi as its ultimate goal.

Sixty permutations: These are all the permutations that can be formed by using the ten heavenly stems and the twelve earthly branches, given the limitation that yang stems can only match with yang branches, and yin stems can only match with yin branches, and vice versa. Each permutation is made of two Chinese characters, one taken from the ten heavenly stems and the other taken from the twelve earthly branches. Thus, Jia (one of the heavenly stems) can only match with either Zi, Ying, Chen, Whu, Shen, or Xu, due to their yang nature. By the same token, Yi (another of the heavenly stems) can only match with either Chou, Mao, Si, Wei, You, or Hai due to their yin nature. This system of permutations is used in traditional China to record not only years, but also months in the year, days in the month, and hours in the day. In fact, the entire Chinese lunar calendar is built on this system of sixty permutations. Since feng shui has a timing dimension, this system has been incorporated into the Chinese geomantic compass.

Sixty-four hexagrams: These hexagrams result from squaring the eight tri-grams of I-Ching. Since each of the trigrams can merge with another including itself, there are altogether sixty-four (8 x 8) hexagrams. The system also represents the cosmology besides the eight trigrams, only in greater detail.

Ten heavenly stems: Contrasted with the twelve earthly branches, these are the ten Chinese characters arranged in the following order: Jia, Yi, Bing, Ding, Wu, Ji, Geng, Xin, Ren, and Kui. Each of these characters or stems belongs to one of the five basic elements, plus a yin or yang nature. Thus, Jia and Yi stand for wood, Bing and Ding stand for fire, Wu and Ji for earth, Geng and Xin for metal, Ren and Kui for water. What is the difference between Jia and Yi, both of which are wood ? The difference lies in the duality of each and all elements. That is to say, each element has a yin side and a yang side. Chinese fathers recognized that almost everything in the universe has in itself both yin and yang natures. Thus, Jia is yang-wood, while Yi is yin-wood. For exactly the same reason, Bing is yang-fire while Ding is yin-fire; Wu is yang-earth while Ji is yin-earth; Geng is yang-metal while Xin is yin-metal; Ren is yang-water and Kui is yin-water. In contrast with the earthly branches, the heavenly stems represent heavenly Qi energy, whereas the earthly branches stand for earthly Qi energy. Together, they form an involved numerical system, on the basis of which the Chinese lunar calenda is set.

Trigrams: These are the eight symbols proposed in I-Ching for divination. As the term implies, each trigram is denoted by three bars, continuous or broken in two. These trigrams are: Qian (denoted by three continuous bars), Dui (denoted by two continuous bars at the bottom and one broken bar on top), Li (denoted by two continuous bars on both ends and a broken one in the middle), Zhen (denoted by two broken bars on top and a continuous one at the bottom), Xun (denoted by two continuous bars on top and a broken one at the bottom), Kan (denoted by a continuous bar in the middle and two broken ones on both ends), Gen (denoted by a continuous bar on top and two broken ones at the bottom), and Kun (denoted by three broken bars). Simplistic as they appear, they are highly rich in connotations and symbolic meaning. Together, they form a representative system of the universe. This system is an integral part of feng shui

theory, indicating the directional relation between a specific locality and its surrounding objects, as well as the relation between individual humans and the environment as determined by individuals' birth year.

In terms of directions, Qian is located in the northwest, Dui the west, Li the south, Zhen the east, Xun the southeast, Kan the north, Gen the northeast, and Kun occupies the southwest. Symbolically, Qian signifies, among other things, the heaven, the emperor, the male, a father, strength, the head, sphere, roundness, horse, and metal. Dui signifies vapor, clouds, the mouth, the tongue, daughter, concubine, and pleasure. Li signifies the sun, fire, heat, light, lightning, brightness, beauty, pheasant, swords, spears, dryness, the heart, crabs, and tortoise. Zhen symbolizes motion, dragon, decision, thunder, feet, development, road, and the eldest son. Xun stands for wind, wood, profit, quickness, length, height, the eldest daughter. Kan indicates water, rivers, oceans, lakes, streams, hidden objects, the moon, the ears, and peril. Gen stands for rocks, hills and mountains, stability, stoppage, gates, a dog, a pig, weight, and the youngest son. To complete the picture of the yin-yang universe, Kun symbolizes Mother-earth, empress, female, a mother, birth, gentleness, and docility.

Twenty-eight constellations: The twenty-eight constellations form an astronomical system in China. Ancient Chinese thought that the stars in the sky could be classified into twenty-eight constellations. They are Jiao, Kang, Di, Fang, Xing, Wei, Ji, Dou, Niu, Nu, Xu, Wei, Shi, Bi, Kuei, Lou, Wai, Mao, Bi, Chi, Chan, Jing, Gui, Liu, Xin, Zhang, Yi, and Chen. Since this is not an exact system of classifying stars, experts differ in their opinion as to where each constellation resides in the heaven. That explains why many discrepancies are found between *Morrison's Dictionary of the Chinese Language* (part II, vol. I, p. 1065) and *Mayers Chinese Reader's Manual* (p. 356).

Twenty-four divisions of the year: In the Chinese lunar calendar, the year is divided into twenty-four sections. Each section or division lasts for fifteen days. Altogether, they make up 360 days for a year. This is five days short of the solar calendar. The Chinese lunar system makes up this deficiency by assigning a repeated month to a certain year once every six years, thus fully recovering the thirty days lost in the previous six-year period. Listed below are the twenty-four Jie's and Qi's in chronological order of the year, inclusive (beginning with the first Jie): Commence of Spring, Rain Water, Resurrection of Hibernation, Vernal Equinox, Clear Brightness, Rains for the Rice; Commence of Summer, Minor Fullness, Grain in Ear, Summer Solstice, Minor Heat, Major Heat; Commence of Autumn, Lingering Heat, Autumnal Equinox, Cold Dew, Falling Frost; Commence of Winter, Minor Snow, Major Snow, Winter Solstice, Minor Cold, and Major Cold.

Useful spirit: An important concept in Chinese divination based on the eight characters of birth. The useful spirit is one of the five elements (water, fire, wood, metal, and earth), which is considered the spirit or force that determines the outcome of the mutual production or mutual destruction among the five elements, and therefore the balance of yin and yang, in the specific horoscope of a person, as determined by the eight characters of birth for that person.

Further Reading

Cai Yuanding. *Fa Wei Lun*. Collected in Ssu Ku Chuan Shu, compiled by Zhu Jianmin. Taipei, Taiwan: Taiwan Commercial Press, 1986.

Chin, R. D. *Feng Shui Revealed*. New York: Clarkson Potter Publishers, 1998.

Craze, Richard. *Practical Feng Shui*. New York: Lorenz Books, 1997.

Dahun, Jiang. *Classics of Watery Dragon* (in Chinese). China: Hua Xia Zhe Li Chan Wei She, 1934.

Guo Pu. *The Book of Burial* (in Chinese). Collected in Ssu Ku Chuan Shu, compiled by Zhu Jianmin. Taipei, Taiwan: Taiwan Commercial Press, 1986.

Lai Wenjun. *Cui Guan Bian*. Collected in Ssu Ku Chuan Shu, compiled by Zhu Jianmin. Taipei, Taiwan: Taiwan Commercial Press, 1986.

Li Mozai. *A Collection of Road-breaking Works* (in Chinese). Shanghai, China: Hui Wen Tang Book Store, 1933.

Lo, Raymond. *Feng Shui and Destiny.* Tynron, 1992.

Rossbach, Sarah. *Feng Shui: The Chinese Art of Placement.* New York: E.P. Dutton, Inc., 1983.

Tin, Li Pak. *Feng Shui: Secrets that Change Your Life.* York Beach, ME: Samuel Weiser, Inc., 1997.

Walter, Derek. *The Feng Shui Handbook: A Practical Guide to Chinese Geomancy.* London: Aquarian, 1991.

Webster, Richard. *Feng Shui for the Workplace.* St. Paul, MN: Llewellyn Publications, 1998.

Wydra, Nancilee. *Feng Shui: The Book of Cures.* Lincolnwood, IL: Contemporary Books, 1996.

Xu, Shanji & Shanshu. *What Every Son Should Know About Geomancy* (in Chinese). Shanghai, China: Shanghai Book Store, 1928.

Yang Yun-song. *Han Long Jin.* Collected in Ssu Ku Chuan Shu, compiled by Zhu Jianmin. Taipei, Taiwan: Taiwan Commercial Press, 1986.

———. *Tian Yu Jin.* Collected in Ssu Ku Chuan Shu, compiled by Zhu Jianmin. Taipei, Taiwan: Taiwan Commercial Press, 1986.

———. *Yi Long Jin.* Collected in Ssu Ku Chuan Shu, compiled by Zhu Jianmin. Taipei, Taiwan: Taiwan Commercial Press, 1986.

Index

237

☽ REACH FOR THE MOON

Llewellyn publishes hundreds of books on your favorite subjects! To get these exciting books, including the ones on the following pages, check your local bookstore or order them directly from Llewellyn.

ORDER BY PHONE
- Call toll-free within the U.S. and Canada, 1-800-THE MOON
- In Minnesota, call (651) 291-1970
- We accept VISA, MasterCard, and American Express

ORDER BY MAIL
- Send the full price of your order (MN residents add 7% sales tax) in U.S. funds, plus postage & handling to:

  Llewellyn Worldwide
  P.O. Box 64383, Dept. K436-7
  St. Paul, MN 55164–0383, U.S.A.

POSTAGE & HANDLING
(For the U.S., Canada, and Mexico)
- $4.00 for orders $15.00 and under
- $5.00 for orders over $15.00
- No charge for orders over $100.00

We ship UPS in the continental United States. We ship standard mail to P.O. boxes. Orders shipped to Alaska, Hawaii, the Virgin Islands, and Puerto Rico are sent first-class mail. Orders shipped to Canada and Mexico are sent surface mail.

International orders: Airmail—add freight equal to price of each book to the total price of order, plus $5.00 for each non-book item (audio tapes, etc.).

Surface mail—Add $1.00 per item.

Allow 2 weeks for delivery on all orders.
Postage and handling rates subject to change.

DISCOUNTS
We offer a 20% discount to group leaders or agents. You must order a minimum of 5 copies of the same book to get our special quantity price.

FREE CATALOG
Get a free copy of our color catalog, *New Worlds of Mind and Spirit*. Subscribe for just $10.00 in the United States and Canada ($30.00 overseas, airmail). Many bookstores carry *New Worlds*— ask for it!

Visit our web site at www.llewellyn.com for more information.

What Your Face Reveals

Chinese Secrets of Face Reading

Henry B. Lin

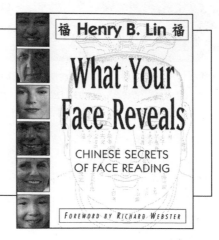

Your forehead may be very promising, but if its color is dark or pale, then summer will be a time of trouble. Your friend with the horse-shaped face is clever, loyal, and will eventually hold a position of great power. Take a good look at your nose—it will tell you whether or not you will be happy in marriage!

The Chinese have been reading faces for more than 3,000 years. Now you can learn how to decode the secrets of fate as written on your face with this simple pictorial guide. Determine the personality of strangers, uncover your future and the future of your loved ones, and use this knowledge to benefit you in work, health, and love.

You will learn how to analyze the shape of the face, its color and spirit, and specific features such as ears, eyebrows, eyes, nose, cheekbones, mouth, teeth, chin, hair, moles, lines, and more. You will also learn a shortcut to face reading with the system of the Twelve Palaces for those times when you only need a broad summary of someone's fate.

1-56718-433-2
264 pp., 7½ x 9⅛, 150 illus. $17.95

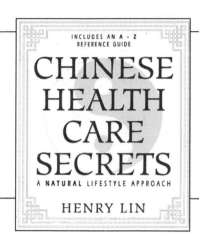

Chinese Health Care Secrets

A Natural Lifestyle Approach

Henry B. Lin

At a time when the medical costs in this country are skyrocketing and chronic disease runs rampant in every walk of life, *Chinese Health Care Secrets* offers a readily applicable, completely natural, and highly effective alternative. It serves as a practical reference on personal health care, as well as a textbook on a health care system from the world's oldest civilization.

It is the Chinese belief that you can achieve optimal health by carrying out your daily activities—including diet, sleep, emotional feeling, physical exercise, and sexual activity—according to the laws of Nature. It is especially effective in treating the degenerative diseases that plague millions of Americans. Many of the techniques have never before been published, and are considered secrets even in China.

Avoid common ailments brought on by aging and modern society when you take charge of your own health with age-old Chinese wisdom, including:

- The secrets of proper diet, sleep and rest, physical hygiene, mental discipline, regular exercise, regulated sex, environmental hygiene
- A list of sixty-five of nature's potent healers
- An A-Z reference guide of special solutions for seventy-six of the most common health problems
- Appendices full of exercises and acupressure points

1-56718-434-0
528 pp., 7½ x 9⅛, illus. $24.95

Feng Shui for Beginners

Successful Living by Design

Richard Webster

Not advancing fast enough in your career? Maybe your desk is located in a "negative position." Wish you had a more peaceful family life? Hang a mirror in your dining room and watch what happens. Is money flowing out of your life rather than into it? You may want to look to the construction of your staircase!

For thousands of years, the ancient art of feng shui has helped people harness universal forces and lead lives rich in good health, wealth, and happiness. The basic techniques in *Feng Shui for Beginners* are very simple, and you can put them into place immediately in your home and work environments. Gain peace of mind, a quiet confidence, and turn adversity to your advantage with feng shui remedies.

1-56718-803-6
240 pp., 5¼ x 8, photos, diagrams

$12.95

To order, call 1-800-THE MOON

Prices are subject to change without notice.